THE ALL-SEASON INVESTOR:
Successful Strategies for Every Stage in the Business Cycle

Martin J. Pring

JOHN WILEY & SONS, INC.

New York • Chichester • Brisbane • Toronto • Singapore

In recognition of the importance of preserving what has been written, it is a policy of John Wiley & Sons, Inc. to have books of enduring value published in the United States printed on acid-free paper, and we exert our best efforts to that end.

Art credited to the *Pring Market Review* was originally produced by the author in the following publication:

Martin J. Pring, editor, *Pring Market Review,* International Institute for Economic Research, P.O. Box 329, Washington Depot, CT 06794.

Library of Congress Cataloging-in-Publication Data

Pring, Martin J.
    The all-season investor: successful strategies for every stage in the business cycle / Martin J. Pring.
        p.   cm.
    Includes index.
    ISBN 0-471-54977-0
    1. Investments.   2. Securities.   3. Business cycles.
    4. Finance,   Public.   I. Title.
    HG4521.P835   1992
    332.6'78—dc20   91-34336

Printed in the United States of America

10 9 8 7 6 5 4 3 2 1

Printed and bound by Courier Companies, Inc.

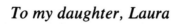

To my daughter, Laura

ACKNOWLEDGMENTS

In putting together a book of this nature, I owe countless people a debt of gratitude. In particular, I would like to thank my colleagues at Pring-Turner Capital, Joe Turner and Bruce Fraser, for their constant encouragement and support and for their help in formulating some of the concepts used in the book.

I would also like to mention Sheila Silvernail for her dedication and diligence in creating many of the charts and for proofing the manuscript, making my job so much easier. Also Renee Pike for help with the risk/reward analysis and many constructive suggestions.

As always, thanks goes to my wife, Danny, for translating the original manuscript into readable English.

CONTENTS

Introduction: What Is Asset Allocation?

The cornerstone of any investment strategy is to maximize return while maintaining a tolerable risk. The process of allocating assets among several investment categories is a way of achieving this goal. The level of "tolerable" risk depends on an individual's psychological makeup, financial position, and stage in life. Younger people can assume greater risks than someone who is retired; a highly paid executive will be less dependent on current portfolio income than will a disabled person on workmen's compensation, and so forth.

Asset allocation can be handled in two steps. The first decision involves a general review of these financial, psychological, and life stage factors to determine overall investment goals. Is your goal current income, capital appreciation, or an acceptable balance? If you decide on capital appreciation, do you have the personality to ride out major declines in the market, or are you the kind of person who would be better off assuming less risk in order to sleep more peacefully? These are decisions that only you can make after careful consideration. Formulating decisions on these overall investment objectives is known as *strategic* asset allocation. It is a process that sets out the broad tone of your investment policy, and

1

one that should be reviewed periodically as your status in life changes. Some guidance on these matters is presented in Chapter 12.

This book, however, is principally concerned with the next step, known as *tactical* asset allocation, in which the proportion of each asset category held in the portfolio is altered in response to changes in the business climate. For instance, a retired person may decide that his or her principal investment objectives are current income and safety. This would not preclude, but would definitely limit, the proportion of the portfolio exposed to the stock market. For this type of investor the range might be 10 to 25 percent. The tactical allocation process would determine whether the equity exposure fell closer to the 10 percent or 25 percent area.

WHY ALLOCATE ASSETS?

There are three principal reasons for an investor to allocate assets: to reduce risk through diversification, to allow for the times when a specific asset is attractive and the times when it is not, and to reduce the emotional aspect of decision making by carefully and gradually shifting emphasis from one type of asset to another. Let's consider each of these reasons in turn.

RISK REDUCTION THROUGH DIVERSIFICATION

It is a well-known investment principle that you shouldn't put all of your eggs into one basket. After all, what might seem to be a no-lose, high-reward situation at the outset may turn out to be a loser in the long run. Investing in more than one vehicle helps to cushion your portfolio in case one of your selections does not turn out to be as profitable as was originally expected. Asset allocation involves a lot more than just buying several different stocks; it also encompasses cash, bonds, and inflation hedge assets. In its purest form the asset allocation process would also include other asset classes such as real estate, oil leases, annuities, and so forth. Because these are not as liquid as assets like equities and bonds, they are not considered in this book.

The simplest way to allocate assets would be to hold small amounts in a variety of financial vehicles and never sell. Such a policy would cushion a portfolio from major stock market declines like the 1987 crash. At the same time it would also participate well in major bull markets such as the 1982–1987 equity boom or the 1978–1980 run up in the price of gold.

There are two problems with this approach. First, a major bull market in a specific asset, such as that for equities in the 1980s, would increase the proportion of that particular asset category well above the original intention. To make matters worse, this over-weighting would occur right at the most inappropriate time—the top of the market! One of the principal objectives of asset allocation is to *increase* the allocation of an asset class in the area of a major *bottom*, not at a market top. Eventually it would become evident that this static approach would have to be adjusted or the portfolio would become skewed toward one particular asset, thereby diluting the beneficial effects of diversification.

The second disadvantage of a static approach is that it consistently fails to take full advantage of major bull markets and does little to provide protection during bear markets. No approach can guarantee full participation in every bull move or liquidation at the beginning of every bear market. Nevertheless, a continuous and conservative alteration in the asset balance as a response to changing economic environments is achievable and can result in superior, although not necessarily spectacular, results.

The idea of improving the risk/reward ratio is a key one in money management. All investments involve some kind of risk, but one of the principal objectives of investing is to limit risk as much as possible while not giving up too much on the reward side. Let's say, for example, that the dividend yield on the Dow Jones Industrial Average (Dow Jones) was less than 3 percent. This falls well below the historical norm and is often associated with bull market peaks. It would, therefore, represent a high risk/reward. On the other hand, a yield of 5 to 5½ percent is unusually generous and normally has been seen only around major market lows. This would represent a low risk/reward and, other things being equal, would justify a larger than normal equity allocation.

If these two extreme examples are plotted on a chart, as in Figure I.1, it is possible to see how an investment goal of maximum return for minimum risk can be achieved. The vertical axis represents the expected reward (an annualized rate of return, for example), so the higher the reward, the closer the plot is to the top of the chart. The horizontal axis measures the risk required to earn that reward. Low risk (more desirable) would be plotted close to the vertical axis while greater risk is plotted to the right. Because the objective is to achieve maximum reward for very little risk, the risk/reward profile for the ideal investment would be plotted somewhere in the top left-hand part of the chart.

Historically, there has been an excellent buying opportunity when equities have yielded 5 percent because the downside risk has

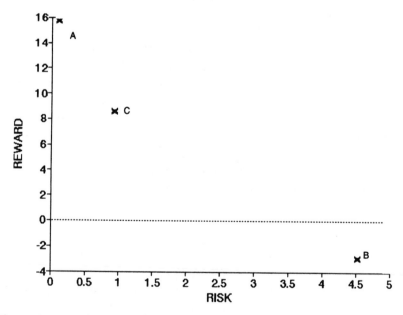

Figure I.1   Risk vs. reward for S&P 500 yield, 1948–1991. (Source: *Pring Market Review*)

been limited and the upside potential substantial. The annualized rate of return for a two-year holding period would be plotted in the diagram at Point A, close to the risk-free area but relatively high up on the reward scale. Conversely, purchasing stocks when the market is experiencing a 3 percent yield has, on average, offered a negative return over a 24-month holding period. This is plotted lower on the return scale and farther out on the risk axis (Point B). Point C represents the risk/reward for the entire period covered (1948–1991). Naturally this falls between Points A and B.

As successful investors, we want to position ourselves toward the top left-hand chart if possible. In investment circles this is known as the *Northwest Quadrant*. In the real world it is not possible to achieve the idealized risk/reward of maximum gains and no risk because there is always a tradeoff. However, there are several techniques that can help you to gravitate toward the North-

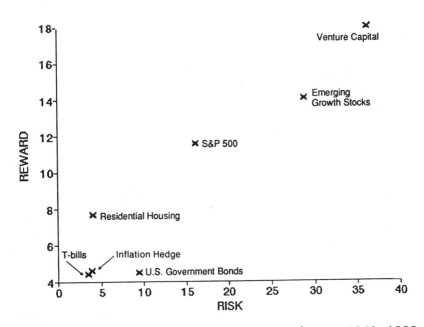

Figure I.2 Risk vs. reward for seven asset classes, 1940–1990. (Source: *Pring Market Review*)

west Quadrant. The first is through diversification. The second is by emphasizing or overweighting an asset at the appropriate time in the business cycle. The third is buying when a particular asset is historically cheap and selling when it becomes overvalued. The latter point is to some extent a corollary of the second. Figure I.2 plots the risk/reward (annualized monthly returns) relationship for various asset classes between 1940 and 1990.

THE SEASONAL APPROACH TO ASSET ALLOCATION

A significant part of this book is devoted to optimizing the tactical allocation of assets within a portfolio on the basis of business cycle conditions. This approach assumes two things. The first assumption is that the business cycle will continue to operate. The cycle has been a fact of life throughout recorded economic history, not only in the United States but in every other capitalist country as well. Typically it encompasses a time span of roughly four years from trough to trough, and is a reflection of human nature in action. Because human nature remains more or less constant, there are few grounds for expecting the business cycle to be "repealed."

The second assumption is that every business cycle progresses through a set, chronological series of events, each of which greatly affects the performance of specific asset classes. Subsequent chapters will describe these events and how they may be recognized. Most importantly, the chronological series of events is very similar to a calendar year moving through the four seasons. Every farmer knows that there is a season for planting and one for harvesting. The same is true for investors because the business cycle provides an optimum time for buying and a propitious one for liquidating each specific financial asset. In farming, if you are familiar with the crops that are suitable for the local soil and climate and know when to plant and harvest, barring an unforeseen natural disaster, it should be possible to obtain reasonable yields. Successful investing is no different. If you have an understanding of the characteristics of the various asset classes and can identify the points in the business cycle when they traditionally do well, it is possible to attain superior returns relative to the risk undertaken.

Unfortunately, the business cycle "seasons" are not as predictable as the calendar year seasons because they vary more in length and intensity. However, the guidelines presented later will provide you with enough information to identify the various seasons and the type of performance to be expected from each asset class during that stage of the cycle. We will discover the time to emphasize bonds or stocks and when it is appropriate to take a more defensive position. For most farmers, winters are a time for less activity because the risk of growing most crops is high. There is also a season in the business cycle when risk taking should be kept at a minimum. This means loading up with cash and waiting for the next opportunity.

During a business cycle, each asset moves through the four risk/reward quadrants indicated in Figure I.1. The objective, subject to the prescribed range established by the strategic allocation, is to assign an asset a very high weighting in the portfolio when it is in its Northwest Quadrant, gradually deemphasizing it as it moves toward the Southeast. These funds are then rotated into another asset that in turn is approaching the Northwest!

PSYCHOLOGICAL ASPECTS OF INVESTING

It is a relatively easy task to gain a theoretical understanding of why markets move up and down. Beating the market on paper is not that difficult, but actually putting that knowledge to work in the marketplace on a day-by-day basis is a much more difficult task. The reason is that as soon as money is committed to an investment, so is emotion. Every time we review the prices of our investments, we subject ourselves to the impulses of fear and greed. These have the effect of deflecting our judgment away from objective criteria to emotional ones. Of course, common sense dictates that periodic monitoring of a portfolio performance is a necessary part of the investment process, but if we get too close to the market, the tendency is to respond to events and prices instead of carefully laid out criteria. The asset allocation approach as described here makes a valuable contribution to this ongoing psychological battle that all investors have to face. First, the very adoption of the principles of allocation implies the establishment of reasonable investment goals and the employment of a plan. If you make a plan and stick to it, you are far less likely to be sidetracked by the latest news and investment fashion. Furthermore, the process of asset allocation involves a slow but steady rotation of asset classes as evidence of changing conditions emerges. This gradual shift means that the emotional ups and downs will also be less intense because the stakes of any specific change will be limited.

History shows that, with few exceptions, the most successful investors have been those who have concentrated on the long term. Today the media have a tendency to glorify the money managers or mutual funds that have outperformed the pack over the latest quarter. But in reality, near-term variations in performance are heavily influenced by chance or by the temporary success of a particular investment philosophy or style. Money managers who specialize in smaller companies are bound to have their performance lifted when these stocks come into fashion. The great temptation is to compare your own performance with the latest investment stars and to reallocate your assets in their footsteps. Studies continually show that, over the long haul, most money managers underperform the market. Perhaps more to the point, those that beat the market in one period have a less than even chance of doing it in the next. In reality, success in any venture is achieved at the margin. The tortoise approach implied by a gradual and continuous reallocation of assets will, in the long run, beat the promise of the investment hare of quick and easy profits.

1
Diversification: The Medicine for Sleepless Nights

Diversification is not only one of the simplest and most logical principles for consistent investment success but an important one as well. Perhaps this concept is so often overlooked by individual investors because of its simplicity in an otherwise complex world.

The justification for diversification rests partly on the factor of chance and partly on protection in the event that our analysis, heaven forbid, should turn out to be incorrect. The purchase of one security or even a portfolio limited to one asset class runs the risk of exposure to an unforeseen or unforeseeable event that could cripple an entire investment strategy. It is certainly true that a portfolio containing 25 stocks will increase the risk that one of them will be adversely affected by a factor of 25, but the odds of the whole portfolio's being wiped out would also be lessened by that amount.

Diversification is often thought of as a technique for spreading risk, but it is, in fact, much more than that. Just as it protects against unfortunate events, diversification can also increase the odds of good fortune. For example, a portfolio containing 10 or 12 stocks will stand a much better chance of being affected by a generous takeover offer, an unexpected technological breakthrough, a big oil strike, or some other beneficial development than one containing just two or three issues.

A further advantage is that diversification allows an investor to make *gradual* changes in a portfolio. For example, market peaks are often confusing affairs as stocks fluctuate in a wide trading band. One by one the indicators fall into place until an overall bearish picture finally becomes clear. The realization that stocks are in a topping out process is a gradual one, so it makes sense to shift the portfolio away from stocks in a step-by-step manner as well. As more factual evidence of a market top is obtained, and individual issues rally to prescribed target ranges, the equity allocation will gradually and deliberately be reduced.

The allocation of assets in a number of different categories achieves diversification, but diversification alone does not necessarily guarantee investment success. For example, if a portfolio is split evenly between bonds, stocks, and cash, it could quite easily lose real purchasing value during a long period of inflation. This would happen because the stock portion, which has traditionally beaten inflation over the long haul, would not be large enough to offset the debilitating effects that inflation would inflict on the fixed income allocation.

WHY DIVERSIFICATION IS NOT ALWAYS PRACTICED

Despite the substantial benefits of diversifying, many investors fail to take advantage of this important and profitable technique. The principal reason stems from the frailty of human nature. The first weakness, which many of us would prefer not to admit, is downright laziness. After all, it is much easier to purchase a stock that has just been painted in glowing terms by a broker or friendly "insider" than to undertake tedious research on a number of different issues from which the final selection will be made.

In a similar vein, many of us are tempted to buy a particular asset theme. "The Fed is pumping up the money supply, OPEC is cutting oil production, and inflation is coming back; so let's buy precious metals." This may be a perfectly legitimate investment idea, but does it mean that we should allocate all of our assets to vehicles that provide an inflation hedge? Perhaps our assumptions are just plain wrong, or conceivably these possibilities have already been discounted by the market. In either case this kind of simplistic one-idea allocation strategy leaves no room for error.

Such situations often arise because an individual's experience and knowledge are limited. People often extrapolate the prevailing set of economic conditions well into the future. The fact that circumstances can and do change is often ignored or conveniently glossed over. For example, we may perceive that inflationary conditions are intensifying as a result of the lagged effect of an easy money policy by the Fed. The decision to buy precious metals may well be the right one, *but only for the time being.* This trend will not continue indefinitely because the economy possesses its own internal correcting mechanisms. For every action there is a reaction, and every inflation breeds its own deflation because as prices rise, so do interest rates. Sooner or later these higher rates make it unprofitable for businesses and undesirable for consumers to borrow, so the economy turns down. When this occurs, inflation hedge assets suffer. Your portfolio might do well for a time, but by putting all of your eggs into an inflationary basket, the end result will be disappointing.

Intellectual laziness also applies to an investor who chooses to concentrate on one specific investment, usually a stock, that he hopes will turn out to be his financial home run. As a result he will have very little, if any, emotional capital left to creatively and objectively examine other possible vehicles. Fear can be just as destructive as greed. When the home run fails to materialize, as is inevitably the case, the investor becomes demoralized. In this kind of emotional state it will be difficult, if not impossible, to make any rational investment decisions. Performance will suffer, and some valuable opportunities will be lost.

Diversification involves a certain degree of patience, thought, and discipline. Unfortunately, in this day of instant analysis and news, not to mention unlimited financial leverage, most of us overlook these virtues on our way to what we (incorrectly) believe to be fast and painless financial rewards.

INFLATION AND VOLATILITY: TWO IMPORTANT RISKS

In the final analysis, the two most important risks to a portfolio are volatility (of the rate of return) and inflation. Experience tells us that over the long run, equities have offered a better rate of return than either cash or bonds. However, it is possible to lose a considerable amount of money over the short term if stocks are bought and sold at the wrong time. Bonds are also subject to volatility as interest rates rise and fall, but all bonds eventually return to par. Even if a bond is purchased at a premium, the interest payments assure a positive overall return if it is held to maturity. Nothing can prevent a default or bankruptcy, but, in general, the longer the holding period for either stocks or bonds, the less important is the volatility risk.

By the same token, inflation is a long-term risk because an environment of rising prices eats away at the purchasing value of the principal. The more substantial the holding period, the greater the loss of purchasing power. Diversification is a useful technique for minimizing both risks. For example, if a portfolio always includes some bonds and equities, the holding period of these core positions is, by definition, a long one, which greatly reduces the volatility risk.

At the same time, part of the portfolio may also be rotated among specific asset classes as the business cycle unfolds. With this combination the investor can hedge against inflation at that time of the cycle when it is most threatening and offset some of the long-term risk. In this way diversification is both a static and a dynamic process.

Diversification can also be used to spread risk for shorter-term periods. For example, you may decide that the outlook for food stocks in general is particularly favorable, especially that of Campbell's Soup. In this instance you are actually making two bets: one for the industry in general and the other specifically for Campbell's Soup. It could turn out that you are correct in your analysis of the food industry, but for some reason Campbell's Soup runs into difficulties of its own and greatly underperforms other companies in the industry. On the other hand, if you invest in several food stocks, you are still exposed to the industry risk, but the individual company risk is spread out among several issues. Under such circumstances, it is unlikely that this diversification will significantly result in a much higher reward, but it will certainly limit the downside potential (i.e., risk) for the investor.

REDUCING RISK FROM INDIVIDUAL COMPANIES (UNSYSTEMATIC RISK)

The approach of diversifying within an industry group can be taken one step further. We all know that putting your eggs into one basket can lead to trouble if the basket breaks, so it is important from an investment point of view to make sure you diversify your portfolio sufficiently in order to avoid being financially crippled if a specific investment turns bad.

Risk associated with individual companies independent of market fluctuations is called "unsystematic" risk. Experts generally agree that risk declines as more stocks are added to a portfolio, but the marginal beneficial effect significantly diminishes as more issues are added. Figure 1.1 indicates that the most substantial reduction

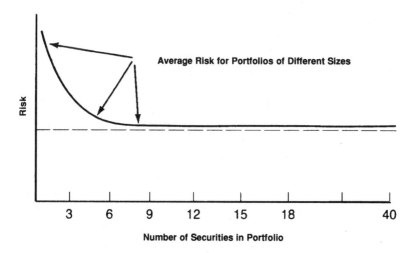

Figure 1.1 Risk reduction through diversification. (Source: *Pring Market Review*)

in risk comes at the early stages when the second and third stocks are added. The marginal benefits are progressively reduced. By the time the twelfth stock is added, there is very little in the way of risk reduction to be obtained. The curve clearly shows that the more stocks in a portfolio, the less susceptible that portfolio is to the fortunes of one particular company. The curve starts to flatten out after 6 issues are included. After this point has been reached, the incremental reduction of risk becomes noticeably lower. In effect, there is a great advantage in diversifying between 1 and 12 issues, but not much more from 12 to, say, 24. Because it takes a lot longer to research 24 than 12 companies, the most efficient approach for most individuals in terms of minimizing risk *and* effort is to limit the stock portion of their portfolio to around 9 to 12 issues because there is little to be gained from additional diversification.

REDUCING RISK FROM GENERAL MARKET FLUCTUATIONS (SYSTEMATIC RISK)

The process of diversifying into a number of different stocks does not in itself eliminate the risk associated with a general market decline, known as "systematic" risk. Indeed, if the portfolio contains 10 stocks, five of which are oils and five of which are oil drillers, it would not provide the kind of risk reduction implied in Figure 1.1. This is because all of these equities, being in similar industries, would be sensitive to changes in the energy industry. If, on the other hand, the portfolio was split into 10 stocks of widely different industries, the advantages of diversification would be significantly enhanced. In this example we are making the assumption that the 10 stocks are an average representation of the equity universe and that all 10 are not about to go bankrupt. The very principle of diversification, though, assumes that one or two might face some trouble. Diversification cushions the portfolio from the risk of individual corporate problems.

The degree of systematic (market) risk from diversification is also a function of the balance of the character of the assets represented in the portfolio. This idea of similar and dissimilar movements in the relative prices of assets, or for that matter between stocks, is known as *correlation*. For example, a well-diversified portfolio includes a number of assets that are not closely *correlated*. If one performs badly, it will be offset by others that do well, i.e., are not correlated. The two assets, therefore, have the effect of counterbalancing each other. It is always important to have some portion of your portfolio oriented toward equities and growth, but making an allocation in other asset classes, such as cash or precious metals, which have a low correlation with equities, gives you some protection.

Balancing the portfolio with a number of instruments that are not closely correlated makes good investment sense. For example, stocks and gold move in different directions over relatively long periods of a year or more. In 1969, stocks lost 8.5 percent, but gold achieved a positive return of over 6 percent. Hedging your bets, i.e., spreading your risk, in these noncorrelated assets makes it possible to significantly reduce your risk.

Table 1.1 shows how well or how poorly the various asset classes (bonds, stocks, and cash) have correlated historically. A reading of 1.00 indicates that the two assets are perfectly correlated, which means that combining them offers only limited benefits. For example, let's suppose you are a conservative investor and require sub-

TABLE 1.1
Correlations of Various Asset Classes

	Aggressive Growth	Corporate Bond	Growth	Growth and Income	Precious Metals	Money Market
Aggressive Growth	1.00	0.40	0.99	0.95	0.42	−0.07
Corporate Bond	0.40	1.00	0.43	0.51	0.07	−0.40
Growth	0.99	0.43	1.00	0.98	0.42	−0.09
Growth and Income	0.95	0.51	0.98	1.00	0.39	−0.08
Precious Metals	0.42	0.07	0.42	0.39	1.00	−0.08
Money Market	−0.07	0.04	−0.09	−0.08	−0.08	1.00

stantial income. This means that you would naturally gravitate to a policy of allocating a high proportion of your assets to corporate bonds. (For this exercise we are ignoring the possibilities of asset rotation around the business cycle and other important considerations, such as psychological ability to bear risk, etc.) In Table 1.1, corporate bonds on the vertical scale, cross-referenced to corporate bonds on the horizontal scale, have a correlation of 1.00. In effect, diversifying into corporate bonds is not going to help because it makes no sense to diversify into an identical item.

On the other hand, in Table 1.1 we can see that corporate bonds correlate only about half the time with growth and income funds, so they would represent a reasonable offset. The relationship between corporate bonds and precious metal funds is even more striking since the correlation has declined to 0.07. This means that they move in the same direction less than 10 percent of the time. The same observation can be made for the relationship between corporate bonds and money market funds. Precious metal funds have the advantage that they are a hedge against inflation, but they produce very little in the way of income. On the other hand, money market funds do produce income but are useless as a long-term inflation hedge.

A diversified portfolio does not necessarily imply lower returns but inevitably guarantees a reduction in risk, provided that the assets in question are not perfectly correlated. *The beneficial effects of diversification are, therefore, best felt when the correlation between asset classes and industry groups is greatest.* This is one reason why an investor is always advised to maintain a portion of the portfolio in each asset class—so that if his judgment of market conditions is wrong, the overall performance is hedged to some extent.

The concept of correlation should also be extended to the equity portion of a portfolio. Many people believe that they are dealing in a stock market, but it is, in fact, a market of stocks. This is because many issues are moving in different directions within any given time frame. It is true that in a bull market most stocks rally and in a bear market most decline, but there remains a substantial amount of difference in the performance of the various industry groups and the stocks that they represent. Even within the stock portfolio itself, it is important to diversify among industry groups that have a low correlation with one another. For example, an industry group rotation develops over the course of the business cycle. At the beginning, when the economy is digging itself out of recession, utilities and other industries whose profits are particularly enhanced by falling interest rates put in their best price performance, and inflation sensitive stocks, such as mines and oils, put in their worst. As the economy moves into the terminal recovery phase, when inflationary pressures are greatest, utility issues start to decline, but the market averages are buoyed by mining and energy issues, which thrive in this kind of environment. A portfolio that is balanced between a number of diverse groups is better positioned to avoid both market and nonmarket risk for virtually the whole cycle.

DIVERSIFICATION CAN ALSO LEAD TO BIGGER GAINS

We can also look at diversification not so much from risk control but from the more positive aspect of spreading the net in order to increase the chances of landing a big fish. Say, for example, we had decided to invest in some fast growing junior companies. One possibility would be to limit the purchase to one or two well-researched candidates. We may find that we now own a future Xerox, but the odds would be pretty slim. On the other hand, an investment in 10 different companies would probably result in one or two very good winners, a couple of mediocre performers, and perhaps one or two major losers. At first glance, you might think that the effect of this combination of winners and losers is more or less a zero sum game. However, this is rarely the case because it is not unusual for a small growth company to increase two or three times in value over a two-to three-year period. On the other hand, losing stocks are unlikely to go out of business, so the strong ones have a tendency to more than outweigh a 40 or 50 percent decline in another of the holdings. Even if we take an extreme case of a bankrupt stock that was purchased for $12, zero is as low as it can possibly get, while it is not unusual for a winning stock to triple or quadruple. In Table 1.2 we

TABLE 1.2
Diversified Portfolio of Aggressive Stocks

	Cost ($)	Gain or Loss (%)	Market Value
Company 1	12	+100	24
Company 2	12	+ 50	18
Company 3	12	−100	0
Company 4	12	− 25	9
Company 5	12	− 33	8
Company 6	12	+ 50	18
Company 7	12	+ 15	13.8
Company 8	12	+ 15	13.8
Company 9	12	+ 15	13.8
Company 10	12	+ 15	13.8
Company 11	12	+ 15	13.8
Company 12	12	+ 15	13.8
Total	**144**		**159.8**
	PROFIT $15.8 (11.0%)		

can see that even with one of the stocks falling to zero and two others experiencing sizable losses, the portfolio still puts in a reasonable performance with an 11 percent gain.

A classic example illustrating the folly of not adopting the principle of diversification was given by that great investment legend Roger Babson in his book *Actions and Reactions*. In the book, Babson recounts how a friend asked him in 1907 to recommend a stock to buy. At the time, Babson was writing a chapter on diversification and had been following 10 stocks, so he recommended all 10 to his friend. The prospect of following all 10 issues was too daunting, so Babson's friend asked him to single out one issue. Babson recalls that during the next two years the average price of the 10 issues gained 50 percent, but the one stock he had singled out did not advance at all. Need we say more!

2
Securities in the Asset Allocation Mix

Before an asset allocation decision can be made, we need to learn a little more about the scope and characteristics of the various instruments that make up a portfolio. The discussion in this book will be confined to bonds, stocks, publicly traded inflation hedge vehicles, and cash. These are described in this chapter under the heading of "securities." These assets can also be purchased in the form of mutual funds, and because these are a very specialized topic in their own right, mutual funds are covered in Chapter 3.

Other asset possibilities include real estate, oil and gas partnerships, art, and so forth. It is important for an investor who might own such assets to take them into consideration when formulating overall investment objectives and strategy. However, the problems of pricing and liquidating them makes it very difficult, if not impossible, to execute the principles of asset allocation set out in subsequent chapters. For example, oil leases or real estate may be excellent long-term investments, but for the most part, they represent specific situations for which pricing data are not readily available. The asset allocation process, as described here, involves the slow but steady rotation of assets. How, for example, can you sell

10 percent of an office building and rotate the proceeds into 5 percent of an old master? Clearly this is an impossible task, so these vehicles have been excluded from the discussion.

This chapter will examine the characteristics of various asset classes, beginning with the safest and gradually proceeding to the more risky vehicles.

CASH

We normally think of cash as some form of deposit in a bank or a money market fund, but definitions of cash can be expanded to include any debt instrument with a maturity of less than one year. Obligations that fall into this definition are called "money market" securities. They qualify as cash because they do not fluctuate much in price and are liquid, i.e., they can easily be bought and sold. Cash instruments can run the gamut from savings or money market deposits to bank CDs, Commercial Paper IOUs, and Treasury Bills.

The prices of fixed income securities are determined by fluctuations in the prevailing level of interest rates. As rates rise, prices fall, and vice versa. The degree of price change for any given interest rate movement depends on the length of time until the due date, known as the *maturity*. The longer the life (maturity), the greater the potential fluctuation. Because money market instruments have very short maturities, market risk is limited. If the instrument is held until maturity, there is, of course, no market risk whatsoever.

Over long periods of time, interest rates can fluctuate a great deal, as indicated in Figure 2.1. Thus, it is possible for instruments with longer maturities to experience significant price fluctuations. The effect of changing interest rate levels and maturity is discussed in the section on bonds later in this chapter.

Some money market instruments, such as savings deposits, pay interest on a monthly basis. The actual amount will be influenced by the prevailing level of interest rates and the size of the deposit. The larger the deposit, the higher the interest rate. Because the principal can be withdrawn at full face value at any time, there is no market

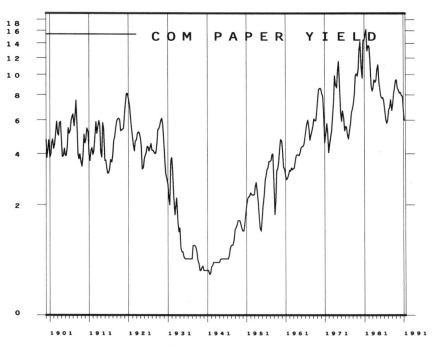

Figure 2.1 Commercial Paper Yield quarterly, 1900–1991. (Source: *Pring Market Review*)

risk whatsoever. However, there is a credit risk due to the ever present, but usually remote, possibility that the institution could default. Because most deposits of this nature are FDIC insured up to $100,000, the possibility of a loss is extremely low.

Certificates of Deposit, or "CDs," are issued for a fixed term by banks and are also FDIC insured up to $100,000.

Treasury Bills are issued by the federal government in denominations of $10,000 and are sold at a discount. For example, a three-month T-Bill might be sold at a price of 98 (i.e., $9,800). This amount, at maturity, would be paid back at full face value ($10,000). In this instance the annualized interest rate would approximate 8 percent, the quarterly 2 percent differential between the price and the maturity value times four. The actual rate would be higher because it is possible to reinvest each quarterly payment at the prevailing rate of interest. This idea of earning interest on interest is known as *compounding*. The major difference between T-Bills and most money market instruments is that they sell at a discount and do not pay interest.

Good quality cash investments have three main advantages. They are liquid, always give a positive return, and are risk free. Their only disadvantage is that the average return is, *for the most part*, much lower than all other forms of investment. The words *for the most part* have been emphasized because there is a time in the business cycle when cash does offer a superior current rate of return, but more about that later.

BONDS

Bonds are longer-term debt obligations that are issued with a repayment date as long as 40 years. Those that mature within two years are known as *short-term bonds*, and those with a lifetime that falls between two and five years are termed *intermediate*. A debt instrument that possesses a maturity in excess of five years is a *long-term bond*. These fixed income securities generally pay interest semiannually. After a bond has been issued by an underwriter, it is freely traded in what is known as the *aftermarket*. When a bond is purchased or sold in the aftermarket, payment will also include an adjustment for accrued interest.

Changes in Interest Rates and Bond Prices

A fixed income security represents an agreement between a borrower and a lender. The borrower agrees to pay back the lender an agreed sum, usually with interest. The agreed sum is known as the *face value* and is almost always equal to the original amount that was lent. The issuing denomination for most bonds is $1,000. The amount of interest is known as the *coupon rate*. Bond prices are usually expressed as a percentage of the face value. In bond terminology the face value is known as *par*.

The prices of debt instruments move inversely with changes in the level of interest rates. The reason for this relationship can be demonstrated by means of an example. Suppose I purchase an 8 percent bond at par. A few months later interest rates rise and are now at 9 percent. My initial reaction might be to sell the bond and purchase another one with the higher 9 percent coupon. Unfortunately for me, everyone else prefers the higher 9 percent rate of interest as well. The only way for my bond to find a willing buyer is for me to sell it at a loss to compensate the buyer for the 1 percent difference in the *current* yield. If the bond matures in one year (for the sake of this example, we will ignore the fact that this is, technically speaking, a money market instrument), the difference would be $10. My bond pays $80, i.e., 8 percent of $1,000, whereas the new bonds yielding 9 percent would pay $90. Because bond prices are expressed as a percentage of the face value, given the prevailing 9 percent rate of interest, the current value of my bond would be 99. If, instead of being a money market instrument, my bond did not mature for 20 or even 30 years, the discount would need to be much greater. Over the life of the bond, the difference in the interest payments would be 20 times $10, or $200. Not only do rising interest rates depress bond prices, but the longer the maturity, the greater the compensation that must be made to a potential purchaser, and therefore the more depressing the effect will be.

The opposite would be true if rates had declined. In that event, my bond would have appreciated in price to compensate me for having to give up a higher rate of current return. The bond would then be said to sell at a *premium* (to its face value). This market reality of premiums and discounts means that the actual return will include some element of capital gain or loss and will therefore differ from the current return. This combination of current income, i.e., the coupon rate plus the discount or less the premium, is known as the *yield to maturity*.

All the calculations for bonds of various coupon rates and prices have already been made. The results are widely published in *yield table books*. In order to establish the yield to maturity (YTM), three pieces of information are needed: the coupon rate, the time remaining to maturity, and the price. Figure 2.2 shows two typical pages nominal yield → 6%

Price	Years to Maturity			
	10	11	12 ←	13
93.50	6.91	6.85	6.80	6.76
94.00	6.84	6.78	6.74	6.70
94.50	6.77	6.72	6.67	6.64
95.00	6.69	6.65	6.61	6.58
95.50	6.62	6.58	6.55	6.52
cost → 96.00	6.55	6.52	6.48 ←	6.46
96.50	6.48	6.45	6.42	6.40
97.00	6.41	6.38	6.36	6.34
97.50	6.34	6.32	6.30	6.28
98.00	6.27	6.25	6.24	6.23

years to maturity / *YTM*

nominal yield → 7%

Price	Years to Maturity			
	5	6 ←	7	8
101	6.76	6.79	6.82	6.84
102	6.52	6.59	6.64	6.67
103	6.29	6.39	6.46	6.51
104	6.06	6.19	6.28	6.35
105	5.83	6.00	6.11	6.20
106	5.61	5.80	5.94	6.04
107	5.38	5.61	5.77	5.89
cost → 108	5.16	5.42 ←	5.60	5.74
109	4.95	5.23	5.44	5.59
110	4.73	5.05	5.27	5.44

years to maturity / *YTM*

Figure 2.2 Bond yield tables for a range of 6 percent (top) and 7 percent (bottom) bonds. (Source: Adapted from Michael C. Thomsett, *Getting Started in Bonds,* John Wiley & Sons, NY, 1991, pg. 55)

from a yield book. Each page makes various assumptions at a specific coupon rate. Some books give calculations based just on round numbers for components, such as 6 percent, 7 percent, 8 percent, etc. Others break it down into fractions or decimals. The example in Figure 2.3 presents data for an 8 percent coupon. In our example, we want to find the yield to maturity, assuming a coupon rate of 8, a price of 95, and a maturity of 15 years. Figure 2.3 shows a yield table for an 8 percent coupon for maturities ranging from 13½ to 30 years. Now look down the extreme left-hand column for the price of 95 and then across to the 15-year column. The yield to maturity is then cross-referenced at 8.6 percent. This same calculation can, of course, be achieved with pocket calculators. Nevertheless, glancing up and down the yield tables gives a good indication of how certain interest rate assumptions might affect prices of differing maturities. Figure 2.3, for example, shows that a price differential of between 90 and 100 for a 20-year maturity would alter the yield from 9.09 percent to 8 percent. This disparity of 1.09 percent is known as a 109 *basis point* difference, a basis point being one-hundredth of a percentage point, or 0.01 percent.

Major Influences on Bond Prices

Three principal factors influence bond prices in general: the maturity, the actual level of interest rates, and the coupon rate.

The Maturity

We have already discovered that the longer the maturity, the greater the movement in bond prices in response to any given change in the general level of interest rates. If an investor feels that interest rates will rise, he or she would be advised to shorten the average maturity of the portfolio. On the other hand, it would make more sense to extend the average maturity if there are indications that interest rates are likely to decline.

The Actual Level of Interest Rates

The higher the actual level of interest rates, the greater a given percentage swing in rates will have on bond prices. Let's compare the effect of a 10 percent increase in interest rates at the 5 percent

Price	Maturity, Yr.															Current Yield
	13½	14	14½	15	16	17	18	19	20	21	22	23	24	25	30	
80	10.86	10.80	10.75	10.71	10.63	10.56	10.49	10.44	10.39	10.35	10.32	10.28	10.26	10.23	10.14	10.00
81	10.69	10.64	10.59	10.55	10.47	10.41	10.35	10.30	10.25	10.21	10.18	10.15	10.12	10.10	10.01	9.88
82	10.53	10.48	10.44	10.39	10.32	10.26	10.20	10.16	10.11	10.08	10.04	10.02	9.99	9.97	9.88	9.76
83	10.37	10.32	10.28	10.24	10.17	10.11	10.06	10.02	9.98	9.94	9.91	9.89	9.86	9.84	9.76	9.64
84	10.21	10.17	10.13	10.09	10.03	9.97	9.92	9.88	9.85	9.81	9.78	9.76	9.73	9.71	9.64	9.52
85	10.05	10.02	9.98	9.95	9.89	9.83	9.79	9.75	9.71	9.68	9.66	9.63	9.61	9.59	9.52	9.41
86	9.90	9.87	9.83	9.80	9.75	9.70	9.65	9.62	9.59	9.56	9.53	9.51	9.49	9.47	9.41	9.30
87	9.75	9.72	9.69	9.66	9.61	9.56	9.52	9.49	9.46	9.43	9.41	9.39	9.37	9.35	9.29	9.20
88	9.60	9.57	9.55	9.52	9.47	9.43	9.39	9.36	9.34	9.31	9.29	9.27	9.25	9.24	9.18	9.09
89	9.46	9.43	9.41	9.38	9.34	9.30	9.27	9.24	9.21	9.19	9.17	9.15	9.14	9.12	9.07	8.99
90	9.32	9.29	9.27	9.25	9.21	9.17	9.14	9.12	9.09	9.07	9.06	9.04	9.03	9.01	8.97	8.89
90½	9.25	9.22	9.20	9.18	9.14	9.11	9.08	9.06	9.04	9.02	9.00	8.98	8.97	8.96	8.91	8.84
91	9.18	9.15	9.13	9.11	9.08	9.05	9.02	9.00	8.98	8.96	8.94	8.93	8.92	8.90	8.86	8.79
91½	9.11	9.09	9.07	9.05	9.01	8.98	8.96	8.94	8.92	8.90	8.89	8.87	8.86	8.85	8.81	8.74
92	9.04	9.02	9.00	8.98	8.95	8.92	8.90	8.88	8.86	8.84	8.83	8.82	8.81	8.80	8.76	8.70
92½	8.97	8.95	8.93	8.92	8.89	8.86	8.84	8.82	8.80	8.79	8.78	8.76	8.75	8.74	8.71	8.65
93	8.90	8.88	8.87	8.85	8.82	8.80	8.78	8.76	8.75	8.73	8.72	8.71	8.70	8.69	8.66	8.60
93½	8.83	8.82	8.80	8.79	8.76	8.74	8.72	8.71	8.69	8.68	8.67	8.66	8.65	8.64	8.61	8.56
94	8.77	8.75	8.74	8.72	8.70	8.68	8.66	8.65	8.64	8.62	8.61	8.60	8.59	8.59	8.56	8.51
94½	8.70	8.69	8.67	8.66	8.64	8.62	8.61	8.59	8.58	8.57	8.56	8.55	8.54	8.54	8.51	8.47
95	8.63	8.62	8.61	8.60	8.58	8.56	8.55	8.54	8.53	8.52	8.51	8.50	8.49	8.48	8.46	8.42
95¼	8.60	8.59	8.58	8.57	8.55	8.53	8.52	8.51	8.50	8.49	8.48	8.47	8.47	8.46	8.44	8.40
95½	8.57	8.56	8.55	8.54	8.52	8.51	8.49	8.48	8.47	8.46	8.45	8.45	8.44	8.43	8.41	8.38
95¾	8.54	8.53	8.52	8.51	8.49	8.48	8.46	8.45	8.44	8.44	8.43	8.42	8.42	8.41	8.39	8.36
96	8.50	8.49	8.48	8.48	8.46	8.45	8.44	8.43	8.42	8.41	8.40	8.40	8.39	8.38	8.37	8.33

Price																
96¼	8.47	8.46	8.45	8.45	8.43	8.42	8.41	8.40	8.39	8.38	8.38	8.37	8.36	8.36	8.34	8.31
96½	8.44	8.43	8.42	8.42	8.40	8.39	8.38	8.37	8.36	8.36	8.35	8.34	8.34	8.34	8.32	8.29
96¾	8.41	8.40	8.39	8.38	8.37	8.36	8.35	8.34	8.34	8.33	8.32	8.32	8.31	8.31	8.30	8.27
97	8.38	8.37	8.36	8.35	8.34	8.33	8.32	8.32	8.31	8.30	8.30	8.29	8.29	8.29	8.27	8.25
97¼	8.34	8.34	8.33	8.32	8.31	8.30	8.30	8.29	8.28	8.28	8.27	8.27	8.27	8.26	8.25	8.23
97½	8.31	8.31	8.30	8.29	8.28	8.28	8.27	8.26	8.26	8.25	8.25	8.24	8.24	8.24	8.23	8.21
97¾	8.28	8.27	8.27	8.26	8.26	8.25	8.24	8.24	8.23	8.23	8.22	8.22	8.22	8.21	8.20	8.18
98	8.25	8.24	8.24	8.23	8.23	8.22	8.21	8.21	8.20	8.20	8.20	8.19	8.19	8.19	8.18	8.16
98¼	8.22	8.21	8.21	8.20	8.20	8.19	8.19	8.18	8.18	8.18	8.17	8.17	8.17	8.17	8.16	8.14
98½	8.19	8.18	8.18	8.18	8.17	8.16	8.16	8.16	8.15	8.15	8.15	8.15	8.14	8.14	8.13	8.12
98¾	8.15	8.15	8.15	8.15	8.14	8.14	8.13	8.13	8.13	8.13	8.12	8.12	8.12	8.12	8.11	8.10
99	8.12	8.12	8.12	8.12	8.11	8.11	8.11	8.10	8.10	8.10	8.10	8.10	8.10	8.09	8.09	8.08
99¼	8.09	8.09	8.09	8.09	8.08	8.08	8.08	8.08	8.08	8.07	8.07	8.07	8.07	8.07	8.07	8.06
99½	8.06	8.06	8.06	8.06	8.06	8.05	8.05	8.05	8.05	8.05	8.05	8.05	8.05	8.05	8.04	8.04
99¾	8.03	8.03	8.03	8.03	8.03	8.03	8.03	8.03	8.03	8.02	8.02	8.02	8.02	8.02	8.02	8.02
100	8.00	8.00	8.00	8.00	8.00	8.00	8.00	8.00	8.00	8.00	8.00	8.00	8.00	8.00	8.00	8.00
100¼	7.97	7.97	7.97	7.97	7.97	7.97	7.97	7.97	7.97	7.98	7.98	7.98	7.98	7.98	7.98	7.98
100½	7.94	7.94	7.94	7.94	7.94	7.95	7.95	7.95	7.95	7.95	7.95	7.95	7.95	7.95	7.96	7.96
100¾	7.91	7.91	7.91	7.91	7.92	7.92	7.92	7.92	7.92	7.93	7.93	7.93	7.93	7.93	7.93	7.94
101	7.88	7.88	7.88	7.89	7.89	7.89	7.90	7.90	7.90	7.90	7.90	7.90	7.91	7.91	7.91	7.92
101½	7.82	7.82	7.83	7.83	7.83	7.84	7.84	7.85	7.85	7.85	7.86	7.86	7.86	7.86	7.87	7.88
102	7.76	7.76	7.77	7.77	7.78	7.79	7.79	7.80	7.80	7.80	7.81	7.81	7.81	7.82	7.83	7.84
102½	7.70	7.71	7.71	7.72	7.73	7.73	7.74	7.75	7.75	7.76	7.76	7.77	7.77	7.77	7.78	7.80
103	7.64	7.65	7.65	7.66	7.67	7.68	7.69	7.70	7.70	7.71	7.71	7.72	7.72	7.73	7.74	7.77
103½	7.58	7.59	7.60	7.60	7.62	7.63	7.64	7.65	7.66	7.66	7.67	7.67	7.68	7.68	7.70	7.73
104	7.52	7.53	7.54	7.55	7.56	7.58	7.59	7.60	7.61	7.62	7.62	7.63	7.63	7.64	7.66	7.69
105	7.41	7.42	7.43	7.44	7.46	7.48	7.49	7.50	7.51	7.52	7.53	7.54	7.55	7.55	7.58	7.62
106	7.29	7.31	7.32	7.33	7.36	7.38	7.39	7.41	7.42	7.43	7.44	7.45	7.46	7.47	7.49	7.55
107	7.18	7.20	7.21	7.21	7.25	7.28	7.30	7.31	7.33	7.34	7.35	7.36	7.37	7.38	7.42	7.48
108	7.07	7.09	7.11	7.12	7.15	7.18	7.20	7.22	7.24	7.25	7.27	7.28	7.29	7.30	7.34	7.41

Figure 2.3 Bond yield table: 8 percent coupon, 13½ to 30 years. (Source: Adapted from Martin J. Pring, *How to Forecast Interest Rates*, McGraw-Hill, NY, 1981, pg. 16)

and 10 percent levels on an instrument with a one-year maturity. We know that the former will pay $50 and the latter $100 in interest over the course of a year. Thus, a 10 percent increase in current coupon rates to 5.5 percent and 11 percent, respectively, will mean that debt instruments paying the new rates will offer a current return of $55 and $110 per annum, respectively. This means that the bond with the 5 percent coupon will have to decline in price to compensate for the higher $5 payout made by new issues: but the other one will have to be discounted more because the difference of $10 is greater. This example featured a one-year maturity, but of course the differences in price movements would be much greater with longer maturities. In effect, the higher the general level of interest rates, the greater the sensitivity of prices will be for any given percentage change in that level.

The Coupon Rate

The lower the coupon rate, the more sensitive bond prices will be to a given change in interest rates. This example differs from the previous one in that we are referring to a change in basis points as opposed to a percentage change in the interest rate level. Let's assume that two 30-year bonds are both yielding 10 percent and that interest rates fall from 10 percent to 8.85 percent. The first bond has a coupon rate of 10 percent and the second has a rate of 8 percent. The yield table indicates that the first bond will respond to the decline in rates by rallying from 100 to 112 and the second from 81 to 91. The increase in actual points is greater for the bond with a 10 percent coupon but in percentage terms, which is what really counts, the bond with the lower coupon rate advances more (12.5 percent compared to 12 percent). In this instance, we are just considering capital appreciation potential. Retired investors requiring high current income would probably wish to forgo the greater leverage and reduced current yield offered by a low coupon bond. If interest rates are falling, an investor would be better off with a bond with a long maturity and a low coupon. The reverse would be true if rates in general were rising.

Influences on the Yield of Specific Securities

The yield of a specific bond is affected by four main influences: the credit rating of the issuer, marketability, maturity, and taxation.

Credit Rating of the Issuer

Generally speaking, the greater the perceived credit risk, the higher the yield.

Marketability

Issues that are actively traded are said to be *liquid*. If a particular bond issue can be easily bought and sold, the risk to the holder, whether a dealer, institution, or individual, is much less. Therefore, the yield will be lower as well. Generally speaking, the larger the issue the greater the liquidity because the ownership is likely to be more widespread. United States Treasury issues, for example, are issued in large quantities and are very liquid. On the other hand, many tax-exempt issues are quite limited in size and distribution. Once they have been placed, they tend to remain in the hands of the original purchaser. As a result, these issues are often extremely illiquid. Quality also has an influence on marketability. When prices decline sharply, bonds of lower quality offer greater risk. Hence, they are less desirable, even when some compensation is made in the form of an existing higher yield structure.

Maturity

Long-term loans are riskier than short-term loans because the longer the period the greater the possibility of something going wrong, and the more substantial is the risk. Longer maturities also have a tendency to become progressively more illiquid as time passes. This factor also adds to the risk content of the yield. The concept of differing yields for different time periods is expressed graphically in Figures 2.4 and 2.5. They show a hypothetical yield

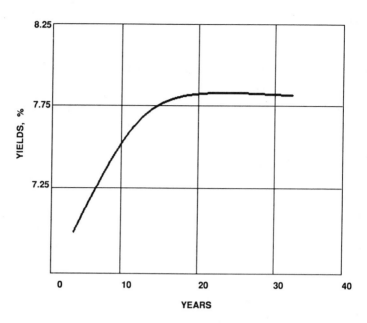

Figure 2.4 Example of a positive yield curve. (Source: *Pring Market Review*)

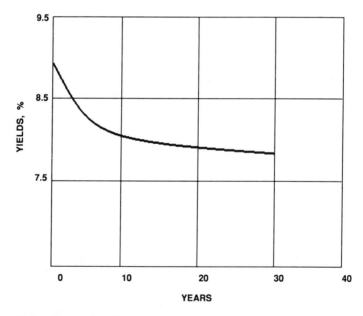

Figure 2.5 Example of a negative yield curve. (Source: *Pring Market Review*)

for securities of a given category, such as Treasury issues for a 30-year time span. Figure 2.4 shows that yields get progressively higher as the maturity increases. This is the normal shape of the yield spectrum when the yield curve is said to have a *positive slope*. When monetary policy is stringent, the slope will invert, or go negative, in the sense that short rates will yield more than longer ones (see Figure 2.5). This is an unusual, but normally temporary event that is almost inevitably followed by a recession. We will have more to say on the yield curve in a later chapter.

Taxation

Taxation has an important effect on the yield structure. Corporate bonds that are taxable at the federal, state, and local levels yield more. Federal interest is not taxable by the states, which means that investors require less in interest compensation. Tax-exempt securities are free from all taxes within the issuing state and normally yield less.

Zero Coupon Bonds

When a bond is issued, the borrower agrees to pay an amount of interest, usually semiannually, together with the principal on the maturity date. In the early 1980s the practice of "stripping" bonds arose. Investment bankers realized that some investors required only current income, i.e., the actual coupons, while others preferred the capital appreciation element or did not require the income immediately. The stripping process involves removing the coupons and selling the interest and capital gain portion separately. Zero coupon bonds, therefore, pay no income. Instead, the investor is compensated by the fact that the bonds sell at a deep discount and will one day mature for the stipulated face value.

Zero coupons come with two advantages. First, in a bull market they appreciate at a much faster rate than coupon bonds. Second, the bonds are priced to sell on the basis of reinvested interest at current, not future, interest rates. Let's look at an example. You buy a 30-year coupon bond at par and the prevailing rate of interest is 9 percent. Two years later rates have dipped to 7 percent. It is true that your bond will have risen in price, but the interest can be reinvested only at the new prevailing rate, i.e., 7 percent. In other words, coupon bonds come with a reinvestment risk. On the other hand, the pricing of zero coupon bonds assumes that the original interest rate will continue throughout the life of the bond.

There are, of course, two sides to every question, and the disadvantage of zeros is that they can fall in response to rising rates just as quickly as they rise when rates fall. By the same token, the coupon bond does at least pay out some current income that can be reinvested at the new, higher rate. This is not possible with zeros. Finally, zero coupon bonds often have a very high spread between the bid and ask price, often as much as 2 to 3 percent. This means that they should be held for long periods; otherwise transaction costs will eat most, if not all, of the profits. Zero coupon bonds are, in effect, a highly leveraged way to play the bond market, but unfortunately, leverage can work both ways. One additional disadvantage of zeros is that the federal government requires taxpayers to calculate the theoretical value of the interest and pay the appropriate tax. Because this is a calculated value, whether the price of the bond rises or falls, the holder is forced to pay tax on income not actually received. This is one of the reasons why zero coupon bonds are more suitable for tax-exempt accounts such as IRAs, pensions, SEPs, etc. Zero coupon bonds are issued and traded in the federal government, corporate, and tax-exempt sectors.

Bond Market Sectors: The Federal Government

The federal sector encompasses all obligations issued or guaranteed by the federal government. Federal obligations trade at lower yields than corporate bonds, partly because they are considered to be of the highest quality and are backed by the full faith and credit of the federal government, and partly because the interest is free from state and local taxes. The spread between equivalent federal and

Aaa corporate issues varies from as little as 20 to as much as 180 basis points. The difference in yield is a function of specific demand/supply relationships between new government and government agency issues, as well as investor preferences for quality throughout the business cycle. During a recession, for example, there may be justifiable investor concern over the credit worthiness of some issues, and investors will require a premium in the yield of the obligations of these corporations to compensate for this perceived risk.

Government bonds are issued in denominations of $1,000, although the investor will always pay a premium on the price in the aftermarket for amounts of less than $1,000,000. Every calendar quarter a government funding takes place when it is possible to purchase bonds on a commission and spread-free basis for amounts as little as $1,000.

The government market is an important benchmark for all other United States dollar-denominated long-term interest rates, and individual maturities are widely quoted in the financial press.

The federal government also guarantees some debt instruments issued by government agencies and other related institutions. Government guaranteed debt normally sells at a slightly higher yield than instruments actually issued by the government. The premium can vary from as little as 20 to as much as 100 basis points. Agency paper can be roughly categorized into two types: those issued by government *owned* agencies and those issued by government *sponsored* agencies. The latter are not actually guaranteed but consist of agencies originally owned by the Treasury whose stock has been transferred to the private sector. These institutions, such as the Federal Home Loan Bank (FHLB) or the Federal National Mortgage Association (FNMA), raise money under the supervision of the Treasury. Actual agency debt would include, among others, obligations issued by the Federal Housing Administration (FHA) or the Government National Mortgage Association (GNMA).

These instruments are quoted in the aftermarket, but because trading activity is much lower than government bonds, the spread between the bid and ask quotations is usually much larger.

The Corporate Sector

The normal reason for issuing a corporate bond is to fund a long-term project, such as a new plant or equipment. As a consquence, the maturity of the bond is often matched with the expected life of the asset. Corporate bonds are quite attractive for tax-exempt accounts because they offer a higher yield than Treasury securities. Corporate bonds generally fall into two categories, secured and unsecured. The former are pledged or secured by a specific asset or set of assets. This could take the form of land, buildings, or even plant and equipment. Unsecured instruments, on the other hand, are limited to a general obligation and are, therefore, backed only by a corporation's ability to generate income.

The job of assessing the credit worthiness of corporations is a very difficult and time-consuming process. Therefore, most investors rely on credit rating services. The two most widely known are Moody's and Standard and Poor's (S&P). Highest quality bonds are rated AAA by Moody's or Aaa by Standard and Poor's. AA and A issues are also considered investment grade, but from there on the trend is down. A corporation is given a BBB rating when it is still financially sound but some doubt exists as to whether it represents a certain degree of speculation. A BB rating is triggered when interest coverage from earnings is low, and B when actual payments could suffer during times of economic softness. Ratings continue on down to C and D benchmarks, which are given to everything from highly speculative issues to those actually in default.

Yields on corporate bonds usually move in sympathy with Treasury securities, although the spread between them will fluctuate, owing to specific supply/demand fundamentals in the various markets. Generally speaking, the higher the quality, the closer the relationship with the government market. In hard economic times, for example, when the fear of default is widespread, the poorer BBB and below issues may actually diverge from the Treasury market until it is clear that either conditions have improved or that the yield structure is now at a wide enough differential to compensate investors for the additional risk.

The corporate market is often divided into three sectors: utility, industrial, and railroad. Utilities have traditionally been regarded as the bellwethers because they are usually high quality due to the stability of their earnings. Another important plus for this sector is the fact that these bonds are usually issued in large amounts because of huge capital requirements. As a result, utility issues are highly liquid and widely quoted, which makes them a convenient investment vehicle for all investors.

The Tax-Exempt Sector

Tax-exempt bonds are issued by state and local governments. The interest from these securities is exempt from federal tax and income tax from the issuing state. Tax-exempt bonds are most suitable for individuals and corporations in the highest tax brackets. Not every bond is exempt from taxes from *every* state and *every* local authority. Therefore, you should always check this before making a purchase. Also, the tax-exempt status may not be recognized by other states, e.g., New York bonds are taxable in New Jersey, and so forth.

Tax-exempt securities are either general obligation bonds, which are backed by the full faith and credit of the issuer, or said to be revenue bonds, where the security comes from the ability of the issuer to generate income from a specific tax or user fee, such as a toll road, water authority, etc. Tax-exempt issuers are classified by the rating services in a similar manner to corporate securities. Bonds with a rating of AAA, AA, or A are generally considered to be safe, whereas a BBB, BB, or B rating denotes various forms of risk. A classification of B indicates that default may be imminent.

Because these bonds offer their holders considerable advantages, the market prices them to yield less than either corporate or Treasury issues. One major problem is that most tax-exempt obligations are not traded as actively as other sectors. This means that they can be highly illiquid. Let's suppose you wanted to dispose of your bonds, and the dealer who purchases them puts them into inventory. The bonds may remain there for some time because of a lack of potential buyers. If the market declines in the meantime, the dealer can be left with a substantial loss. This potential risk requires some compensation, which takes the form of a very wide spread between the bid and asking prices. This clearly works to the disadvantage of the investor who does not buy and hold for the long term.

Treasury Versus Non-Treasury Issues

Treasury issues are widely quoted, highly liquid, and are bond market leaders, and, therefore, are our preferred vehicle for asset allocation. Treasury issues have an additional advantage because most series are noncallable. Many bond issuers have a clause written in the bond covenants that some or all of an issue can be redeemed either at the issuer's option or completely at the discretion of the issuer. This means that if interest rates fall sharply, the bondholder will be forced to sell the bonds back to the issuer at a specified price. The problem is that the holder of the bond is not then in a position to reinvest the proceeds at the original high rate of interest but at the greatly reduced new current level. This disadvantage does not occur with *most* Treasury issues because they cannot be called. Callable and noncallable issues are differentiated in the financial press by the fact that noncallable issues have one date immediately following the month, and callable issues have two dates. In Figure 2.6, for instance, the bonds with one date (e.g., Aug. 05 and Feb. 06) are noncallable, and the one with two dates (i.e., Aug. 03–08) is callable. The first number, 03 (i.e., 2003), is the

Treasury Bonds, Notes, and Bills

Rate	Maturity Mo./Yr.	Bid	Asked	Change	Asking Yield
10¾	Aug. 05	119 : 09	119 : 13	−10	8.39
9⅛	Feb. 06	106 : 28	109 : 00	−11	8.30
8⅛	Aug. 03–08	100 : 12	100 : 16	−13	8.31

Figure 2.6 Callable vs. noncallable issues.

date when the government has the right to call the bond, and the second number, 08 (i.e., 2008), is the maturity date.

During the recessionary part of the business cycle, credit risks are greatest, and this forces up the yields on poorer quality instruments in general. This may or may not represent a real risk for a specific issue. But no matter whether it is real or perceived, it is possible for one or two well-published defaults to affect a number of issues. The problem is that many investors do not have the time or resources to investigate whether the risk is real or implied and are, therefore, much better off with Treasuries. A final advantage of federal government obligations is that tax-exempt and corporate issuers could flood the market with securities and push down prices. This situation is unlikely to happen in reverse because it is more likely that a spate of Treasury issues would depress the prices of the other sectors, rather than resulting in Treasury yields rising *above* those of corporate and tax-exempt issues.

Convertible Bonds

Some corporate bonds give the buyer the option to hold them until maturity or convert them into common stock. These are known as convertible bonds. Normally they are junior debentures and are not secured by anything other than a promise to pay. If so, the holder will rank below all other bondholders should the company go bankrupt. Your first task when selecting a convertible bond is, therefore, to satisfy yourself on the company's financial stability. Because of the conversion feature the convertible bond represents one important exception to the normal rule—the lower the yield, the lower the risk.

Convertible bonds trade off two things, the price of the common stock and the general level of interest rates. If the stock price rises, the bond will, too. However, the bond's appreciation will be slower than the stock's at the beginning because of the conversion premium. If the price of the stock falls sharply, the bond will also decline in price. However, once the conversion premium becomes too high and the yield rises close to the level of other debt securities, the bond's price will be influenced more by changes in the general level of interest rates. Convertible bonds, therefore, tend to be far less volatile than the underlying common security but more volatile than ordinary bonds. When you are considering convertible bonds, it is important to learn what the conversion privileges are, how long they are in effect, whether there is any clause that forces conversion, and whether the conversion features protect holders in the event of stock distributions, new issues, etc.

Convertible bonds can be of great benefit for those seeking a compromise between growth and income.

STOCKS

Common Stocks

The purchase of common stocks makes the holder a partial owner in a company. Stockholders do not receive a guaranteed specified amount like bondholders. Instead, the expected return is based on anticipation of future dividend growth and expectation that this will also be translated into a capital gain. Dividends represent a residual after bond interest and other expenses have been paid, which makes equity ownership more risky than owning bonds.

The average annual total return on blue chip stocks since the mid-1920s has been approximately 10 percent. This is an average number, which means that there have been some periods when equities have given a negative return and some when the rewards have been substantially greater. Between 1926 and 1990 investors would have made money in 45 years and lost money in 20. When broken down into monthly time periods, equities lose money about 30 percent of the time. History tells us that generally speaking, the longer you can hold on to your equity position, the greater are your odds of obtaining a positive return. For example, the largest annual loss of 43.3 percent occurred in 1931, and the worst losing streak over a five-year period was 48.9 percent; however, for 10 years it was only 8 percent. If an investor held on for 15 years, there is no period in which the portfolio would have lost money! In terms of odds, the chances of losing money over 1, 5, 10, and 15-year periods drops from 31 percent to 14 percent, 4 percent, and zero, respectively.

The stock market is not a homogeneous vehicle; it is really a market of stocks. Some equities, such as electric utilities, are purchased as much for their current dividend yield as for potential capital appreciation. At the other end of the spectrum, companies that are growing at a rapid rate do not pay out much in the form of dividends but plough profits back into the company. Investors purchase these issues purely for capital gain and, to some extent, the future income stream. Because these growth equities do not pay high dividends, there is not much downside protection in the event of unexpectedly bad news. These securities, therefore, have a tendency to be much more volatile than the more sedate but slower moving utility sector. Their main advantage comes from superior long-term performance.

Valuing Stocks

Establishing when individual equities are over- or undervalued falls out of the scope of this book. However, it is important for any investor to have some understanding of the guidelines that determine whether equities are cheap or expensive.

Price/Earnings Ratios

Price earnings ratios, or P/Es as they are more commonly called, measure the relationship between the price of the stock and the after-tax earnings of each share. In effect, the ratio indicates how many dollars investors are prepared to pay for one dollar's worth of earnings. P/Es for individual companies are influenced by a number of factors, but generally speaking, the two most important ones are speed and consistency of growth. A company that has experienced and is likely to continue to experience a fast rate of earnings growth will, other things being equal, sell at a higher P/E ratio than a slow growing company that has experienced erratic earnings fluctuations. This influence of expected growth is also an important factor in valuing the market as a whole. If corporate profits in general are expected to rise, the P/E multiple that the market puts on the S&P Composite will tend to be higher than if the outlook is uncertain. The general level of P/Es is also influenced by interest rates. The two move inversely so that when interest rates rise, P/E ratios in general will fall. This occurs for two reasons. First, rising interest rates sooner or later adversely affect profits and, therefore, prospects for growth. Second, rising rates mean that bonds become increasingly attractive as an alternative investment to stocks, and money flows out of equities into the fixed income market.

Prices are usually related to earnings on what is termed a 12-month *trailing* basis. This means that the earnings part of the calculation is based on the total for the most recent four quarters. General market P/E ratios have experienced tremendous fluctuations over the last 50 years, but generally the market is considered to be overvalued when the P/E on the S&P Composite is above 22 and undervalued when less than 11. The average is about 14. Figures 2.7 and 2.8 show some historical perspective. The dashed lines indicate the over- and undervaluation extremes. It is apparent from the relationship between the level of the P/E and the market itself that an extreme reading does not necessarily guarantee that the market will reverse direction. It is amazing how, during a bear market, "cheap" stocks have a habit of getting cheaper. Valuation measures are, therefore, more useful in pointing up periods when the probabilities favor buying or selling.

Interpreting the quality of earnings can be a very difficult task. An investor is really interested in identifying profit trends based on day-to-day operations (operating earnings). However, in many cases the actual reported numbers are distorted by changes in accounting conventions, one shot gains from the sale of an asset, special charges or writedowns due to plant closings, inventory revaluations, etc. Other distortions could arise because of an increase in potential share dilution as a result of the issuance of warrants, etc. All or any of these factors can make superficial earnings comparisons with previous years or other companies in the industry misleading. Many of these discrepancies can be discovered

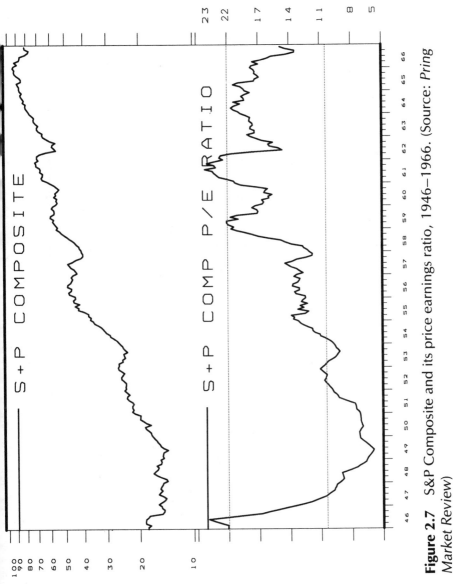

Figure 2.7 S&P Composite and its price earnings ratio, 1946–1966. (Source: *Pring Market Review*)

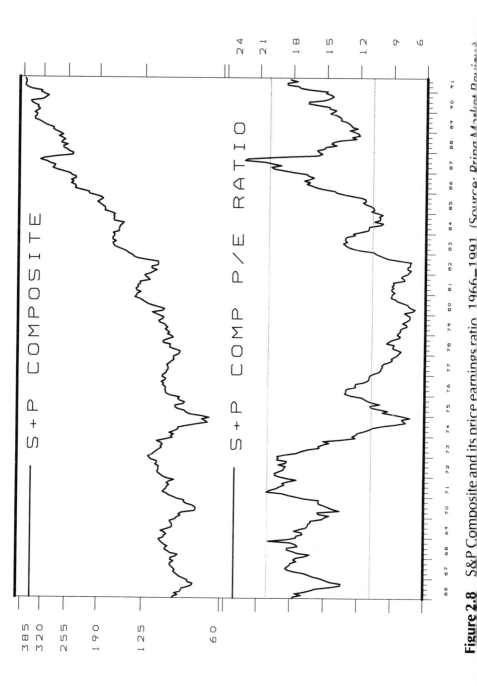

Figure 2.8 S&P Composite and its price earnings ratio, 1966–1991. (Source: *Pring Market Review*)

from the notations that accompany financial statements. A quicker method is to find out from your broker or subscribe to a service such as Value Line, where these distortions will be discussed.

There are a number of ways in which P/E analysis can help in investment endeavors. We know from an earlier discussion that a review of the historical multiple range for a stock, industry, or even the market itself can point in the direction of over- or undervaluation. This knowledge can be combined with the business cycle analysis, discussed in later chapters, to decide to what extent the equity allocation of your portfolio should be expanded or contracted.

The next step is to discover the most attractive sectors. This involves the comparison of the P/E ratio of specific industry groups, such as automobiles, pharmaceuticals, etc., with their historic norms and also with the relationship of their P/Es to the P/E of the overall market. The idea is not only to identify groups that are cheap relative to their own historic valuation range, but to go through this process for their relationship to the market itself. Let's suppose that the food and automobile groups are both currently selling at a multiple of 7 and that they have historically ranged between 6 and 16 times earnings, and 5 and 12 times earnings, respectively. On this basis they each represent good value. However, it is possible that this analysis is being done at a bear market low, in which case many groups will also be offered at bargain prices. How do we tell which one offers the superior value? Part of the answer requires the comparison of the current multiple of the two groups with their historical relation to the multiple of the whole market. Let's suppose that the ranges for the food and automobile groups have traditionally fluctuated between a 30 percent discount and a 10 percent premium, and a 50 percent discount and a 5 percent premium, respectively. If the current market multiple is 10, it would mean that each group, with a P/E of 7, is trading at a 30 percent discount to the market. With a 32 percent discount, foods would represent the better value because this group was at the bottom of its historical range. On the other hand, automobiles would be roughly on par with their normal relationship to the market. Supplementary analysis to the P/E ratio comparison would also be necessary before a final conclusion should be made, but it is certainly a useful starting point for filtering out promising candidates. In this respect it is always important to address the question of whether there are any factors that justify the current low valuation, such as a company or industry maturing to such an extent that previous growth rates are now unattainable. In such instances the chances are that a permanent downward revision in the multiple will have taken place.

The third step involves a repeat of the previous comparison, but this time it involves the specific stocks that make up the previously selected industry groups. In this instance the current P/E of the stocks would be compared both with that of their own historical range and as a relative historical measure to the P/E for that industry. In this exercise more attention would have to be paid to the quality of the earnings of the individual companies than to the industry as a whole, where aggregate earnings data may well cancel out the discrepancies of the individual companies.

Multiple Revisions, Profit Growth, and Capital Appreciation

If you purchase a company at the low end of its historical multiple range in anticipation that it will be reevaluated by the market to the higher end, it is reasonable to expect the price of the stock to appreciate. This upward multiple revision is only part of the story because profits should also increase. Table 2.1 shows how various assumptions of upward multiple revision and profit growth can affect the price of a stock.

TABLE 2.1
Potential Growth Using Various Profit and P/E
Multiple Assumptions

Year	Earnings	Price/Earnings Multiple			
		5	10	15	20
1	$1.00	$ 5.00	$10.00	$15.00	$20.00
5	$2.00	$10.00	$20.00	$30.00	$40.00
10	$4.00	$20.00	$40.00	$60.00	$80.00

Other Valuation Yardsticks

There are many other methods of valuing equities, but an in-depth examination does not fall within the scope of this book.

Convertible Stocks

Convertible preferred shares represent a compromise between a fixed income and a growth security. These issues normally pay a fixed dividend but give the holder the option to convert them into common shares. Because preferred shares typically rank ahead of common ones for dividend payment purposes, they are more secure. Furthermore, if a common share dividend is passed, there is no obligation from the company's point of view to make up for the discrepancy. In many cases preferred shares are cumulative. This means that if the company does fall on bad times and omits a preferred dividend, it is obliged to make up these arrears before common shareholders may again start to receive dividends. The yield on a preferred share is usually much more generous than on a common share and is therefore more attractive to investors seeking a relatively high rate of current return.

Because preferred shares are also convertible into common ones, the investor has a stake in the company's growth prospects as well. With convertible securities the investor can, in some respects, have his cake and eat it. Normally, the conversion privilege will change over time. When the security is first issued, the conversion level will usually be pegged somewhere above the prevailing level of the common stock. The convertible will, therefore, be priced more on its investment value, i.e., in relation to the yield on nonconvertible preferreds. As the price of the common increases, the convertible price also advances and is then said to trade off its conversion value. In an efficient market the convertible preferred will always trade at a premium to the common because of its higher and more secure dividend, but as the price of the common advances that premium will slip. On the other hand, when the common price falls sharply and the conversion possibility becomes less of a factor, the preferred will trade more off its investment value. It will be more protected from a severe downside buffeting than the common shares because of its generous yield. When you purchase a convertible preferred, it is always important to understand the nature of the conversion privileges and how long they will remain in force. In many instances the conversion features will become less generous as the years progress. You should also check to see whether the conversion feature protects holders, in case more common shares are issued. The more shares that are issued, the greater the dilution effect and, therefore, the less attractive the conversion feature will be.

Convertible preferreds are not for everyone but are particularly attractive to risk-averse investors who also need to protect themselves against the loss of purchasing value that arises from inflation.

3
Mutual Funds

Mutual funds evolved at the turn of the last century. They were originally trusts established by bankers and other financial intermediaries as a way of providing affordable professional money management to the small investor. The first fund as we know it today was formed in 1924 by the Massachusetts Investors Trust, which gave its shareholders the right to redeem their shares at net asset value. Today the range of products offered by the industry has grown from a general equity fund to those that specialize in virtually all conceivable areas, both in the United States and around the world. Mutual funds fall into two principal categories, open- and closed-end.

CLOSED-END FUNDS

Closed-end funds are pools of professionally managed investment capital that have a fixed number of shares that can be purchased only from other shareholders. They trade on an exchange or over-the-counter just as any other share, but instead of being in the business of manufacturing or producing a service, the fund is involved in the investment and management of a portfolio of securities. The nature of the portfolio depends upon the mission of the fund. Some are balanced between equities and bonds. Others might be limited to equities, equities in a specific country, and so forth. Figure 3.1 compares the price performance of a specific fund (the U.K. Fund) to an index related to their investment objective (the U.K. market). For a full description of its investment objective (the U.K. market), limitations, and fees charged by the investment managers of a specific fund, you need to consult the original prospectus or one of the many mutual fund reference books.

There are two important factors to take into consideration when purchasing a closed-end fund. First, does the fund's investment objectives correspond to your own? For instance, it does not make

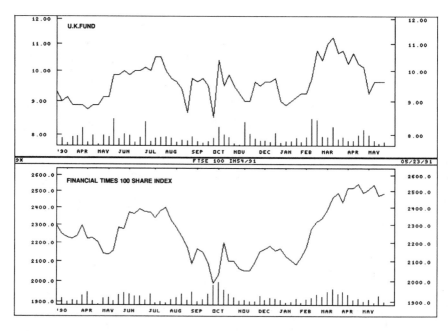

Figure 3.1   Price performance of closed-end funds: United Kingdom Fund vs. United Kingdom Stock Market. (Source: *Pring Market Review*)

much sense to invest in an equity fund if you believe that a bear market has just begun, or in a gold fund if your analysis shows that a recession is just around the corner.

Second, the quoted price of a closed-end fund is not only influenced by the (net asset) value of the underlying portfolio, but can also be subject to wide fluctuations around that value as market participants continually reassess the fund's prospects. Sometimes the net asset value of the outstanding shares is below the quoted price, in which case it is said to be trading at a *discount*. On other occasions, the book value is above the market price, and the fund is trading at a *premium*. The net asset value (NAV) is calculated as follows:

$$\text{Net Asset Value} = \frac{\text{Total Value} - \text{Liabilities}}{\text{Shares Outstanding}}$$

This value is computed daily and can be obtained from publicly offered data bases, such as Commodity Systems Incorporated (CSI), Warner, Dow Jones, etc. *Barron's* also reports the relationship between NAV and price. One would naturally expect the price of the fund and the NAV to be identical, for, after all, if the fund were liquidated, the proceeds would roughly equal the NAV. However, funds can and do fluctuate a great deal around their NAVs for a number of reasons. For example, a fund may be invested in an industry or country that has temporarily fallen out of favor with the investment community. This often happens with bond funds during strong periods of price inflation. On the other hand, the fund could sell at a premium because it is a specialized vehicle for which there are few, if any, alternatives. This could take the form of a country fund, such as the Korea Fund, which has typically traded above its NAV since it is the only way for the average United States investor to participate in the Korean stock market (due to legal restraints affecting foreign investors). Other funds might sell at a premium because they have specialized management that cannot easily be duplicated. An example might be emerging growth companies in a highly technical field. Generally most funds sell at a small discount to NAV. Since the discount or premium represents a rough guide to sentiment, it is generally a good idea to buy a fund when it is trading far below its normal discount or premium, and to sell when the reverse condition holds true. Current premium/discount information is published in *Barron's* on a weekly basis, but historical ranges are harder to come by. Another useful source would be a closed-end mutual fund reference book such as *The Complete Guide to Closed-End Funds,* 2nd ed., by Frank Cappiello, W. Douglas Dent, and Peter W. Madlem (International Publishing Corporation, Chicago, 1990).

We will establish our own principles for allocating assets in subsequent chapters, but fluctuations in discount/premium relationships can be used to develop low risk profitable strategies. While at the University of Alabama, Assistant Professor Seth Copeland Anderson tracked several different closed-end investment fund strategies over three different periods. Essentially, the approach involved the investment of equal amounts of a hypothetical portfolio into several closed-end funds. Purchases were made when the discount of an individual fund fell to a specific level, and it was sold when it reached a predetermined goal.

The results are summarized in Table 3.1. In fact, an investor would have made money during this period just by adopting a simple buy/hold approach, regardless of whether the money was exposed to the funds or the overall market. Nevertheless, the table shows that all of the trading strategies would have beaten the market. The only one that would have been beaten by a buy/hold strategy was to buy at a 30 percent discount and sell when it reached a 15 percent discount in the 1965–1969 period.

These possibilities are described not so much as a strategy that should be followed in isolation, but as one that could be integrated with the business cycle asset allocation approach described later. For example, if our analysis of the economic, financial, and technical conditions indicates that the environment is favorable for equities, it makes a great deal of sense to search out closed-end equity funds selling at a discount of 20 percent because this was the entry point that tested best.

TABLE 3.1

Results of Eight Trading Strategies (Seth Copeland Anderson)

Buy at Discount from Net Asset Value of	Sell When Discount Narrows to	Average Performance		
		July 1965 to Dec. 1969	Jan. 1969 to Dec. 1976	Jan. 1977 to Aug. 1984
5%	0%	+114%	+105%	+260%
10%	5%	+129%	+110%	+262%
15%	10%	+147%	+104%	+334%
20%	10%	+136%	+ 83%	+387%
20%	15%	+135%	+126%	+448%
25%	10%	+171%	+ 61%	+404%
25%	15%	+123%	+ 86%	+387%
30%	15%	+ 49%	+ 98%	+344%
Buy and Hold (No Trading)		+ 86%	+ 51%	+273%
Standard & Poor's 500 Index		+ 24%	+ 49%	+126%

Source: *The Complete Guide to Closed-End Funds*, 2d ed., by Frank Cappiello, W. Douglas Dent, and Peter W. Madlem, 1990. Adapted from a 1986 article in the *Journal of Modern Portfolio Management* by Seth Copeland Anderson.

OPEN-END FUNDS

The second type of mutual fund is the open-end variety, where there is normally no limitation on the number of shares that can be issued. Purchase and sales prices of open-end funds are based specifically on the NAV. Therefore, the funds never sell at a premium or discount. Open-end funds are not publicly traded but are bought and sold through the fund companies directly or through a sales agent, such as a stock broker. Open-end funds are either *load* or *no-load*.

Purchasers of loaded funds pay a sales charge, or load, in order to participate. The load can be as little as 1 or 2 percent or as much as 8 percent. In addition to the load, all funds have a management charge, which varies from 0.5 to 1 percent of the net asset or liquidation value of the fund. The management fee is often a function of the volatility of the fund. For instance, money market funds, which invest only in short-term money market instruments, do not require as much attention as a portfolio comprising a number of very small companies; hence, their management fees will be less than a highly specialized fund.

Other things being equal, investors are better advised to buy no-load funds, which incur no sales charge. Independent research has shown that there is no difference in the performance of load and no-load funds as a class. Because 100 percent of the purchase price of a no-load fund goes to work immediately and nothing is eaten up in distribution charges, it means that on a net basis no-load investments will perform better. This comparison is shown in Figure 3.2. It is important to note, for example, that if $1,000 is invested in a mutual fund with an 8.5 percent load or commission, only 91.5 percent of the original investment will be invested; hence, the fund has to appreciate by 9.29 percent (i.e., $85 divided by $915) just to break even. Because the average historical return from equities is just under 10 percent, this means that anyone paying a load charge of 8 percent is effectively giving up a full year of prospective return.

In some isolated cases, it might make more sense to invest in a loaded fund. For instance, the Fidelity Select Funds permit their investors to switch between over 20 specialized industry funds for a

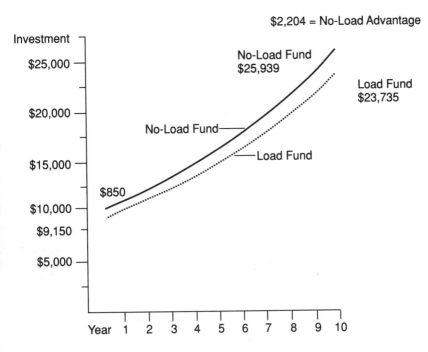

Figure 3.2 Comparison of a $10,000 investment in two mutual funds that are each growing 10 percent per year, compounded annually. (Source: Adapted from Sheldon Jacobs, editor, *The Handbook for No-Load Fund Investors,* The No-Load Fund Investor, Inc., Hastings-on-Hudson, NY, 1990, pg. 27)

nominal fee, but there is a load of 3 percent (2 percent initial, 1 percent on redemption) to move in and out of the family. Because the select concept is a unique way of participating in so many specialized choices, the limited cost of entry represents an exception to the rule. This would be especially true for active investors who are continually rotating their portfolios between various industry groups because they would probably find that these same switches using individual stocks would incur much higher transaction costs overall.

Mutual funds are quoted in the financial press with a bid/ask price as shown in Figure 3.3. No-load funds can be identified by the

	Net Asset Value (NAV)	Offer Price	NAV Chg.
Shearson Funds:			
PrcM	12.23	12.87	−.16
PrnRT	10.90	NL	−.02
PrinII	7.91	NL	−.01

Figure 3.3   Mutual fund quotations.

symbol under the offer price. Some no-load funds have hidden fees, such as redemption charges. Therefore, a prospective investor should always check the full extent of potential charges by carefully studying the fund's prospectus. Once the proper documents have been signed, switching between funds sponsored by the same company is usually as simple as a toll free telephone call. To move money between different companies is more involved unless it is done by check. The problem then becomes one of timing because the mutual fund companies require several days for the check to clear before the account is credited. Many investors prefer to deal with one or two large companies that offer a full line of potential investment candidates.

ADVANTAGES OF MUTUAL FUNDS OVER INDIVIDUAL STOCKS

Mutual funds have the following advantages over individual securities.

1. Performance figures are readily available for analysis.
2. Funds can negotiate lower transaction costs than individual investors.
3. Funds are already diversified.
4. Purchase and redemption can be made easily for a nominal fee.
5. Mutual funds have professional, experienced management.
6. The risk/reward ratio of a specific fund can be determined quickly and accurately.

The main disadvantage of owning a mutual fund is the cost of management. However, this expense will usually be offset by better performance or lower transaction costs than an individual might incur. Certainly, the nominal management fee for mutual fund ownership compares very favorably with those charged by investment advisors for smaller accounts.

The ownership of equities involves two major risks, market and company. The first arises from the possibility that the market itself will decline. This invariably means that the prices of most shares will also lose ground. The second is that an individual company might run into trouble. Equity mutual funds offer immediate diversification, which extends protection against company risk.

The process of diversification is more complicated than just owning a number of different stocks. A more effective method involves investment in equities of different industries that are subject to different economic stimuli and are therefore likely to behave differently at different times. This is known as balancing the portfolio with securities that have a low correlation. For example, financial stocks, such as insurance companies, tend to do better at the beginning of a bull market, and inflation sensitive groups, such as energy, often put in their best performance at the tail end of the cycle. The idea of balancing the portfolio with assets that do not correlate well is discussed in greater detail in Chapter 4.

In any event, the purchase of a mutual fund gives three advantages: a level of diversification that could be achieved only through the purchase of many different individual securities; avoidance of the high transaction costs and time-consuming research associated with the individual acquisition of many securities; and lower minimum cash requirements favor the smaller investor.

USING MUTUAL FUNDS TO OBTAIN INVESTMENT OBJECTIVES

One of the goals of this book is to describe some useful pointers for setting up and carrying out asset allocation investment objectives. This section examines some classifications of mutual funds that can be used to accomplish this goal.

When we look at the vast array of available funds, it is evident that they cover the entire investment spectrum, from ultrasafe Treasury Bill funds to those specializing in highly speculative small company equity funds. This idea is shown graphically in Figure 3.4.

THE MUTUAL FUND PROSPECTUS

A mutual fund prospectus is usually a dry but indispensable document. It is necessary not only because it is a government requirement that a prospective purchaser receive one, but also because it contains pertinent information that a prospective investor will find informative. For example, it discloses the investment objectives of the fund, together with its portfolio restrictions, management fees, and expenses. Potential risks are also mentioned, as are redemption fees and procedures. When totaled, the sum of all fees, expenses, etc., typically come out at about 1 to 1½ percent of net assets. The prospectus also contains information on the latest portfolio holdings, together with some idea of the turnover rate. The portfolio, of course, changes over time, but the prospectus at least gives the purchaser some idea of the potential quality and diversity.

One of the most useful pieces of information contained in the prospectus is the fund's investment objective. Usually the title of the fund will tell you most of what you want to know, but it is always a good idea to check with the prospectus to make sure.

CATEGORIES OF MUTUAL FUNDS

Money Market Funds

Money market funds invest in short-term or money market debt instruments. The objective of these funds is threefold: capital preservation, liquidity, and a high level of current income commensurate with the funds' investment objectives. Under normal economic conditions these funds are quite safe because they are well diversified in a wide variety of securities and issuers. Those with the

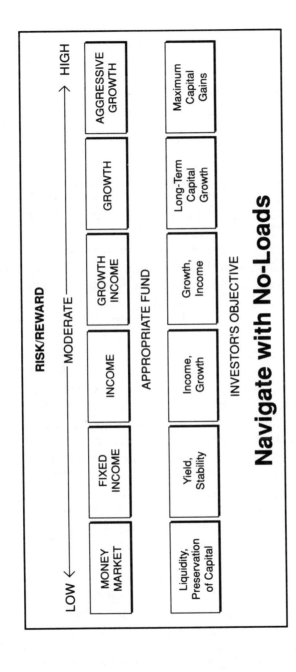

Figure 3.4 Risk vs. reward for various types of funds. (Source: Adapted from Sheldon Jacobs, editor, *The Handbook for No-Load Fund Investors*, The No-Load Fund Investor, Inc., Hastings-on-Hudson, NY, 1990, pg. 34)

highest safety margin of all invest solely in Treasury securities. Safety and return are usually a trade-off, so these funds also yield less than those exposed to corporate issues. Money market funds can usually be redeemed by writing a check on the account in a manner similar to a savings account at a bank, but the funds almost always offer a higher yield.

The second function of a money market account is a convenient place to park cash reserves when alternative investment vehicles are not attractive. The principal disadvantage of a money market fund is that it is not FDIC insured, unlike most bank accounts. By the end of 1991, a default of this kind had never occurred from a shareholder perspective, although one or two funds that had experienced defaults from specific issues decided to absorb the loss in order to maintain shareholder confidence. An obvious way for an investor to avoid a potential risk of this nature is to buy a fund that limits its exposure to federal government short-term obligations, such as the Fidelity Spartan U.S. Government Money Market Fund or the Benham Capital Preservation Trust. The possibility of the federal government's defaulting on its obligations always exists, but it is a more remote risk than a corporation's reneging on its IOU.

Money market funds also invest in tax-exempt securities. Such funds are usually set up for specific states, and their dividends are exempt from federal taxes, as well as state and local taxes for that particular state. Prospective investors are advised to investigate the prospectus to make sure that *all* income qualifies for this tax-exempt status. It is important to make this check because fund managers may occasionally consider the paper of a specific state to be of questionable investment grade and prefer to substitute that for (partially taxable) investments of other states.

In recent years international money funds investing in specific currency denominations have begun to emerge. They will gain popularity in the future for two primary reasons. First, these funds offer investors a convenient opportunity to diversify away from the dollar. Second, these vehicles are in a position to achieve superior nominal returns in countries where the interest rate structure is higher than that of the United States. No reward comes without some degree of risk, and in this case, potential currency risk could offset some of the beneficial effects of higher overseas interest rates. It is unlikely that such funds would actually experience negative returns because foreign currency exposure would always be offset by hedging strategies in order to protect the principal value when denominated in dollars.

Bond Funds

Bond funds are tailored to a wide variety of investment objectives, from high-quality, low-risk Treasury obligations to high-yield, high-risk junk bond funds. Tax-exempt bond funds, based on principles similar to tax-exempt money market funds, are also available. International bond funds, specializing either in a global portfolio or that of a specific country, began to emerge in the mid-1980s and will undoubtedly grow in popularity in the current decade.

Bond funds specialize in all three sectors of the bond market: federal government, corporate, and tax-exempt. The latter two categories can be further subdivided by quality. For example, some funds just specialize in junk bonds (called *high yield* in fund jargon) while others are oriented to issues of AAA quality. Some government funds invest solely in government backed mortgage certificates (GNMA, or *Ginnie Mae*). These certificates are originally issued by an FHA authorized mortgage broker and sold to the fund. Although they have a stated maturity of 20 to 30 years, care has to be paid to the nature of the portfolio because some of the mortgages in the portfolio are prepaid when interest rates experience a substantial decline. This means that the average life of a typical certificate often falls well short of its stipulated maturity. This represents a major disadvantage for the investor because it means that high yields cannot always be "locked in."

An important factor in the risk/reward of bond investments is the length of maturities in the portfolio. A mutual fund company often markets several different funds, each of which is targeted to a different range of maturity. In this way an investor is in a better position to assess the degree of risk associated with a particular fund's average maturity.

The most radical example of this phenomenon is marketed by the Benham Group, which offers a complete family of zero coupon (Target Maturity) bond funds. These maturities range from four to as many as 30 years. Because zero coupon bonds pay no interest, they fluctuate a great deal more in price than coupon bearing instruments. This means that the spread between the bid and ask quotations can be extremely high for the small amounts in which individual investors typically deal. Because the Benham funds are no-load, these transaction costs, where the spread can often be in the 10 percent range, are avoided. This alternative makes a great deal of sense to anyone moving in and out of such instruments on a regular basis. On the other hand, an investor who plans to hold a zero coupon bond for a long period or even to maturity is probably better off buying the bond itself, because a mutual fund management fee of about ½ of 1 percent will add up over a number of years.

In a straight comparison of bonds vs. funds, the bond funds offer diversification, require smaller transaction costs, and are run by professional management who can take advantage of temporary price discrepancies between issues. There are two principal disadvantages. The first is the management fee, usually about ½ to ¾ percent per annum. The second is that substantial amounts of new money flow into the fund during a bond market. This has the effect of diluting the performance from that of an individual bond because this money is eventually put to work at higher prices.

Equity Funds

Equity funds come in many different varieties. In a broad sense, they can be divided into Conservative, Index, Growth, Aggressive Growth, Industry Group (Sector), Gold, and International.

Conservative funds are just that—portfolios limited to equities of the highest quality, i.e., those that have strong balance sheets and consistent earnings growth. Such issues are usually highly liquid and include dividends as an important component of total return. Conservative funds parallel or underperform the market on the way up, but they are far more stable in a declining market.

Index funds are a relatively new addition. They were introduced for those investors who track the S&P Composite or other market averages and require a portfolio of stocks that closely parallels the performance of the average in question. The Vanguard Index Fund was one of the first to be introduced, but in recent years others, such as Fidelity's Spartan Market Index, have been added. This type of fund, provided it is no-load and has insignificant management expenses, offers the individual investor an inexpensive opportunity to duplicate a market index without the necessity of having to buy all of its components and make periodic adjustments as the composition of the average is altered.

Growth funds are sometimes called *long-term growth* funds because their objective is to offer the type of long-term growth sought by conservative investors. Their portfolios are usually too large to maintain the faster growth normally achieved by the more aggressive funds. The investment objectives set out in the prospectus typically emphasize capital gain over current income.

Aggressive growth funds take the biggest risks, and by the same token, experience the greatest volatility, both on the up side and down side. These funds usually perform best in a bull market environment. Even so, one of the keys to even better performance is whether the trend of smaller capitalization stocks relative to the blue chips is a positive one. Figure 3.5 shows the ratio of the Russell 2,000 vs. the Russell 1,000. The former is a proxy for smaller companies favored by the aggressive growth funds. The Russell 1,000, on the other hand, is constructed from the 1,000 companies with the largest capitalization. The line in the lower panel is a ratio between the two. When the line is above its 40-week moving average (MA), it indicates that the smaller stocks are outperforming their blue chip counterparts and vice versa. A rising trend in this ratio, therefore, indicates that an investment in a *typical* aggressive growth fund is likely to outperform a more conservative fund. The word *typical* is highlighted because it is quite possible that several funds in the aggressive category may be in the wrong stocks entirely. All the rising ratio tells us is that the environment for aggressive funds relative to blue chips is positive.

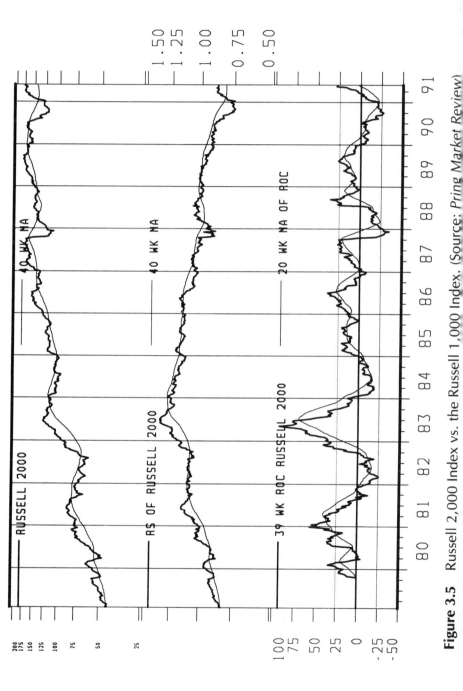

Figure 3.5 Russell 2,000 Index vs. the Russell 1,000 Index. (Source: *Pring Market Review*)

Sector Funds

A later chapter will explain that the stock market experiences an internal rotation between the various industry groups. For instance, at the beginning of the business cycle financial stocks, such as insurance companies, tend to outperform the market, whereas mines and energy issues do better at the end when inflationary pressures are intensifying. Not all groups fit conveniently into this rotation process, and it is more complex than described here. Nevertheless, it is important to note that there is a wide diversity in the performance of various sectors throughout the cycle. Some mutual fund companies have recognized this fact and offer funds that are targeted to specific industries or sectors. The performance of these sector funds will depend to a large part on the general environment for the group as a whole. By investing in these groups, the individual investor has the opportunity of hiring professional management, who should be in a better position to select the better performing issues in the group. Provided that purchase of the fund does not involve a high load, the modest management fee is a small price to pay for the time and effort involved in the research required to sift out the best companies in the industry.

Gold Funds

Gold funds are really a special type of sector fund because they invest primarily in gold shares. For those times in the business cycle when gold is an appropriate asset to hold, these funds represent an efficient vehicle for participation. Gold funds have the inherent advantage over bullion in that they do offer some current return in the form of dividends. This has been particularly true of funds specializing in South African gold shares where payout has traditionally been much greater than in North America or Australia.

4

The Power of Compounding

When most of us consider return, it is only natural that our first thoughts should turn to capital appreciation. That is because capital gain is the form in which the most spectacular short-term gains are achieved. Current income usually takes a back seat, and in some cases gets no consideration at all. This is a shame because the compounding factor of interest and dividends can be a significant ingredient in the long-term performance of a portfolio. For it to be really effective, compounding requires a great deal of time. Unfortunately, in this day of instant analysis and fast track results, this kind of patience and discipline is beyond the scope of most investors. Compounding also lacks the appeal of growth oriented assets and is, quite frankly, not a very exciting proposition.

The term *compounding* usually refers to interest earned on principal, and accumulated interest reinvested from prior periods. However, over long periods of time the compounding element of dividends can also be a significant element in the ultimate total return. The compounding feature of dividends is normally a more dynamic process than that for interest. It is not just a question of reinvesting the fixed dividend each quarter, but in many instances dividend payments are periodically increased. If a dividend doubles over a five-year period, so does the yield on the original investment.

A gradually rising dividend stream is, therefore, a valuable aid to an investor concerned about keeping up with inflation. This growth element is something that is just not available to investors in fixed income instruments.

COMPOUNDING WITH FIXED INCOME SECURITIES

An investor receiving interest or dividends is faced with a choice. The proceeds can either be consumed or reinvested. Obviously the portfolio will grow faster if the current income is reinvested. However, the positive effect is actually greater than might first appear because compounding results in the payment of interest on interest. Table 4.1 shows the difference between a compounding and straight-yield approach. In column four, the cumulative total increases only by the amount of the payment. In column seven, on the other hand, growth is faster because the proceeds are reinvested, and the interest earns interest on interest. Initially there is

TABLE 4.1
Comparison Between Yield on Single Payout and Reinvested Payout at 8 %

	Capital Value	Single Payout Annual Payout	Cumulative Total of Payouts	Reinvested Payout Annual Payout	Capital with Payout Reinvested	Cumulative Total of Payouts
Year 1	$10,000	$800	$800	$800	$10,800	
Year 2	$10,000	$800	$1,600	$866	$11,664	$1,664
Year 3	$10,000	$800	$2,400	$933	$12,597	$2,597
Year 4	$10,000	$800	$3,200	$1,008	$13,605	$3,605
Year 5	$10,000	$800	$4,000	$1,088	$14,693	$4,693
Year 6	$10,000	$800	$4,800	$1,175	$15,869	$5,868
Year 7	$10,000	$800	$5,600	$1,270	$17,139	$7,138
Year 8	$10,000	$800	$6,400	$1,371	$18,510	$8,509
Year 9	$10,000	$800	$7,200	$1,481	$19,990	$9,990
Year 10	$10,000	$800	$8,000	$1,599	$21,590	$11,589
Total	$100,000	$8,000	$44,000	$11,591	$156,457	$55,653

not much difference between the two results, but with the passage of time the variation in performance is considerable. This is because the longer the period, the greater is the proportion of current income earned by the previously reinvested payments.

This table assumes that the interest is paid annually, but in fact, most bonds pay interest on a semiannual basis. This is important over a long period because it means that half the income is available for reinvestment six months earlier than if the whole sum was paid out once each year. Table 4.2 shows this difference. Figure 4.1 compares the difference on two investments paying monthly and annually. Both begin with $1,000, but you can see that the benefits of monthly reinvestment result in a final return of $7,328 compared

TABLE 4.2
Table of Annual Yield Equivalents
(Yield Based on Annual Compounding Equivalent to Stated
Semiannual Yield)*

Semiannual Yield	Annual Yield	Semiannual Yield	Annual Yield	Semiannual Yield	Annual Yield
3	3.02	7	7.12	11	11.30
3¼	3.28	7¼	7.38	11¼	11.57
3½	3.53	7½	7.64	11½	11.83
3¾	3.79	7¾	7.90	11¾	12.10
4	4.04	8	8.16	12	12.36
4¼	4.30	8¼	8.42	12¼	12.63
4½	4.55	8½	8.68	12½	12.89
4¾	4.81	8¾	8.94	12¾	13.16
5	5.06	9	9.20	13	13.42
5¼	5.32	9¼	9.46	13¼	13.69
5½	5.58	9½	9.73	13½	13.96
5¾	5.83	9¾	9.99	13¾	14.22
6	6.09	10	10.25	14	14.49
6¼	6.35	10¼	10.51	14¼	14.76
6½	6.61	10½	10.78	14½	15.03
6¾	6.86	10¾	11.04	14¾	15.29
7	7.12	11	11.30	15	15.56

* The nominal annual yield tabulated here assumes semiannual compounding. If interest were compounded only once a year, the nominal rate would be slightly higher. For example, an 8 percent yield assuming semiannual compounding is equivalent to an 8.16 percent yield assuming annual compounding.

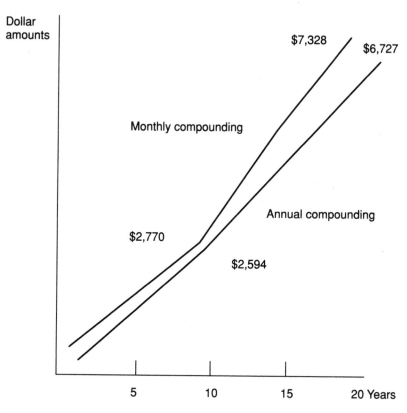

Figure 4.1   How compounding is affected by the frequency of payout.

to the annual contribution, which nets $6,727. The widening differential between the two series demonstrates quite clearly that two factors influence the significance of the compounding effect. These are the overall time period and the frequency of payment. The longer the holding period and the more frequent the payment, the greater the ultimate return.

A third factor is the nominal interest rate. Obviously, the higher the rate, the greater the return. Figure 4.2 compares the results of three different interest rate assumptions and indicates, as would be

Figure 4.2 How compounding is affected by the coupon rate.

expected, that the end results are substantially influenced by the coupon rate.

In this example we have assumed that the coupon and reinvestment rates are the same, but in practice the prevailing interest rate will vary from that of the coupon. Another complicating factor arises from the fact that it is not always possible to reinvest all the proceeds from an interest payment. Let's take the example of a $50,000 bond with an 8.5 percent coupon where payments are made semiannually. Each payment will consist of 4.25

percent of the value, i.e., half of 8.5 percent, which in dollar terms is $2,150. Because bonds are usually issued in denominations of $1,000, it means that the surplus of $150 over the $2,000 amount cannot be reinvested at the prevailing rate for long-term bonds. Therefore, it will have to be parked temporarily in a money market fund or a savings account.

A final complication arises from the fact that the investor will have to pay an additional commission to buy these new bonds. Because the amount of the bond purchase will be small, the commission costs will be proportionately large. One solution would be to invest in a no-load bond mutual fund, where it is possible to reinvest all the proceeds from the dividends without having to pay a commission cost. Even this situation will not be a *pure* compounding play because all such funds charge some kind of management fee.

Perhaps the cleanest solution to the reinvestment problem comes from zero coupon bonds, where the compounding effect not only is built into the price of the bond but is also predictable. This is because the market price of a zero coupon bond assumes that the prevailing interest rate will be the reinvestment rate for the remaining life of the bond. Purchasers of zero coupon bonds do not have to worry about reinvesting the interest payments because this is, in effect, automatically accomplished. There is, therefore, no reinvestment risk or additional commission cost that needs to be considered. The lack of periodic interest payments makes zero coupon bonds extremely sensitive to changes in the general level of interest. Therefore, they represent a highly leveraged way of playing the bond market. This volatility is of little importance to an investor who plans to hold a zero coupon bond to maturity because all bonds will eventually be redeemed at face value. However, the prices of zero coupon bonds can and do fluctuate a great deal more than regular coupon paying issues over the course of a business cycle. The rewards can be considerable for investors who time the cycle correctly but disastrous for those who do not.

If an investor knows that a specific sum of money will be required within a prescribed time period, such as college expenses, zero coupon bonds are an ideal investment because both the maturity and the redemption value of the bond are known in advance. It is important to remember that the theoretical accumulation of interest payments for zeros is taxable in the year incurred. For a tax-free account, such as a pension, Keogh, or IRA, or a nontaxable bond as issued by state and local authorities, this is of no consequence. However, for other accounts the holder is required by law to pay taxes for funds not yet received, in effect reducing the compounding effect of reinvested interest by the amount of the tax.

REGULAR CONTRIBUTIONS AND COMPOUNDING

Investing a lump sum and watching the investment compound is only one alternative. Many individuals set up investment plans that call for regular fixed contributions. Over time the compounding effect of this approach can result in significant gains. Figure 4.3 shows three investment plans, each requiring a $50 monthly contribution to a money market fund. Each series assumes that reinvestment is automatically achieved at the same interest rate. There is not a great deal of difference for the first few years, but with the passage of time, the effect of interest earning interest becomes more pronounced. The difference between 5½ percent and 10 percent is considerable. In reality, the reinvestment rate would fluctuate throughout the 20-year period, so this is not a realistic comparison. Nevertheless, the example does show that modest regular contributions can add up over the years, even with low interest rate assumptions.

The importance of the time element in compounding is shown in Table 4.3, which is based on statistics provided by Market Logic (3471 North Federal Highway, Fort Lauderdale, FL 33306). The Investor A columns assume that an IRA investor makes seven equal payments of $2,000 between the ages of 19 and 25 for a total of $14,000. At that point the contributions cease, and the compounding is left to do its job. Investor B is represented in the other two columns. She delays making any contributions until age 26 but more than makes up for this tardiness through a regular deposit of $2,000 for 39 years. Her total contributions will be $80,000. Logic would

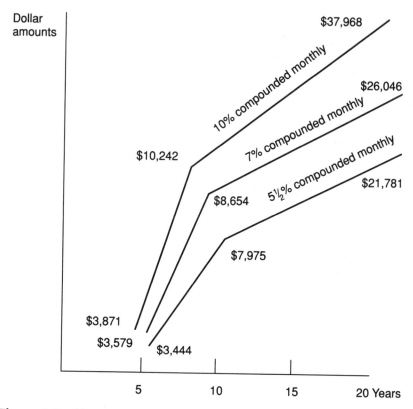

Figure 4.3   How compounding is affected by the reinvestment rate.

tell us that the second investor will make more money than the first simply because she has contributed about six times as much in annual payments. The reality is quite different. It is the early bird that gets the worm. This portfolio, which assumes a 10 percent rate of reinvestment, gains by over 66 times to $930,000 while the second investor's portfolio is limited to an 11-fold increase of $894,000. The reason is that the first investor already had $20,872 working for him before the second one had even made the first contribution. The amounts would be different with alternative interest rate scenarios,

TABLE 4.3
Regular Contributions and Compounding

| Age | Investor A | | Investor B | |
---	Contribution	Year-End Value	Contribution	Year-End Value
8	0	0	0	0
9	0	0	0	0
10	0	0	0	0
11	0	0	0	0
12	0	0	0	0
13	0	0	0	0
14	0	0	0	0
15	0	0	0	0
16	0	0	0	0
17	0	0	0	0
18	0	0	0	0
19	2,000	2,200	0	0
20	2,000	4,620	0	0
21	2,000	7,282	0	0
22	2,000	10,210	0	0
23	2,000	13,431	0	0
24	2,000	16,974	0	0
25	2,000	20,872	0	0
26	0	22,959	2,000	2,200
27	0	25,255	2,000	4,620
28	0	27,780	2,000	7,282
29	0	30,558	2,000	10,210
30	0	33,614	2,000	13,431
31	0	36,976	2,000	16,974
32	0	40,673	2,000	20,872
33	0	44,741	2,000	25,159
34	0	49,215	2,000	29,875
35	0	54,136	2,000	35,062
36	0	59,550	2,000	40,769
37	0	65,505	2,000	47,045
38	0	72,055	2,000	53,950
39	0	79,261	2,000	61,545
40	0	87,187	2,000	69,899
41	0	95,905	2,000	79,089
42	0	105,496	2,000	89,198
43	0	116,045	2,000	100,318
44	0	127,650	2,000	112,550
45	0	140,415	2,000	126,005
46	0	154,456	2,000	140,805
47	0	169,902	2,000	157,086

(continued)

TABLE 4.3 (*Continued*)

Age	Investor A		Investor B	
	Contribution	Year-End Value	Contribution	Year-End Value
48	0	186,892	2,000	174,995
49	0	205,518	2,000	194,694
50	0	226,140	2,000	216,364
51	0	248,754	2,000	240,200
52	0	273,629	2,000	266,420
53	0	300,002	2,000	295,262
54	0	331,091	2,000	326,988
55	0	364,200	2,000	361,887
56	0	400,620	2,000	400,276
57	0	440,682	2,000	442,503
58	0	484,750	2,000	488,953
59	0	533,225	2,000	540,049
60	0	586,548	2,000	596,254
61	0	645,203	2,000	658,079
62	0	709,723	2,000	726,087
63	0	780,695	2,000	800,896
64	0	858,765	2,000	883,185
65	0	944,641	2,000	973,704
Less Total Invested:		(14,000)		(80,000)
Equals Net Earnings:		930,641		893,704
Money Grew:		66-fold		11-fold

but the principle that a few early contributions are more valuable than many contributions made later still holds true. Younger readers should bear this in mind because every year you delay making contributions, you increase the sacrifice required in later years to catch up.

THE COMPOUNDING EFFECT OF DIVIDENDS

The first criterion in selecting individual equity issues is usually based on the potential for capital appreciation, and current return usually takes a back seat. For a patient, income conscious investor, though, dividend growth and its compounding effect can make a very valuable contribution to total return. In this respect, Table 4.4 shows the compounding effect of a $10,000 investment in three stocks with different yield and growth characteristics. All the examples assume that the companies are showing consistent growth and that none of them are cyclical in nature. It is further presumed that the stock with the highest current dividend yield also has the slowest dividend growth, whereas the company with the lowest yield has the highest dividend growth rate. This assumption is made on the basis that a corporation that pays out more will generally have less cash flow to use for expansion than one that is more miserly in its dividend distribution policy. It is also true to say that high yields do not always result from higher dividend payout from profits, but this is normally the case. In the first example, it is assumed that a company pays an initial dividend of $400 (i.e., 4 percent of $10,000) and that the dividend is increased by a factor of 5 percent per

TABLE 4.4
Compounding Effect of Dividend Payouts

Year	Company A Initial Yield 4% Dividend Increases 5% Per Annum	Company B Initial Yield 2.5% Dividend Increases 10% Per Annum	Company C Initial Yield 1.0% Dividend Increases 15% Per Annum
1	$400	$250	$100
2	$420	$275	$115
3	$441	$303	$132
4	$463	$333	$152
5	$486	$366	$175
6	$511	$403	$201
7	$536	$443	$231
8	$563	$487	$266
9	$591	$536	$306
10	$621	$589	$352
11	$652	$648	$405
12	$684	$713	$465
13	$718	$785	$535
14	$754	$863	$615
15	$792	$949	$708
16	$832	$1044	$814
17	$873	$1149	$936

Source: Pring-Turner Capital Group

annum. From a purely income point of view, the higher yield and the lower growth rate compare very favorably in the early years and only after year 12 or year 17 do the higher growth companies come into their own. We should also note that in general faster growing companies will also increase more in value, but that is another story because this exercise is done from the aspect of an income conscious investor with greater interest in the compound features of dividend growth. Higher yielding, slower growing corporations will also be associated with significantly reduced volatility. This investment characteristic is sought by more conservative investors.

CONSISTENTLY MODEST RETURNS VERSUS VOLATILE RETURNS

We have already discovered that small changes in the reinvestment rate of interest payments can result in significant differences in portfolio returns over a 10-year period and that this effect is magnified the longer the time span. We can also relate this idea to the compounded total return for the portfolio as a complete entity.

In this respect, Table 4.5 sets out the compounded total return for a portfolio over a 25-year period using several different growth scenarios. It is indeed impressive to see how an incremental increase in the average compounded return from 7 percent to 10 percent results in a difference between $10,000 growing to $19,700 and $25,900. The important point to bear in mind is that it is not necessary to take big risks in order to obtain big gains when time is on your side. You may think that it is necessary to obtain high returns of 15 percent, 20 percent, or even 25 percent in order to build wealth, but this is definitely not the case. You stand a far better chance of achieving a superior long-term financial goal by using the asset allocation strategies outlined here. They can help you achieve an incremental improvement in the average annual return better than going for the high risk, fast buck. Table 4.5 shows quite clearly that a seemingly small increase in growth can result in substantially better long-term results.

It is also important to remember that if you go for fast, aggressive

TABLE 4.5
Compounding of $10,000 Using Various Assumptions

Years	6%	7%	8%	9%	10%	11%	12%	13%	14%
1	10,600	10,700	10,800	10,900	11,000	11,100	11,200	11,300	11,400
5	13,400	14,000	14,700	15,400	16,100	16,900	17,600	18,400	19,300
10	17,900	19,700	21,600	23,700	25,900	28,400	31,100	33,900	37,100
15	24,000	27,600	31,700	36,400	41,800	47,800	54,700	62,500	71,400
20	32,100	38,700	46,600	56,000	67,300	80,600	96,500	115,200	137,400
25	42,900	54,300	68,500	86,200	108,300	135,900	170,000	212,300	264,600

Source: Pring-Turner Capital Group

TABLE 4.6

Comparison of a Consistent Modest Growth Rate with an Erratic Growth Rate

Year	Example A		Example B	
	Growth Rate Per Annum	Cumulative Value	Growth Rate Per Annum	Cumulative Value
0	0%	100	0%	100
1	8%	108	20%	120
2	8%	117	20%	144
3	8%	126	20%	173
4	8%	136	20%	207
5	8%	147	−35%	136
6	8%	159	20%	162
7	8%	171	10%	178
8	8%	185	−15%	151
9	8%	200	20%	181
10	8%	216	10%	200

Source: Pring-Turner Capital Group

gains, the volatility factor also increases. We all like upside volatility, but downside volatility is something most of us could do without. Let's look at this compounding question from another aspect by comparing a consistent 8 percent tortoise with a more aggressive financial hare. Column 2 under Example A in Table 4.6 represents the change in value of an initial investment of $100 and assumes a consistent 8 percent annualized growth rate. Column 2 under Example B, on the other hand, presents the picture of a more aggressive investor who is able to achieve 20 percent gains in six out of 10 years. You would think that this would be enough to beat the 8 percent investor, but we also have to remember that where there is substantial gain, there is also plenty of risk. It is, therefore, reasonable to assume that even the most savvy investor will experience a couple of years of losses. It turns out that these are the only periods that he is beaten by the 8 percent tortoise, but this is sufficient to result in a poorer performance overall. If the actual percentage gains of the two investors are summed and averaged, the aggressive investor actually wins with an average annual increase of 9 percent compared to 8 percent. Why then is the more conservative investor ahead at the finish? The answer is that it takes a larger percentage increase to come back from a loss. For example, in Year 5, when the aggressive portfolio loses 35 percent, it needs to grow by 54 percent to get back to the break-even point. When we also consider that the tortoise takes far less risk than the hare and still puts in a better performance, the case for slow but steady returns becomes very appealing.

5

Manage Risk, and the Profits Take Care of Themselves

Calculations about potential reward usually receive top priority when a new investment strategy comes under consideration. This has traditionally been the case, but the financial boom of the 1980s and its promises of fast and easy profits placed even greater emphasis on performance. The media routinely bombard us with stories glorifying the latest 6- or 12-month investment performance of the best money managers and mutual funds, so it is easy for anyone to draw the conclusion that they are falling behind in the investment game. The commentators seldom discuss the amount of risk required to achieve those gains, whether the investment style of those particular managers has stood the test of time, or if it is a flash in the pan.

History tells us that market environments rarely remain the same for long. For example, between 1975 and 1982 the so-called small growth stocks, as measured by Standard and Poor's *Low Priced Stock Index,* were stellar market performers, so money managers whose investment style was suited to this sector naturally performed very well. Between 1983 and late 1990 the tables were turned because blue chips, as reflected in Standard and Poor's *High*

Grade Stock Index or the Dow Jones, did much better. As a result money managers concentrating on this sector were far more successful than those whose investment style was less aggressive. This relative performance is illustrated in Figure 5.1, where a rising line favors speculative, low-priced stocks and a falling line represents the blue chips.

Studies of comparative returns indicate that the stock market has outperformed bonds, cash, and gold over the last 100 years. In their book *Diversify,* Gerald W. Perritt and Alan Levine (Longman, 1990) point out that the performance of stocks in any given period has fluctuated from a gain of 31 percent to a loss of 11 percent. This translates into a risk, or margin of error, of 21 percentage points. They also estimated that the average rate of return for government bonds has been 4.3 percent, but the risk is less than half, at 8.5

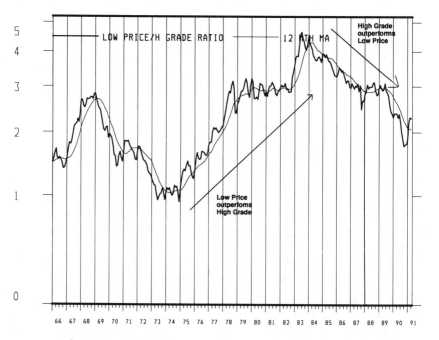

Figure 5.1 Low price vs. high grade stock ratio, 1966–1991. (Source: *Pring Market Review*)

percent. Three-month Treasury Bills averaged 3.5 percent, with a margin of error of only 3.4 percent.

INFLATION AND VOLATILITY

In the long term there are two broad risks that have to be dealt with—inflation and volatility. Inflation is like a slow cancer that eats away at the real purchasing value of a portfolio. Notwithstanding the risk of default, the inflationary peril is the principal long-term hazard faced by bondholders. The business cycle approach to asset allocation helps to warn of periods when inflationary pressures are likely to be most intense, so bond allocations can be trimmed accordingly. Stocks, on the other hand, have been a good long-term hedge against inflation, but if held for short periods, such as one or two years, their principal investment risk is volatility. We shall see later that the longer the holding period, the smaller is the risk from volatility. This is one of the primary reasons why, from a risk management point of view, it is always important to hold a core equity position no matter how bad the immediate cyclical environment may appear.

In this chapter we will examine four basic types of risk that are more applicable to the two- to three-year holding period typically associated with business cycle investing. We will also discuss how they can be managed to achieve a better balance of risk/reward. In this context risk can be broken down into the following categories— security, market, opportunity, and emotion. Before we examine them individually, let's review and elaborate on the discussion in the Introduction concerning the graphic representation of the risk/ reward relationship.

VISUALIZING RISK/REWARD

In Figure 5.2 reward is represented on the vertical scale and risk is on the horizontal scale. The ideal investment would be plotted in the top left-hand corner because this is the point at which reward is the

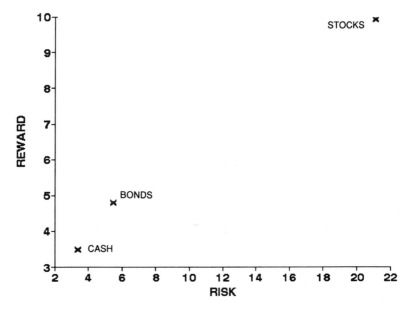

Figure 5.2   Risk vs. reward of stocks, bonds, and cash, 1926–1987.
(Source: *Pring Market Review*)

greatest and risk is the smallest. This area is commonly referred to
as the *Northwest Quadrant*. In reality, it is usually impossible to
obtain large returns without first exposing oneself to high risks.
Three portfolio alternatives—stocks, Treasury Bonds, and Treasury Bills (cash)—are shown according to their historical (1926–
1987) risk/reward attributes.

Cash is represented by three-month Treasury Bills and is plotted
closer to the horizontal axis than the other markets because of the
lower return generated. The market risk associated with Treasury
Bills is minimal, and there is very little risk of a default; so these
instruments are also plotted close to the horizontal, risk axis.
Stocks offer greater potential but are more risky, so they appear
farther away from both the horizontal and vertical axes. Twenty-
year government bonds fall somewhere in between, for although
there is a small risk of default, there is still some market risk due to
interest rate fluctuations.

The reward is calculated by averaging the performance of the three markets each year, including reinvested dividends and interest. Risk is assessed by comparing the difference between the best and worst performing years and treating them as a standard deviation. For example, since 1926, stocks have earned 10 percent on average, they are plotted in Figure 5.2 at 10 percent on the vertical, reward scale. (This risk/reward figure and Figure I.1 in the Introduction differ because they are calculated for different time periods.) On the other hand, their performance in any given period has fluctuated from a gain of 31 percent to a loss of 11 percent. This translates to a risk, or margin of error, of 21 percent. These are average risk and return figures, but your objective in managing a portfolio should be to allocate assets to those markets where the risk/reward ratio is more favorable than normal and to reduce exposure to those markets believed to be less favorable than average. Our principal objective is to offer some rough guidelines as to how risk can be managed in order to position each asset class toward the Northwest Quadrant.

SECURITY RISKS WITH FIXED INCOME SECURITIES

Credit Quality

The major forms of security risk for fixed income securities are credit quality, reinvestment, and volatility. The credit risk and return associated with Treasury Bills is very low. At the other extreme junk bonds offer a high reward but are much more vulnerable to default. Good quality corporate and tax exempt bonds fall into the middle of the range. In a general sense, credit risk is greatest when the economy is slowing down or in recession. Prudent risk management practices, therefore, dictate that a much higher proportion of a portfolio's assets should be exposed to good Aaa quality bonds in such periods. The time to sacrifice quality and go for a higher yield is during a recovery, when the risk of default is significantly lower. An alternative method of risk management is to diversify your portfolio into several issues, so that if one company defaults, your risk exposure is limited.

Reinvestment Risk

Reinvestment risk occurs when a bond is *called* after the general level of interest rates has fallen sharply. Most corporate bond covenants have a clause that enables the issuer to call or retire a portion or even the entire issue. This option is usually exercised when interest rates have fallen a great deal because the issuer is then able to reborrow the money at a lower rate. The problem is that you, the holder, can reinvest only the proceeds according to the new, lower interest rate structure. The best way to manage this reinvestment risk is to make sure that your purchases are limited to instruments that do not have a call feature, e.g., most United States government bonds. Reinvestment risk also occurs in a limited sense with non-callable bonds when interest rates fall appreciably. The bond being held still pays interest at the original rate, but the reinvestment of these proceeds can be made only at the new, lower levels. This problem can be overcome by purchasing zero coupon bonds since a constant and predictable reinvestment rate is built into their price. The drawback, as discussed in greater detail in Chapter 2, is that zeros are a lot more volatile than regular bonds. If you plan to hold them to maturity, this is not a concern, but if you find yourself trading them on a regular basis, volatility could be a major problem.

Volatility Risk

The primary risk associated with individual fixed income securities is a function of the coupon and maturity concepts that were discussed at length in Chapter 2. Volatility risk associated with specific securities, as opposed to market risk, can also be a function of the quality and size of the specific debt issue in question. Lower quality bonds tend to be more volatile in price than higher quality issues. This is because they are more sensitive to uncertainty, so the slightest hint of default or even a late interest rate payment, etc., can affect the price (shown in Figure 5.3). The upper panel represents the relationship between Treasury issues and Aaa Corporate yields, and the lower one is the ratio of Treasuries to Baa Corporate. Note how the Baa bonds fluctuate a great deal more against the Treasur-

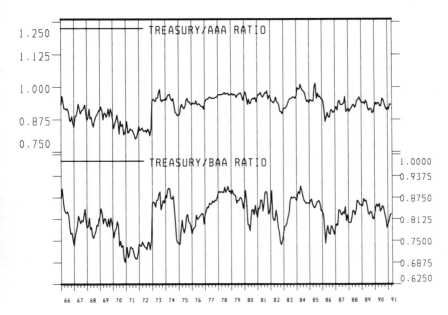

Figure 5.3 Treasuries vs. Aaa Corporate Yields and Treasuries vs. Baa Corporate Yields, 1966–1991. (Source: *Pring Market Review*)

ies than the higher quality series. Another factor that influences volatility is the size of a bond issue. Generally speaking, the larger the size the more liquid the issue is likely to be because of the greater potential number of market participants. In many ways liquidity is a self-feeding process because people who are contemplating an investment are attracted to instruments with known liquidity because of the lower transaction costs (i.e., narrower spreads) with which they are associated.

SECURITY RISKS WITH EQUITIES

Quality

Holding good quality equity issues can be every bit as important in controlling risk in the equity market as is quality in the fixed income market. This results from the combination of two important facts.

First, good quality issues are more resilient during a market decline, and second, the more substantial the decline in price, the greater the percentage advance required to return to the former level. For example, if you own a stock that falls from $100 to $80, this represents a decline of $20, or 20 percent. To get back to the $100 level will still require a $20 gain but the *percentage* will increase to 25 percent, i.e., $20 divided by the new lower capital value of $80.

Standard and Poor's rates stocks according to the stability and quality of their earnings in a way similar to the bond classification discussed in Chapter 2. From the point of view of risk management, there are two things to note. First, higher quality companies, i.e., those rated A− or better, are generally more liquid than those with a lower rating. Second, as the quality deteriorates, losses in bear markets increase. Figure 5.4 shows these various classifications and Figure 5.5 shows how they fared during the 1969–1970 bear market.

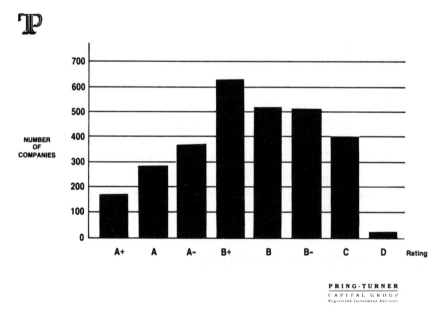

Figure 5.4   S&P quality rating. (Source: Pring-Turner Capital Group, Investment Advisors, Walnut Creek, CA)

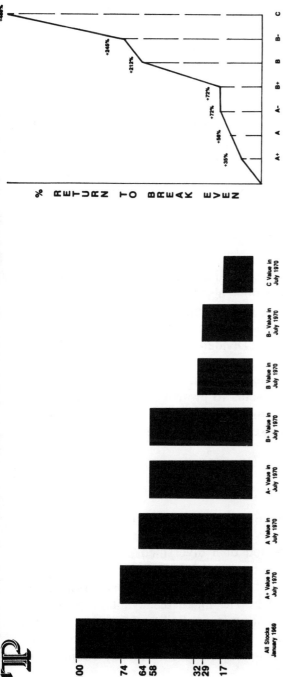

Arithmetic losses require geometric gains to recapture bear market losses.

PRING·TURNER
CAPITAL GROUP
Registered Investment Advisors

This chart demonstrates that in a bear market most stocks decline, but quality stocks retain more of their value. The importance of capital preservation during a bear market can be appreciated from the right hand chart, which shows that only a 35% increase in A+ quality stocks would have been required after July 1970 to eliminate the damage of the bear market, but since C quality stocks lost 83% of their value, they would have needed to increase by 488% just to return to break-even.

Figure 5.5 Quality control: Retention of value by quality rating during the 1969–1970 bear market (left), and bear market and quality controls (right). (Source: Pring-Turner Capital Group, Investment Advisors, Walnut Creek, CA)

The diagram shows that A+ quality stocks lost only about 25 percent, whereas C issues gave up 83 percent of their value. Figure 5.5 takes this exercise one step further by showing the amount of gain required to wipe out the damage caused by the bear market for each category. In this example, the C issues had to increase by 488 percent in order to return to their bull market peaks, yet A+ rated stocks had to advance only by 35 percent to reach the same point. From a risk management point of view, the odds clearly favor investments in better quality issues during a bear market.

Reinvestment Risk

Not only is a high level of current income (dividends) an important contribution to total return, but it also helps to stabilize a portfolio's performance. First, capital gains in and of themselves can be an elusive affair because paper profits can quickly turn into realized losses during a bear market. Dividends, on the other hand, represent actual money payments that can be reinvested, which of course boosts the compounded rate of return. Second, provided the dividend is safe, a high yield helps to protect a stock's price on the downside. Overall returns might be superior in a more speculative stock, but the risk undertaken would be higher as well.

Volatility

Volatility risk is something that is associated more with stocks than bonds. There are two ways in which it can be viewed. The first relates to the holding period of a diversified portfolio, and the second relates to the characteristics of the individual issues.

Over very long periods of time, equities offer a superior rate of return over bonds and cash. The major disadvantage of holding stocks is the relatively high short-run volatility of principal value. If you know that you are going to need a substantial amount of money in the next six months, it makes little sense to buy equities. Although the long-run performance of stocks is better than other investments, the volatility risk is extremely high over a short period such as six months, so in most situations the potential reward would be outweighed by the risk. Unfortunately, many of us concentrate far too much on the short term, overlooking the fact that paper losses in the stock market are not necessarily permanent.

The volatility risk is reduced if the time horizon is expanded. For example, from 1926 to 1991 stocks outperformed Treasury Bills about 60 percent of the time, based on a one-year holding period. However, if the holding period is increased from one to five years, the superior equity performance increases from 60 percent to 70 percent of the time. This number improves as the holding period is increased, eventually reaching a total of 100 percent over a 20-year span. It is worth noting that even in the worst 10-year holding period, which includes the Great Depression, stocks lost only a miserly 1 percent. Obviously a strategy of allocating assets around the business cycle does not indicate such a long holding period. However, all of the allocations discussed in Chapter 12 include a minimum base position for all assets at all times, even when the environment is generally unfavorable. This recognizes that the time element is an important one in the risk management process.

The most widely used measure of volatility is known as a *beta value*, which measures the response of a specific issue to changes in the overall market. For example, if you own a portfolio that moves in approximately the same proportion as the Standard and Poor's (S&P) Composite (i.e., the market), it would have a beta value of 1.0. If the beta value of your portfolio or stock mutual fund was 1.25, the implication is that it would appreciate 25 percent more than the S&P during a rally, but decline 25 percent more in a decline. Beta values are widely published and can also be obtained from a broker or mutual fund representative. Knowing the beta value of an investment puts you in possession of a powerful risk management tool. If you think that the market is likely to rally, it would be appropriate to increase the beta quotient and take more risk. It is important to note, though, that a high beta does not guarantee a faster rate of appreciation in a bull trend; it merely tells us that the stock in question is more volatile than the market as a whole and, therefore, potentially more sensitive to any given bullish stimulus.

MARKET RISK WITH FIXED INCOME SECURITIES

Market risk for a fixed income security is a direct function of the length of its maturity and changes in the general level of interest rates. Three-month Treasury Bills mature in 90 days, so there is very little market risk due to changes in the interest rate structure. At the other extreme, 30-year zero coupon bonds pay no interest, so their price fluctuates much more dramatically with changes in the prevailing level of interest rates. Table 5.1 shows the change in value of the price of a bond using several maturity and interest rate change assumptions. Note how a 30-year zero loses about 25 percent of its value when interest rates climb from 8 to 9 percent, whereas the loss is less than 10 percent for a 10-year maturity. On the other hand, if rates fall, the gain in the longer maturity is much greater. Managing the maturity of the bond portion of a portfolio clearly requires careful consideration of the future course of interest rates.

One of the principal objectives of asset allocation based on business cycle conditions is the reduction of market risk; this will be discussed later. However, a number of individual indicators also demonstrate risk limitation characteristics.

Bond Versus Commodity Prices

One of the most consistent and timely leading indicators of the bond market is the trend of commodity prices. The relationship is far from perfect, but in most periods the reward to risk ratio of a bond portfolio has historically been better when the *CRB Spot Raw Materials Index* (a widely published indicator for commodity prices) has been below its 12-month moving average than when it has been above it. Figure 5.6 shows the risk/reward for bonds for

TABLE 5.1

Zero Coupon Bond Sensitivity to Interest Rate Changes

Cost of 1,000 Principal of Zero Coupon Bonds at Various Interest Rates and Various Durations

Maturity	4%	5%	6%	7%	8%	9%	10%	11%	12%	13%
0	1,000	1,000	1,000	1,000	1,000	1,000	1,000	1,000	1,000	1,000
1	962	952	943	935	926	917	909	901	893	885
2	925	907	890	873	857	842	826	812	797	783
3	889	864	840	816	794	772	751	731	712	693
4	855	823	792	763	735	708	683	659	636	613
5	822	784	747	713	681	650	621	593	567	543
6	790	746	705	666	630	596	564	535	507	480
7	760	711	665	623	583	547	513	482	452	425
8	731	677	627	582	540	502	467	434	404	376
9	703	645	592	544	500	460	424	391	361	333
10	676	614	558	508	463	422	386	352	322	295
11	650	585	527	475	429	388	350	317	287	261
12	625	557	497	444	397	356	319	286	257	231
13	601	530	469	415	368	326	290	258	229	204
14	577	505	442	388	340	299	263	232	205	181
15	555	481	417	362	315	275	239	209	183	160
16	534	458	394	339	292	252	218	188	163	141
17	513	436	371	317	270	231	198	170	146	125
18	494	416	350	296	250	212	180	153	130	111
19	475	396	331	277	232	194	164	138	116	98
20	456	377	312	258	215	178	149	124	104	87
21	439	359	294	242	199	164	135	112	93	77
22	422	342	278	226	184	150	123	101	83	68
23	406	326	262	211	170	138	112	91	74	60
24	390	310	247	197	158	126	102	82	66	53
25	375	295	233	184	146	116	92	74	59	47
26	361	281	220	172	135	106	84	66	53	42
27	347	268	207	161	125	98	76	60	47	37
28	333	255	196	150	116	90	69	54	42	33
29	321	243	185	141	107	82	63	48	37	29
30	308	231	174	131	99	75	57	44	33	26

Source: *Pring Market Review*

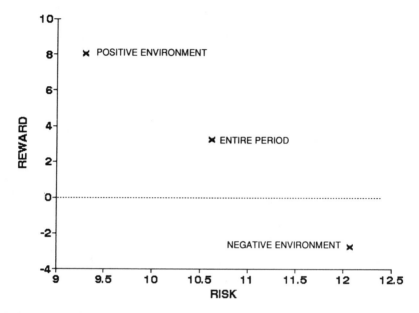

Figure 5.6   Risk vs. reward of long-term government bonds relative to commodity prices, 1948–1990. (Source: *Pring Market Review*)

the period 1948–1990, showing the risk/reward when commodity prices were below their moving average (i.e., declining), and above the average (i.e., rising). Figures 5.7 and 5.8 show these two series in graphic format. A bond investment in a falling commodity environment pushes the risk/return ratio closer to the Northwest Quadrant than average or inflationary periods (see Figure 5.2). Clearly all bond investment decisions should not be based on the direction of the trend of commodity prices. Even so, this exercise does demonstrate how a very simple technique can greatly improve the risk/ reward ratio. In general, it makes sense to extend maturities and allocations when commodity prices are falling and to reduce exposure when they are rising.

Figures 5.9 and 5.10 show the relationship between government bond prices and manufacturing capacity. This is an economic series that indicates the amount of slack in the manufacturing sector and is

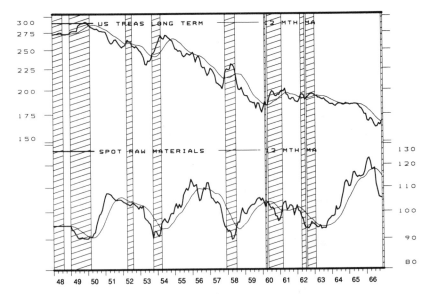

Figure 5.7   United States Treasury long-term government bonds and Spot Raw Materials, 1948–1966. Shaded areas show when the Treasury Bond Index is above its 12-month-moving average (MA) and the Spot Raw Materials Index is below its 12-month MA. (Source: *Pring Market Review*)

published monthly by the Commerce Department. Manufacturing has slipped in economic importance in the last few decades, but the indicator still appears to maintain a fairly close correlation with progress in the bond market. The idea is that manufacturers find less resistance to price increases when capacity is tight, which translates into higher inflation and lower bond prices. Conversely low utilization rates indicate a weak economy and the inability of manufacturers to raise prices. The dividing line between a positive and negative environment for the debt market appears to be 82 percent. The shaded areas on Figures 5.9 and 5.10, therefore, indicate when manufacturers are operating at less than this amount. A quick glance at both charts shows that this approach works reasonably well, capturing nearly all of the bond market rallies. Every indicator

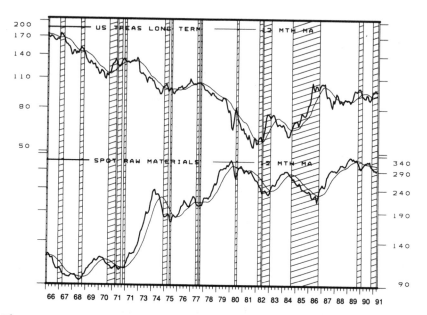

Figure 5.8 United States Treasury long-term government bonds and Spot Raw Materials, 1966–1991. Shaded areas show when the Treasury Bond Index is above its 12-month moving average (MA) and the Spot Raw Materials Index is below its 12-month MA. (Source: *Pring Market Review*)

fails from time to time, and this one is certainly no exception. In 1958, for example, a very low level of capacity did not stop a fairly sharp decline in bond prices. Most of the time, though, this simple approach is successful in helping to define when bond market risk is above or below the norm. In this respect, Table 5.2 indicates that the annualized rate of return during favorable periods is 3.36 percent compared to −6.66 percent in times of *tight* capacity. Equally important, the volatility (risk) experienced in achieving these superior results is only 11.16 percent compared to unfavorable periods of 13.46 percent. Volatility in this and subsequent tables in this chapter is measured as an average deviation from a 12-month

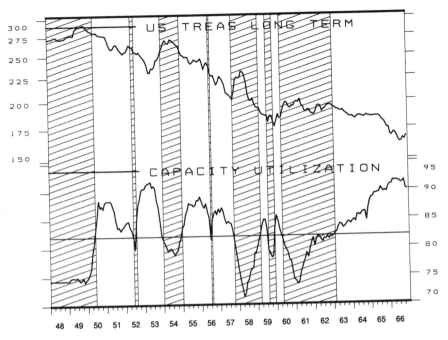

Figure 5.9   United States Treasury long-term government bonds and capacity utilization, 1948–1966. Shaded areas show when capacity utilization is 82 percent or lower. (Source: *Pring Market Review*)

rate of change. Figure 5.11 shows the performance of this approach in graphic format.

Another simple but effective technique for controlling risk and enhancing gains is to invest in bonds when the Discount Rate is below its 12-month moving average. This approach is shown in Figures 5.12 and 5.13, where the shaded areas again flag favorable periods. The Discount Rate indicator offers an even better risk/reward ratio; the average annualized return is over 12 percent with a somewhat low volatility (risk) of 6 percent. On the other hand, unfavorable periods generate a loss of 7 percent with a substantial increase in volatility of nearly 15 percent (see Figure 5.14 and Table 5.3).

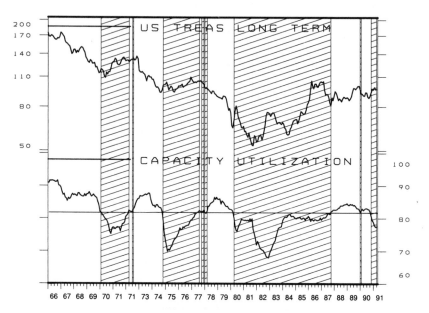

Figure 5.10 United States Treasury long-term government bonds and capacity utilization, 1966–1991. Shaded areas show when capacity utilization is 82 percent or lower. (Source: *Pring Market Review*)

TABLE 5.2

United States Treasury Long-Term and Capacity Utilization, 1948–1991

	Annualized Return (Based on a 2-Year Holding Period)	Annualized Risk	
Favorable periods for bonds	3.36	11.16	When capacity utilization is 82% or lower
Entire 43 years	−1.76	12.27	
Unfavorable periods for bonds	−6.66	13.46	When capacity utilization is greater than 82%

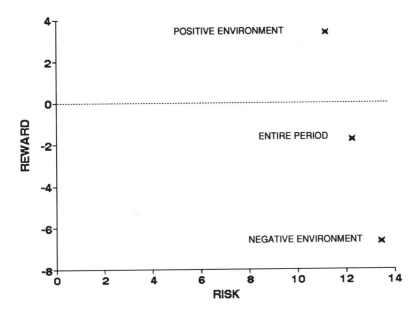

Figure 5.11   United States long-term government bonds and capacity utilization, 1948–1991. (Source: *Pring Market Review*)

MARKET RISK WITH EQUITIES

The same principle of isolating favorable and unfavorable environments through Discount Rate changes also applies to the stock market. Bearish periods occur after the Discount Rate has been raised three times following a series of cuts and remain in force until the rate is lowered. Bullish periods are signaled from the time of the first cut until the third in a series of consecutive hikes takes place. Table 5.4 shows that this simple approach would require little risk and a substantial reward. Figure 5.15 shows this simple rule in a graphic format.

This is not the only rule to use for stock market investments, but it is quite clear from the position of the plots that this approach greatly increases the potential rewards, but at a lower level of

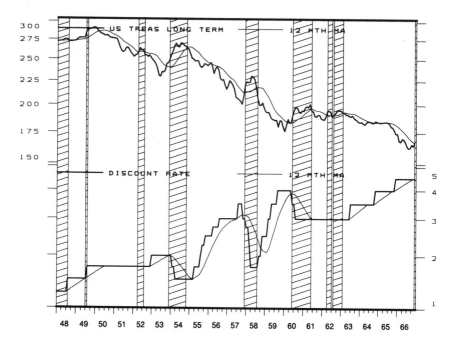

Figure 5.12 United States Treasury long-term government bonds and Discount Rate, 1948–1966. Shaded areas show when the Treasury bond price is above its 12-month moving average (MA) and the Discount Rate is below its 12-month MA. (Source: *Pring Market Review*)

overall risk. Clearly, if you want to roll the dice and expose yourself to some higher beta stocks, it is important to wait for the Discount Rate to be cut first.

Another method of filtering favorable and unfavorable periods for equity ownership is to relate the sensitivity of stock prices to changes in interest rates. For example, we know that falling interest rates are always positive for stock prices, but what is unclear is the time lag between the cyclical peak in rates and the final low in equity prices, because it varies considerably from cycle to cycle. For example, stocks and interest rates both reversed their cyclical trends in October 1966; yet in the 1981–1982 period there was a lag

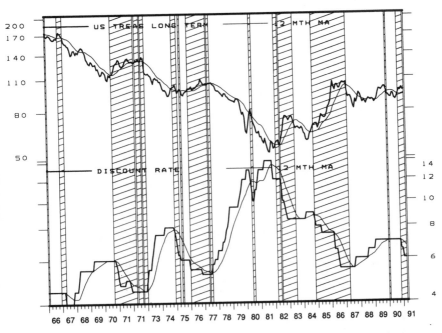

Figure 5.13 United States Treasury long-term government bonds and Discount Rate, 1966–1991. Shaded areas show when the Treasury bond price is above its 12-month moving average (MA) and the Discount Rate is below its 12-month MA. (Source: *Pring Market Review*)

of almost a year between these two events. One way to take advantage of this known relationship and yet avoid the pitfalls of being too early is to invest in equities when they begin to show a positive response to a decline in rates, and vice versa.

History tells us that 12-month moving average crossovers by the S&P Composite have been the most consistently reliable of any time span in identifying bull and bear trends in the stock market. Favorable periods for equity ownership under this approach require the yield on three-month commercial paper to be below its 12-month average and for the S&P Composite to be above its 12-month moving average. All other conditions are regarded as unfavorable.

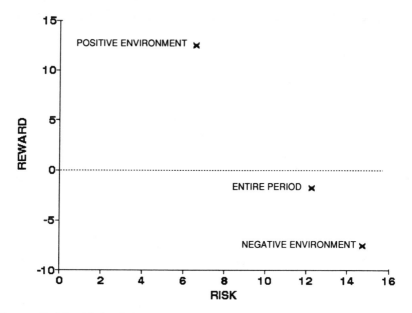

Figure 5.14   United States Treasury long-term government bonds and Discount Rate, 1948–1991. (Source: *Pring Market Review*)

TABLE 5.3
United States Treasury Long-Term and Discount Rate, 1948–1991

	Annualized Return (Based on a Two-Year Holding Period)	Annualized Risk	
Favorable periods for bonds	12.52	6.59	When long-term Treasury is above its MA and Discount Rate is at or below its MA
Entire 43 years	−1.76	12.27	
Unfavorable periods for bonds	−7.56	14.73	When long-term Treasury is below its MA and Discount Rate is at or above its MA

TABLE 5.4
Discount Rate Principle Applied to the Stock Market

Bearish Periods

Date of Third Hike	S&P at Third Hike	Date of First Cut After Third Hike	S&P at First Cut After Third Hike	Gain or Loss (%)
Sept. 1955	44.34	Nov. 1957	40.35	−9.00
Mar. 1959	56.15	June 1960	57.26	1.98
Dec. 1965	91.73	Apr. 1967	90.96	−0.84
Apr. 1968	95.67	Nov. 1970	84.28	−11.91
May 1973	107.22	Dec. 1974	67.07	−37.45
Jan. 1978	90.25	May 1980	107.69	19.32
Dec. 1980	133.48	Dec. 1981	123.79	−7.26
Feb. 1989	293.40	Dec. 1990	328.33	11.91

Bullish Periods

Date of First Cut	S&P at First Cut	Date of Third Hike After Cut	S&P at Third Hike After Cut	Gain or Loss (%)
Feb. 1954	26.02	Sept. 1955	44.34	70.41
Nov. 1957	40.35	Mar. 1959	56.15	39.16
June 1960	57.26	Dec. 1965	91.73	60.20
Apr. 1967	90.96	Apr. 1968	95.67	5.18
Nov. 1970	84.28	May 1973	107.22	27.22
Dec. 1974	67.07	Jan. 1978	90.25	34.56
May 1980	107.69	Dec. 1980	133.48	23.95
Dec. 1981	123.79	Feb. 1989	293.40	137.01
Dec. 1990	328.33			

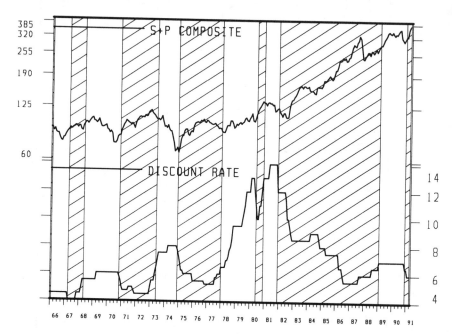

Figure 5.15 S&P Composite and Discount Rate, 1966–1991. Shaded areas represent points between the first Discount Rate cut after a series of rises and the third hike following a series of cuts. (Source: *Pring Market Review*)

The results (shown in Figures 5.16 and 5.17 and Table 5.5) are quite spectacular since the annualized return jumps from a 1948–1991 average of 8 percent to 24 percent (see Figure 5.18), but equally as important, investors are faced with considerably less volatility (risk), i.e., 4.75 vs. 12.36.

Valuation is another important concept that can be used in market risk containment. There are many different ways of valuing stocks. The most common are price/earnings ratios (discussed in Chapter 2), price to book value, price to free cash flow, and so forth. My particular favorite is the dividend yield because the receipt of dividend payments is the ultimate reason for owning stocks, and dividends are not subject to accounting gimmickry as are earnings,

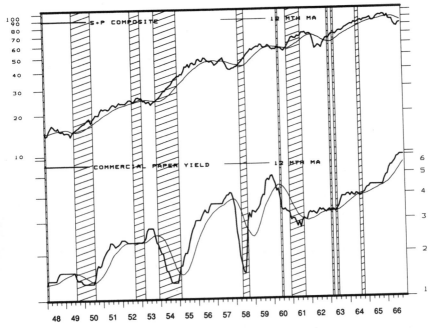

Figure 5.16 S&P Composite and Commercial Paper Yield, 1948–
1966. Shaded areas show when the S&P Composite is at or above its
moving average (MA) and the Commercial Paper Yield is below its
MA. (Source: *Pring Market Review*)

cash flow, book value, and other valuation measures. Directors are
reluctant to alter dividend payment policies, so when they are
raised or lowered it provides an important clue to management's
confidence in the company's prospects. Figures 5.19 and 5.20 show
the dividend yield for the S&P Composite since 1948. When the
yield is less than 3 percent, it is generally a risky time to own
equities. In some periods, such as 1963–1965, this low yield did not
prevent the market from advancing, but in most instances the risk
clearly outweighed the reward. It is also important to remember
that a low yield of dividends does not offer much in the way of
downside protection. On the other hand, when the yield has risen to
the five to six percent area it has proved to be a low risk/high reward

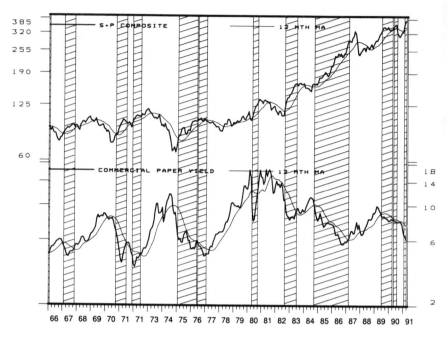

Figure 5.17 S&P Composite and Commercial Paper Yield, 1966–1991. Shaded areas show when the S&P Composite is at or above its moving average (MA) and the Commercial Paper Yield is below its MA. (Source: *Pring Market Review*)

TABLE 5.5
S&P Composite and Commercial Paper Yield, 1948–1991

	Annualized Return (Based on a Two-Year Holding Period)	Annualized Risk	
Favorable periods for equities/shaded	24.33	4.75	S&P Composite is at or above its MA and CP Yield is below its MA
Entire 43 years	8.02	12.36	
Unfavorable periods for equities/unshaded	1.08	15.48	S&P Composite is below its MA and CP Yield is above its MA

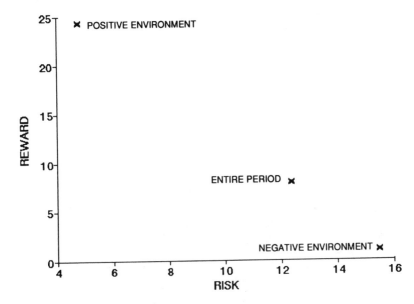

Figure 5.18 S&P Composite and Commercial Paper Yield, 1948–1991. (Source: *Pring Market Review*)

opportunity historically. Even when the market does not immediately respond, such as early 1981, the generous dividend yield provides a just reward for your patience.

The results of these over- and undervaluation approaches are shown in Tables 5.6 and 5.7 and are represented graphically in Figures 5.21 and 5.22.

OPPORTUNITY RISK

We almost always judge the performance of an investment in terms of whether or not it generates a profit. Perhaps more consideration should be given to the rate of return on alternative investments. For example, a positive return can always be obtained from holding cash. The money market or savings account in question might be

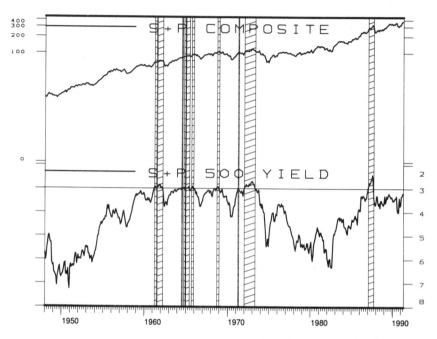

Figure 5.19 S&P 500 Composite and S&P 500 Composite yield, 1948–1991 (3 percent or less). Shaded areas show when the S&P Composite yield is below 3 percent. (Source: *Pring Market Review*)

safe, but it is important to remember that the very act of holding cash means that the opportunity to earn potentially greater rewards from bonds or stocks is lost. For example, conditions may encourage us to maintain most of our assets in cash because we feel that interest rates will continue to rise and put downward pressure on bond prices. We also feel comfortable in a money market fund because the rate of return is (at least temporarily) above, say, the average compound rate of return for equities of 10 percent. If our expectations are incorrect and interest rates plummet, as they usually do at primary peaks, then a nice juicy 10 percent yield may soon fall to 7 percent or even 6 percent. In effect, by remaining in high yielding money market instruments, we run the risk of not locking in

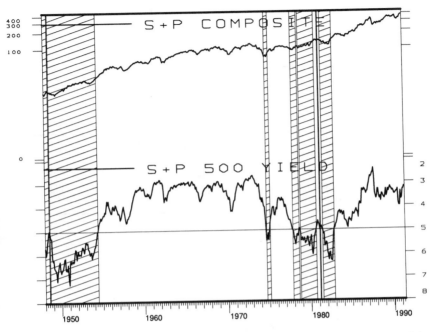

Figure 5.20 S&P 500 Composite and S&P 500 Composite yield, 1948–1991 (5 percent or greater). Shaded areas show when the S&P Composite yield is above 5 percent. (Source: *Pring Market Review*)

TABLE 5.6
S&P 500 and S&P 500 Yield, 1948–1991
(3% or Less)

	Annualized Return (Based on a Two-Year Holding Period)	Annualized Risk
Periods when the yield is greater than 3%/unshaded	9.94	0.48
Entire 43 years	8.62	0.92
Periods when yield is 3% or less/shaded	−2.92	4.52

TABLE 5.7
S&P 500 and S&P 500 Yield, 1948–1991
(5% or Greater)

	Annualized Return (Based on a Two-Year Holding Period)	Annualized Risk
Periods when yield is 5% or greater/shaded	15.76	0.10
Entire 43 years	8.62	0.92
Periods when the yield is less than 5%/unshaded	6.19	1.20

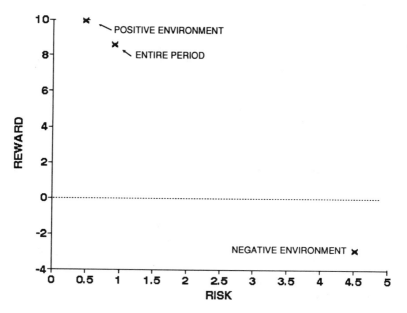

Figure 5.21 S&P 500 Composite and S&P 500 Composite yield, 1948–1991 (3 percent or less). (Source: *Pring Market Review*)

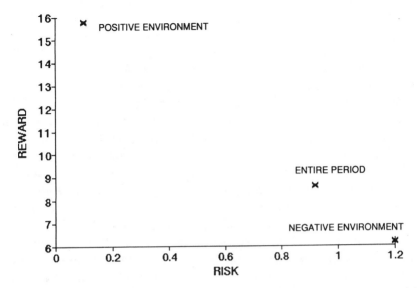

Figure 5.22 S&P 500 Composite and S&P 500 Composite yield, 1948–1991 (5 percent or greater). (Source: *Pring Market Review*)

a high yield in the bond market. A better approach would be to gradually rotate from cash to bonds. In this way the risk of lower bond prices would be reduced, but so too would the opportunity risk of being unable to lock up some high long-term yields.

Possibly the greatest opportunity cost of holding cash occurs when stocks are experiencing a bull market. Between 1982 and the summer of 1987, for example, a portfolio totally exposed to cash would have gained about 50 percent, but one oriented to equities (with dividends reinvested) would have returned over 250 percent. In this case the opportunity cost of remaining solely in cash would have been considerable.

EMOTIONAL RISK

One of the most important aspects of investment is the *sleep at night factor*. It makes little sense to embark on a potentially high yielding instrument if the slightest setback causes you to sell at the wrong time. It is very important for each of us as individuals to assess the amount of risk that we can deal with comfortably and the kind of rewards commensurate with those risks. Obviously an investment objective and related risk absorption will very much depend on our individual financial position, emotional makeup, and stage in life. Worrywarts should not expose themselves to a lot of risk, and neither should retirees whose main source of income comes from investments. By the same token, you might be one of those people who have an aggressive, energetic nature and decide to (uncharacteristically) invest in ultrahigh quality "dull" blue chips during the early stages of a bull market. The chances are that you will be disappointed with the performance of these investments and decide to move into more aggressive stocks after prices have moved substantially higher, exactly at the wrong time. Had you defined your level for risk tolerance and tendency to jump in at a moment's notice at the outset, your success rate would undoubtedly have been better. In the first place, you could have designed your original portfolio to be a little more aggressive, to some extent satisfying your desire for the fast track. Perhaps more importantly, establishing a realistic assessment of your risk tolerance at the outset would remind you of the dangers of making a sudden and risky switch later on.

If you find you are always changing your mind, the chances are that you do not have a sense of perspective. The key is to set realistic goals and slowly work toward them. Make gradual and systematic changes in your portfolio, not large or frequent ones.

Another problem common to many investors is that they are able to make an investment based on sound logic but have no idea under what conditions it should be liquidated if their expectations are not realized. Establishing benchmarks for these situations, therefore, is a mandatory requirement for risk control. Benchmarks convert the investment from an open-end risk into a manageable one. It doesn't matter whether such yardsticks are based on market prices, economic indicators, valuation measures, etc. The important point is that they should represent logical, soundly based criteria that not only help to define the risk in question, but also enable the investor to sleep more easily at night in the full knowledge that the risk is limited.

DIVERSIFICATION

A basic principle of risk management is diversification. We all know that putting your eggs into one basket can lead to trouble if the basket breaks, so it is important from an investment perspective to make sure you diversify your portfolio sufficiently to avoid being financially crippled if a specific investment turns bad. This subject is covered at length in Chapter 1 but is mentioned here as a reminder that no risk management program is complete without some attention to diversification.

The degree of risk reduction is not only a function of the types of asset included in a portfolio, but the makeup of the bond and stock component as well. For example, an industry group rotation develops over the course of the business cycle. At the beginning, when the economy is digging itself out of recession, utilities and other industries whose profits are particularly enhanced by falling interest rates put in their best price performance. As the economy moves into the terminal recovery phase when inflationary pressures are greatest, utility issues put in a relatively poor performance. On the other hand, this type of environment favors mining and energy issues that usually come to the fore. A portfolio that is balanced between a number of diverse groups is, therefore, better positioned to avoid market risk.

Another method of achieving risk reduction is to balance the portfolio with a number of instruments that are not closely correlated. The most obvious example of a noncorrelation develops between stocks and cash during an equity bear market. In this situation stocks are losing money, and the compounding effect of cash gives it a positive rate of return. Generally speaking, bonds and precious metals do not correlate with stocks. There are certain periods in the business cycle when they do, but it is usually in the most risky periods for equity ownership that they do not. This is precisely when the stabilizing influence of diversification is most needed. The day of the 1987 market crash probably gives us the most extreme example of the usefulness of combining assets with a low correlation. At the close of Black Monday, equities lost over 20 percent of their value, but government bonds had actually risen by just under 1 percent. The advantage of constructing a portfolio from noncorrelating assets can also be extended to embrace non–United States securities. For example, Ibbotsen Associates of Chicago published a study that showed that between 1977 and 1986 United Kingdom and Japanese government bonds had negative correlations with United States Treasuries. Since the returns of United States and overseas bonds were similar, a globally balanced bond portfolio would have resulted in a similar gain to a purely United States one, but with a dramatically reduced risk.

SUMMARY

The first step in the risk management process is to establish a personal tolerance for risk based on your financial position, stage in life, and emotional makeup. This permits realistic goal setting and the creation of a plan to achieve the objectives. The next step involves the determination of the types of assets that you would like to include in your portfolio, e.g., bonds, stocks, precious metals, foreign markets, cash, etc. Remember, it is important to limit yourself to those asset categories with which you feel comfortable. Do not try to follow too many vehicles because this will inevitably lead to confusion or the failure to give them the attention they deserve. For example, it is often a better idea to consider two or three mutual funds specializing in blue chips, growth stocks, and foreign markets, rather than to try to follow 20 or 30 individual stocks. This way it is not only possible to be well diversified, but it is much easier to participate in three different specialized areas should you feel the need. Finally, it is important to arrive at maximum and minimum allocations for each asset. These allocations are then raised or lowered within your guidelines as your assessment of the economic and financial environment changes.

6
The Business Cycle and Asset Allocation

The economic history of the last 200 years reveals a consistent repetition of a pattern of alternating prosperity and recession known as the business cycle. This experience is not limited to the United States but has occurred with regularity in all countries for which detailed records are available. Economic data before the eighteenth century are less precise, but there is little in the records to refute the existence of a cycle. Why there is a business cycle and what its importance is for asset allocation are two key questions that will be discussed in this and the next two chapters.

The business cycle is commonly assumed to last for four years from trough to trough. In actual fact, the average duration is closer to 41.6 months, or a little under four years. Economists have also noticed several other cycles in business activity. In his book *Business Cycles*, Joseph Schumpeter combined what he considered to be the three dominant ones (i.e., Kondratieff, Juglar, and Kitchin) into one single long-term cycle (see Figure 6.1). Our main concern here is with the four-year, Kitchin cycle, but it is worth looking briefly at Schumpeter's ideas because they offer some valuable long-term perspectives. They, in turn, will give us some useful clues to the characteristics of the prevailing four-year cycle.

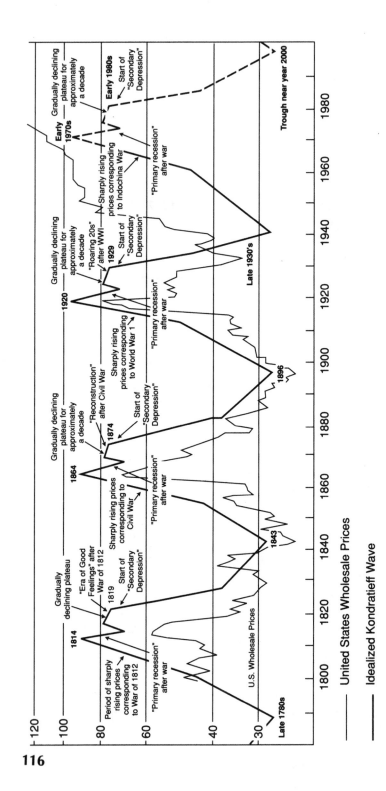

Figure 6.1 The Kondratieff wave, based on annual averages with a ratio scale of 1967 = 100. (Source: Adapted from Martin J. Pring, *Technical Analysis Explained*, McGraw-Hill, NY, 1991. Original source: *The Media General Financial Weekly*, June 3, 1974)

THE LONG (KONDRATIEFF) WAVE

The diagram shown in Figure 6.2 is a graphical representation of the sum of the 50- to 54-year Kondratieff, the nine-year Juglar, and the four-year Kitchin cycles. It is important to note that the diagram

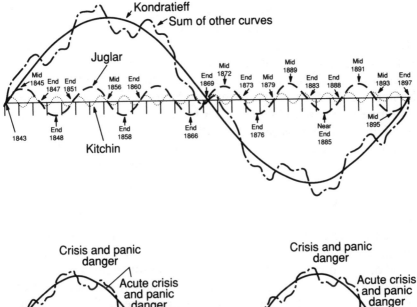

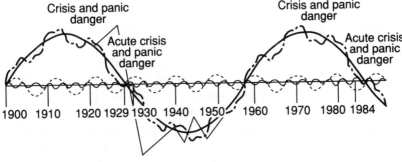

Figure 6.2 Schumpeter's model of the nineteenth-century business cycle (top) vs. the twentieth-century business cycle and crisis points, calculated path (bottom). (Source: Adapted from Martin J. Pring, *Technical Analysis Explained*, McGraw-Hill, NY, 1991. Original source: T. J. Zimmerman, *Geschichte der theoretischen Volkswirtschafts-lehre*, in an unpublished paper by P. E. Erdman)

was originally constructed in the 1930s; everything after this point has been projected on the basis of Schumpeter's ideas. Because the Kondratieff wave is the one with the greatest long-term effect on financial markets, it is worth further consideration.

Nikolai Kondratieff was a Russian economist who was commissioned by the communist government in the 1920s to prove that capitalism would not work. Kondratieff's theory showed that, far from being self-destructive, the capitalist system actually had the ability to cleanse and renew itself, eventually moving on to greater strength. For this astute and courageous conclusion, Kondratieff was rewarded with permanent exile to Siberia.

He observed that the capitalist economy went through a long business cycle lasting approximately 50 to 54 years. The wave was effectively the embodiment of a long-term cycle in innovation and technology, and was strongly influenced by emotional trends in business activity. The cycle was also characterized by long-term swings in prices and interest rates as inflationary and deflationary forces continually battled to get the upper hand. There were, according to Kondratieff, three phases to the cycle. An *upwave* lasted approximately 15 to 20 years and occurred when technology conceived in the previous cycle was adopted into the economy. As a result, each successive (four-year) business cycle achieved a higher level of economic activity than its predecessor because the technology improved and confidence grew. Confidence was important because it meant that business people were more and more willing to take risks. The upwave was associated with a successively higher standard of living, but this did not come without a price. In a general sense, interest rates and price inflation also moved higher in each successive cycle. Because the purchasing value of money depreciates in periods of inflation, it pays to borrow. This means that the system typically becomes top heavy with debt as the upwave draws to a close. In effect, the prosperity associated with the tail end of the upwave is largely built on borrowed money as people, businesses, and often governments take on far more debt than they can reasonably expect to service. It is important to note that the long period of prosperity characterized by the upwave also encourages individuals and businesses to take less care in their planning as they extrapolate the prosperous past into an uncertain future. As a result, long-wave peaks are distinguished by an excess of manufacturing capacity. This is especially true of the mining and energy sectors, which are usually the primary beneficiaries of the commodity price boom that develops at the tail end of this period.

The *downwave* also lasts for about 15 to 20 years and is symptomatic of a period in which these debt burdened balance sheets are slowly and painfully improved. During this stage, each successive business cycle is associated with a trend of lower commodity prices and interest rates as the deflationary effect of the excessive manufacturing capacity and contraction in debt is experienced. Once this cleansing process has run its course, a firm foundation is then in place for the next upwave.

Kondratieff also noted that the rising and falling parts of the cycle were separated by a period of fairly stable prices that provided an interregnum between the inflationary times of the upwave and the sharp deterioration in living standards associated with the declining part of the cycle. He called this middle phase the *plateau period*. It was also associated with what appeared to be great prosperity. Under the surface, things were not so rosy as the legacy of the debt burden and excess plant capacity, accumulated in the previous phase, prevented many industries from fully participating in the recovery. The long period of prosperity associated with the plateau period meant that many of the remaining economic sectors also moved into a state of chronic overcapacity. For example, the 1920s represented a plateau era. During this time many industries, such as farming and shipbuilding, were barely able to survive. However, the general feeling one gets from the stock market boom and the depiction of the period as the Roaring Twenties is one of great prosperity. By the end of the decade, the automobile industry, one of the leading sectors during the plateau phase, had the capacity to produce 6.4 million cars annually, yet the best previous year for sales was only 4.5 million.

Kondratieff made his observations in the 1920s and was able to identify only two complete waves in the United States. Even though events since then appear to fit the theory quite well, his conclusions, except in a most generalized way, should be treated with some degree of caution. The nature of the economy has changed considerably since Kondratieff first drew his conclusions. One of the key changes has been the role and size of governments. They have increasingly become a stabilizing force through the adoption of safety nets that reduce some of the debilitating effects of unemployment. Central banks have also become a lot more sophisticated and adept in both anticipating areas of financial vulnerability and taking action to avoid precipitating a financial collapse. The makeup of the economy is also quite different because it is no longer dominated by cyclical industries, such as farming. It is now more influenced by service industries, which are far less sensitive to cyclical swings. Whether they will be immune to secular forces, though, is another question. This is relevant to asset allocation because the long wave has a very important influence on the character of an individual business cycle. For example, during the upwave, the trend of interest rates has an upward bias in each succeeding cycle. During the postwar period until 1981, for instance, the cyclical peaks and troughs of interest rates moved progressively higher (see Figure 6.3). On the other hand, rates were in a declining trend from 1920 to the early 1940s. In effect, during the postwar period until 1981, each bull market in rates associated with the four-year business cycle was longer than bear markets. (During the 1920–1940 downwave, the opposite was generally true.) Figures 6.4 and 6.5 show that the reverse set of circumstances ruled for commodity prices. *The position of the economy in relation to the long wave, therefore, has important implications for the way in which assets might be allocated during the course of a specific four-year cycle.* I shall have more to say on that later.

THE FOUR-YEAR (42-MONTH) KITCHIN CYCLE

The Kitchin cycle is the one that we normally refer to as the four-year, or Presidential, cycle. Figure 6.6 shows an idealized business cycle in which the two troughs are separated by 42 months. The sine curve represents the growth path of business activity, and the horizontal line separates the period of expansion from one of economic

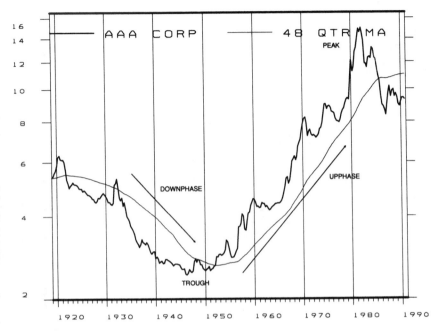

Figure 6.3   Corporate bond yields, 1919–1991. (Source: *Pring Market Review*)

contraction. In reality, the economy comprises many different industries and segments that are actually moving in different directions most of the time. For example, the level of housing starts is extremely sensitive to interest rate changes, so housing is the first sector of the economy to enter the recessionary phase. More often than not, the housing industry is the first area of the economy to bottom, typically when the overall level of business activity is still contracting. On the other hand, capital expenditure, especially that associated with the mining and agricultural industries, is a lagging indicator. It is often still growing in the early phase of a recession. This is because decisions to expand capacity are made when plants are running close to their physical limit, i.e., after the business cycle has been underway for some time. Furthermore, the implementation of such decisions requires considerable time for planning and financing.

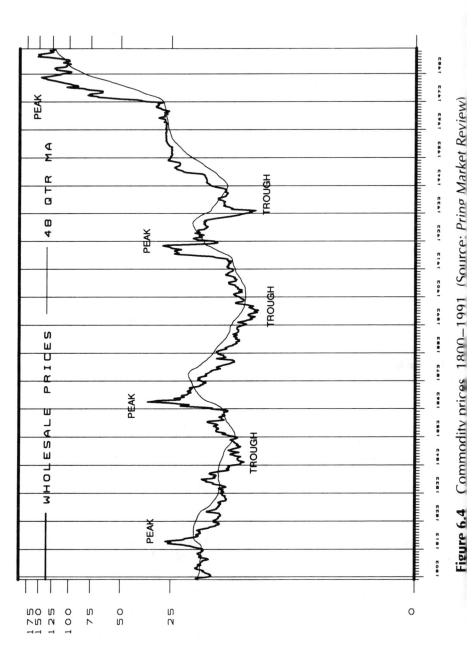

Figure 6.4 Commodity prices 1800–1991 (Source: *Pring Market Review*)

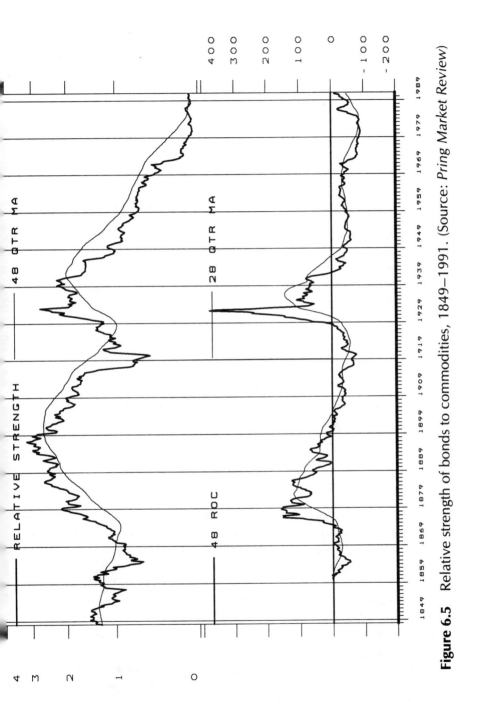

Figure 6.5 Relative strength of bonds to commodities, 1849–1991. (Source: *Pring Market Review*)

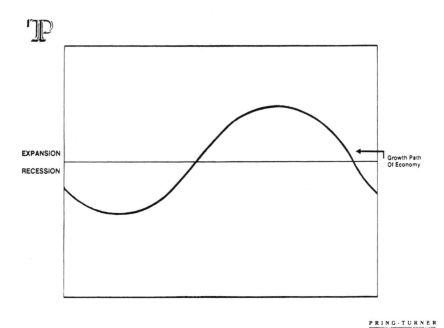

Figure 6.6 Peaks and troughs of the financial markets and how they relate to the business cycle. (Source: Pring-Turner Capital Group, Investment Advisors, Walnut Creek, CA)

The growth curve shown in Figure 6.6 is, therefore, a proxy for those indicators that move coincidentally with the economy, such as industrial production, etc. When the sine curve is above the horizontal equilibrium line and rising, it implies that the economy is growing at a faster and faster rate. The topping-out process in the curve does not indicate a recessionary period, merely that the growth rate is slowing. Eventually, the curve stalls completely and crosses below the line, which indicates that the economy is in a contracting or recessionary phase.

When the curve is below zero and falling, downside momentum is expanding, i.e., the economy is contracting at a faster and faster rate. Before business activity starts to expand, downside momentum must first bottom, gradually dissipating until the curve moves into positive territory and signals the beginning of a new recovery.

HOW THE MARKETS FIT INTO THE BUSINESS CYCLE

It was mentioned earlier that the course of the three asset classes—bonds, stocks, and inflation hedge investments—is strongly influenced by the business cycle. A review of the last 200 years of financial market history indicates almost without exception that there is a definite chronological sequence of events that takes place during the course of the business cycle. This progression consists of a bottoming in bond prices (peak in interest rates), then equities, and finally in commodities. It continues with the peaking out of bond prices (interest rates troughing), then stocks, and finally commodity prices. This idealized sequence is shown in Figure 6.7. It is fairly consistent, but the magnitude of the individual bull and bear markets varies from cycle to cycle. The leads and lags between the peaks and troughs also change. For example, bonds and stocks bottomed almost simultaneously in October 1966, yet in 1981–1982 the two troughs were separated by almost a year.

Knowledge of this rotation principle and the ability to obtain some kind of anchor, however approximate, on the prevailing stage of the business cycle, has tremendous significance for the asset allocation process. If we have a clear idea that the economy is in a recession, then it is normally safe to buy bonds. This is especially true if it has also been established that stocks and commodities are in a bear market. In effect, this progression of financial market turning points provides us with the basis for a framework or map, which can be used to formulate a more effective investment strategy.

These relationships and their implications will be examined in the next three chapters, but first let's look at how and why these relationships occur and how the business cycle influences market activity.

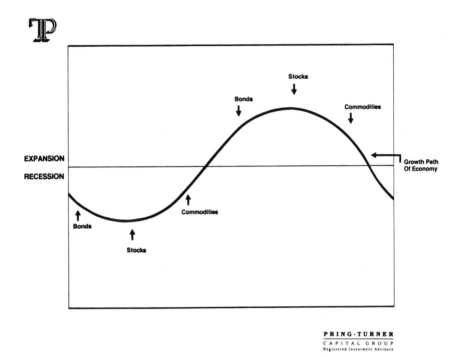

Figure 6.7   Peaks and troughs of the bond, stock, and commodity markets and how they relate to the business cycle (down arrows indicate market peaks and up arrows indicate market troughs). The sine curve represents the growth path of the economy over the course of a business cycle. In almost every business cycle since the beginning of the nineteenth century, this market sequence (bonds, stocks, and commodities) has repeated. (Source: Pring-Turner Capital Group, Investment Advisors, Walnut Creek, CA)

STEPS IN THE SEQUENCE

Interest Rates Peak

The cycle begins as bond prices bottom out, and interest rates peak. An interest rate is the price of credit and, like any other price, is determined by the interaction between supply and demand. A fun-

damental shift in this supply balance has to materialize before interest rates reverse their upward trend. This almost always occurs
after the economy has entered a recessionary phase.

The Money Supply Increases

The Federal Reserve is the key player on the supply side. The
Central Bank is engaged in a continual battle as it alternatively fights
inflation or recession. When it becomes increasingly evident that
the economy is in serious trouble, the Fed reverses its role as
inflation fighter and takes on the unemployment battle. In effect,
this results in a policy reversal from tight to easy monetary policy.
The Fed usually moves with a lag because it takes some time before
all the economic numbers are reported and digested. Also, the
Central Bank does not reverse policy very often. Thus, when a
switch is made, the authorities are careful to ascertain that they do
not give the impression of indecisiveness by subsequently reversing
themselves.

As soon as the Fed realizes that recession is a serious problem, it
starts to inject liquidity (cash) into the system through the purchase
of Treasury Bills (known as *open market* operations). This, along
with other measures, such as reducing the reserve requirements in
the banking system, has the effect of increasing the supply of credit.
This increased credit availability makes possible a decline in the
federal funds rate and later the Discount Rate. It is important to note
that the Fed can directly control the trend of short-term interest
rates over the near term through its influence on the supply side. On
the other hand, it can affect yields at the long end only *indirectly*
because that is the prerogative of the market itself. If participants
feel that monetary policy is too easy and will later result in inflationary conditions, bond yields will remain high relative to short-
term rates and vice versa. In effect, if short rates fall against long
rates investors will extend the maturities of their portfolios. That
much is within the power of the Fed. However, if investors feel that
the risk of a resurgence of inflationary pressures and lower bond
prices is high, they will forgo the (relatively) tempting prospects of

longer-term maturities in favor of the safety of shorter-dated securities.

Demand for Credit Declines

Recessionary conditions also reduce the demand for credit as businesses and consumers retrench. Loan demand normally peaks two to three months into the recession. It would be reasonable to expect credit growth to crest as soon as the economy begins to contract.

This is not normally the case because corporations usually find themselves in a cash squeeze at this stage in the cycle. The squeeze is caused by the sharp decline in sales as the economy rolls over. Businesses try very hard to liquidate unwanted inventory but can never move fast enough to compensate for the reduced revenues. As a result, they are forced to borrow in the money markets for a temporary period, which artificially pushes up rates. This process, known as *involuntary inventory accumulation,* usually lasts for about six weeks and is shown in graphic form in Figure 6.8. It is almost like a corporate margin call, and because the cash flow deficit (the shaded area in Figure 6.8) has to be financed at any price, this is a main reason why interest rate peaks usually have the appearance of a sharp spike.

Equities Bottom Out

Once interest rates have peaked (bond prices bottomed), it is only a matter of time before equities also experience a low. This occurs when stock market participants conclude that rates have fallen sufficiently for a recovery to take place. Equities are then accumulated in anticipation of the upswing. If the recession has been particularly severe, it means that corporations have been more aggressive in cutting costs and lowering their break-even levels. As a consequence, the rebound in stock prices is normally much greater, and the initial rally in the equity market can be explosive. Two examples that come to mind are the January 1975 and August 1982 stock

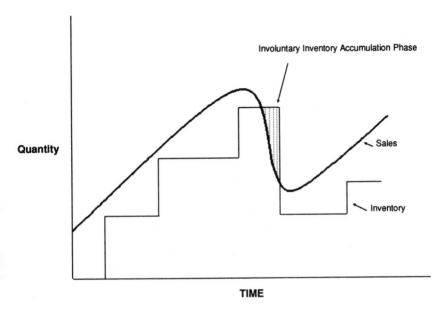

Figure 6.8 Involuntary inventory accumulation phase. (Source: *Pring Market Review*)

market rallies. One clue as to whether the initial rally will be above or below average can be gleaned from the lag between the low in bond prices and that of stocks. Generally speaking, the longer the lag, the greater the implied severity and duration of the recession. In 1877 for example, the lag was four years and was followed by a doubling of stock prices. In 1920 and 1982, the bottom in bonds and stocks was separated by about a year, and both periods were associated with a longer than average bull market in equities.

Commodities Bottom Out

At this point, bonds and stocks are both rising, but commodities are still experiencing a bear market. It is not until the recovery has been under way for a few months that they reach their final low. Typically, the commodity markets bottom after the sine curve has crossed above the recession/expansion line. Occasionally, the actual price low occurs during the terminal phase of the recession, but even so, commodities usually remain in a wide trading range and only embark on a sustainable advance once the recovery is underway. Early recessionary bottoms in the commodity markets usually occur when the previous recovery has been characterized by an unusually large commodity boom. Under such circumstances, the final peak in commodity prices is associated with a speculative froth, as both individuals and corporations attempt to cash in on the boom. This means that the tail end of the commodity cycle is exaggerated, as is the subsequent margin liquidation. Speculators who enjoyed the commodity boom are forced out at any price, which means that commodities are liquidated well below their true economic value. This temporary oversupply is quickly corrected, and prices bounce back. However, until a reversal in the economy results in a more substantial demand for commodities, prices make little net upside progress.

Interest Rates Trough Out

At this point all three markets are in a rising trend, but all good parties come to an end, and this one is no exception as the period of falling interest rates draws rapidly to a close. Gradually the reported economic data improve, and it becomes evident that the recovery has taken hold. The Central Bank abandons its role as recession fighter. Its policy at this stage does not immediately move to one of tightness, but more toward neutrality. At the same time, confidence returns to businesses and consumers who are now willing to take on more debt. Because the supply of credit is less expansive and demand has increased, interest rates (the price of credit) bottom out. Interest rate troughs are usually gradual affairs, looking something like saucers when shown in graphic form. This contrasts with cyclical peaks, which are associated with the frenzied pace of borrowing activity that characterizes the involuntary inventory accumulation phase and are, therefore, much sharper, parabolic affairs.

Rising rates at this stage in the cycle reflect stable, controlled but definitely improving business conditions and do not adversely affect the stock market. This is because equity investors are interested in corporate profits. Provided profits can rise at a faster clip than interest rates and rising rates are not a threat to the recovery, the stock market continues to advance.

Equities Peak

At some point, though, rising rates do adversely affect the economy, and stock market participants anticipate potential economic weakness, selling equities in a similar way to which they had earlier discounted the recovery. Even though stocks are falling, the economy itself continues to expand, using up what little excess manufacturing and labor market capacity that still exists. As a result, demand for commodities outstrips the available supply. Through the price mechanism, quantities are then rationed by higher prices.

Commodity Prices Peak

Eventually inflation gets the attention of the Fed, which adopts a restrictive monetary policy. This, and a continued expansion in loan demand, puts renewed upward pressure on interest rates. Finally, the strain on the system brought about by higher rates succeeds in breaking the back of the recovery. In turn, this causes commodity prices to peak. Sometimes this event takes place at the tail end of the recovery, occasionally in the first few months of the recession. All three markets are now in a bear phase and ready for a new cycle to begin.

RECENT HISTORY OF THE SEQUENCE IN ACTION

Figures 6.9 and 6.10 show the three markets between 1969 and 1991. The arrows on Figure 6.9 connect the cyclical peaks, while Figure 6.10 accomplishes the same thing for the bottoms. The consistent

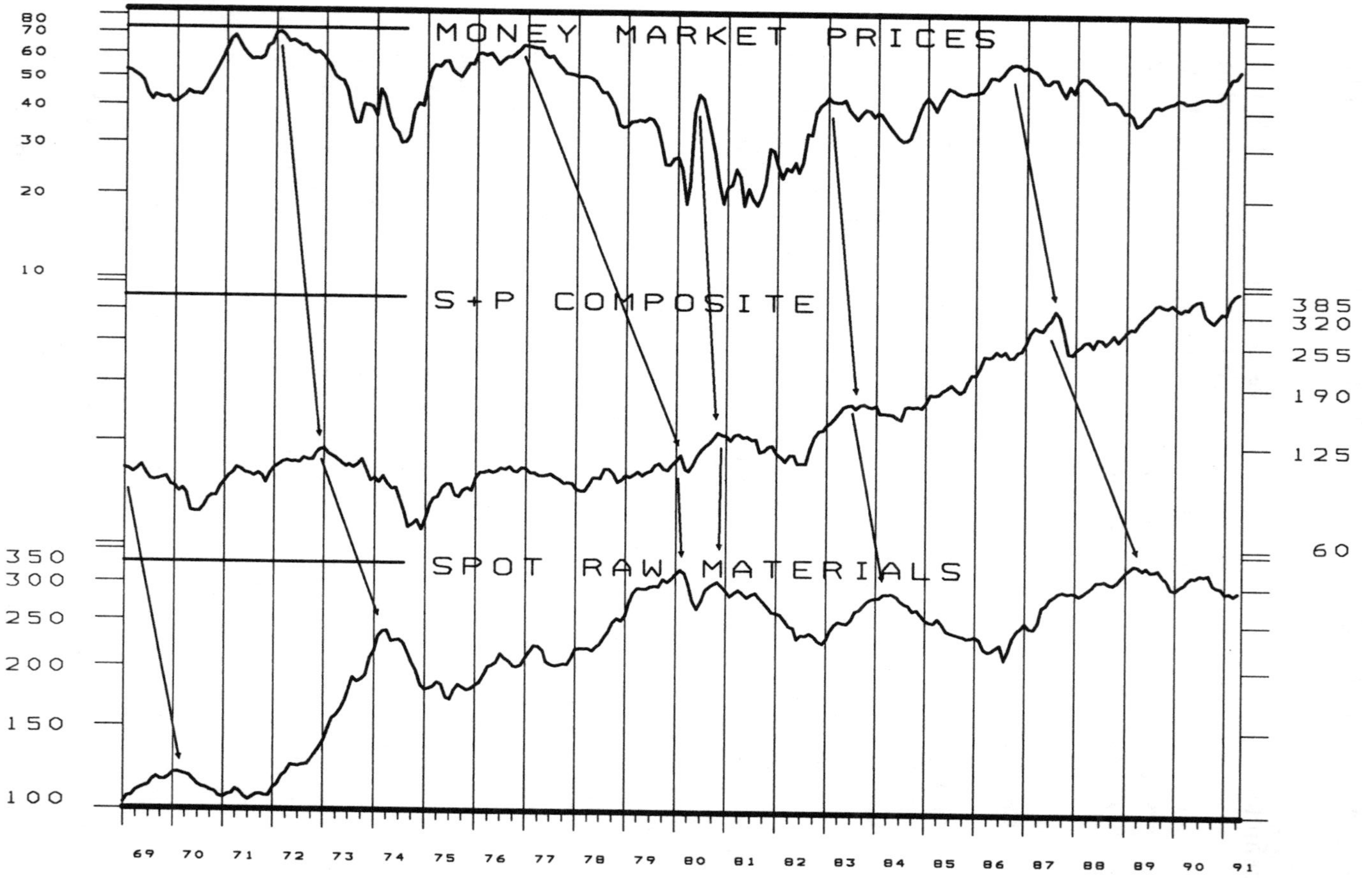

Figure 6.9 The business cycle sequence showing market tops, 1969–1991. (Source: *Pring Market Review*)

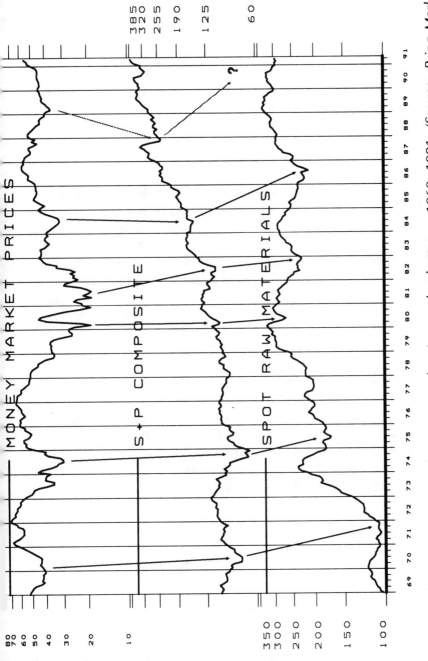

Figure 6.10 The business cycle sequence showing market bottoms, 1969–1991. (Source: *Pring Market Review*)

movement of the arrows to the right indicates the chronological sequence between money market price, equities, and commodities. Note how the lags are different in each cycle. Occasionally, the sequence breaks down entirely as it did in 1988–1990, but this is the exception rather than the rule.

THE CHARACTER OF BULL AND BEAR MARKETS

The magnitude of the cyclical advance and decline in each market is determined by the characteristics of the recovery/recession cycle, which is largely influenced by the prevailing stage of the Schumpeter model described earlier. Generally speaking, during the inflationary sequence (upwave) of the long wave, bull markets in commodities and bear markets in bond prices tend to be fairly lengthy, whereas the tables are completely turned in the deflationary (down) wave. We shall discover later that each business cycle has an inflationary and deflationary part, just like the long wave. Consequently, during a Kondratieff upwave the inflationary portion of the business cycle predominates, but in the downwave, it is the deflationary part that experiences greater magnitude and duration. This means that inflation-predominated cycles are usually associated with superior performance by energy and mining stocks, but in the downwave the stellar performers tend to be concentrated in the defensive areas. Natural beneficiaries include defensive issues, such as foods and interest sensitive groups in the stock market. This environment is also favorable, of course, for bonds.

THE DOUBLE CYCLE

Occasionally, the trough between recessions extends well beyond the normal 41-month periodicity. In this event, the economy and financial markets undergo what I call a *double cycle,* where the contraction in business activity is replaced by a *slowdown in the growth rate,* rather than a contraction. A hypothetical example is shown in Figure 6.11. In economic jargon, this phenomenon is

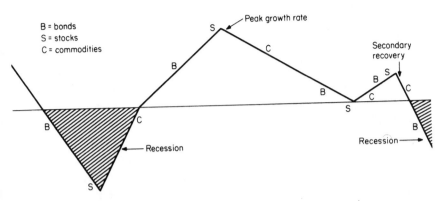

Figure 6.11 Growth track of the economy in a double cycle. (Source: Martin J. Pring, *Technical Analysis Explained*, McGraw-Hill, NY, 1991, pg. 27)

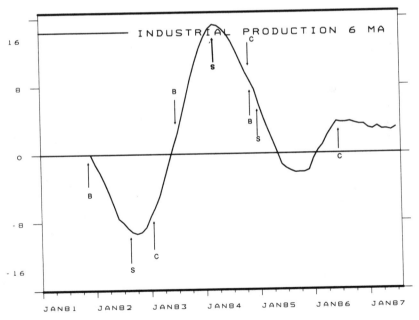

Figure 6.12 Financial market turning points vs. industrial production. (Source: *Pring Market Review*)

known as a *growth recession*. It has developed more frequently in the postwar era, due to the commitment of governments to a full employment policy.

Interestingly, the financial market sequence described above also occurs during the double cycle. In this respect, Figure 6.12 shows the approximate peaks and troughs of the three markets superimposed on a representation of industrial production between 1981 and 1987.

The most recent example of a double cycle occurred in the 1980s during the so-called rolling recession. All sectors and regions of the United States moved into the recovery stage in the early 1980s, but by the 1985–1986 period, the farm, energy producing, and rust belt areas of the country experienced an extremely sharp recession. Because other regions were quite buoyant, the aggregate economy did not slip into recession, but the internal distortions were so great that the financial markets experienced a couple of minicyles.

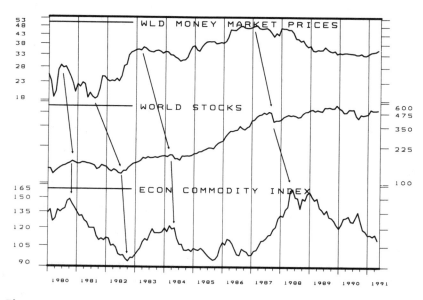

Figure 6.13   Global markets and the business cycle sequence at market tops, 1980–1991. (Source: *Pring Market Review*)

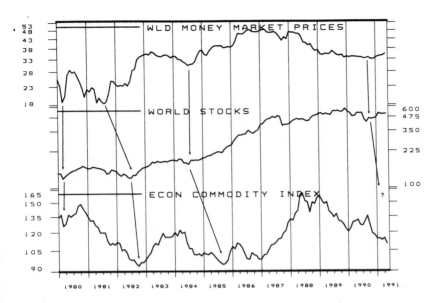

Figure 6.14 Global markets and the business cycle sequence at market bottoms, 1980–1991. (Source: *Pring Market Review*)

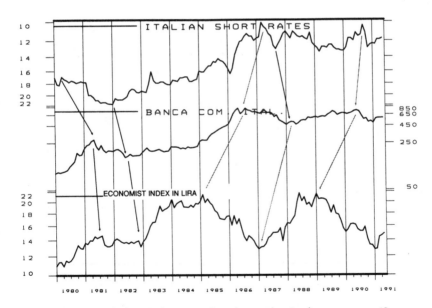

Figure 6.15 Italian markets vs. the chronological sequence. (Source: *Pring Market Review*)

THE BUSINESS CYCLE IN OTHER COUNTRIES

This concept also appears to work for the global economy. Figure 6.13, for example, shows world short-term interest rates (plotted inversely to correspond to prices), world stocks, and world commodities. The arrows connect the market peaks. Figure 6.14 shows the same three markets, this time joined by the bottoms. Unfor-

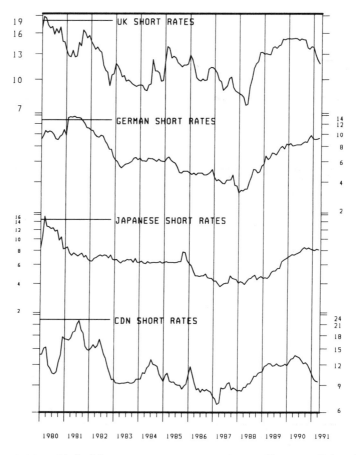

Figure 6.16 Global interest rates, 1980–1991. (Source: *Pring Market Review*)

tunately, this financial market sequence does not appear to operate as consistently in other countries as it does in the United States and the world as a whole. Figure 6.15, for example, shows the three markets in Italy between 1980 and 1991. You can see how the chronological progression works very well between 1980 and 1982, but beginning in 1983, it breaks down completely. This type of inconsistency is apparent in most countries. One probable reason

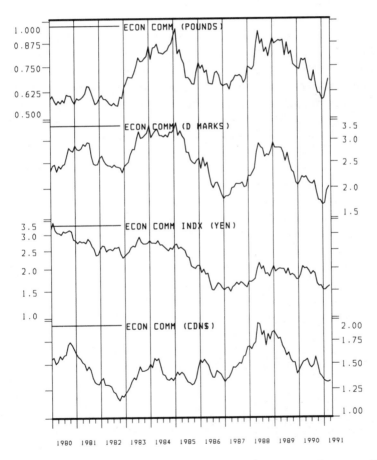

Figure 6.17 Global commodity prices, 1980–1991. (Source: *Pring Market Review*)

for this is the greater impact of foreign trade on most economies relative to the United States. It is true that the amount of foreign trade in the United States has grown rapidly, but by 1991 exports as a share of GNP were roughly 7 percent. This compares to 19 percent for the United Kingdom, 27 percent for Germany, and 10 percent for Japan. The greater influence of foreign trade means that the monetary policy of most countries is affected by external factors relatively more than that of the United States. The effect of this is to uncouple the financial markets from their normal chronological sequence.

Even though the chronological sequence of the financial market rotation may not work well for individual countries, the broad swings of interest rates and commodity prices in the principal industrialized countries are very similar, as shown in Figures 6.16 and 6.17. This means that investors in non–United States markets should still keep an eye on global trends because sooner or later they are likely to have an impact on that country.

7
Tracking the Typical Cycle

The previous chapter introduced the concept of the business cycle, explaining how the economy alternates between recovery and recession. Although it is popularly termed the four-year cycle, statistics from the beginning of the nineteenth century show that the average period from trough to trough is actually closer to 41 months. Sometimes the cycle lasts much longer. For example, the 1980s were dominated by a cycle that began in late 1982 and extended for nearly eight years. This may appear to contradict the existence of an approximate four-year periodicity, but when economic data are more closely examined, it is apparent that this whole period actually encompassed two complete cycles. The difference was that the recessionary phase of the cycle was replaced by a slowdown in the growth rate. Economists use the term *growth recession* to describe this type of phenomenon. In effect, the so-called rust and inflation belts suffered a very deep recession during the mid-1980s, but the majority of the country held up quite well. The net result was that the growth rate of the United States economy slowed, but business activity did not actually contract. Extralong expansions of a similar nature also occurred in the 1920s and 1960s.

Due to this somewhat extended cycle, it was argued in the late 1980s that the business cycle had ceased to exist. These doubts were encouraged by many inaccurate predictions of impending recession. Sophisticated new theories arose justifying the demise of the cycle. The world, it was argued, was now so integrated that weakness in one country or continent would be offset by strength in another, in a similar manner to the mid-1980s regional correction in the United States. Others pointed out that the service sector, which is not subject to sharp cyclical fluctuations, was now the predominant force in the economies of most of the principal industrialized countries. These factors, and the stabilizing force of government safety nets, would ensure the repeal of the business cycle. The problem with any of these explanations is that they do not address the main cause of business cycles—human nature.

WHY BUSINESS CYCLES REPEAT

Human nature is more or less constant. The alternation between recovery and recession is caused by people responding to certain incentives (the recovery) and then repeating the same sort of mistakes that cause the slowdown or recession. As Dr. Richard Coghlan puts it in his book *Profiting from the Business Cycle* (McGraw-Hill, London, 1992): "The regularity is in the pattern of these reactions, not in the cycle itself."

There is no single pattern that is repeated exactly; if so, the forecasting process would be all too easy. This is because people tend to learn from their experience and do not usually repeat the same mistakes in consecutive cycles. It is this learning process that contributes greatly to the variation of each cycle. There is also a constant process of renewal and replacement as fresh participants bear the responsibilities of business decision making, and old hands retire from the scene. The consistent feature is that each generation has to learn for itself. Even though the basic elements and the process of the business cycle are more or less constant, new factors have to be taken into account. These changing elements have the effect of altering the timing and direction of economic events. Examples include international political events, the timing of elections, weather extremes, and so forth.

One example of the kind of mistake made by businesses occurs toward the end of the cycle. Companies typically plan major expansions when profits are greatest. This is usually the wrong time because everyone else in the industry is responding in a similar manner. As a result, capacity in the industry starts to exceed demand, profits decline, workers are laid off, and the economy contracts. This is just one example of the kind of mistake that is made, and we must remember that each cycle experiences different distortions in different industries to different degrees. The important point is that generally people respond to comparable economic events in broadly similar ways. At the beginning of the cycle decisions are made with prudence, but success gradually translates to overconfidence and finally to greed as businesspeople become carried away with their own success.

From an investment point of view there is little advantage in understanding the repetitive characteristics of business activity unless this knowledge can be used to pinpoint the prevailing stage of the cycle and its implications for individual markets or financial assets. The calendar year goes through four distinct seasons, each of which is suitable for different activities. For instance, seeds are planted in the spring and harvested in the summer or fall. The business cycle also goes through its own seasons in which there is an appropriate time to buy a specific asset and one to sell it. For example, the best time to buy bonds has traditionally been the middle of a recession, whereas liquidation has been more appropriate about one to two years into the recovery. It is often a good time to buy about six months before the recovery starts, while a good time to take profits has often been six to nine months before the onset of the next recession. How do we recognize the current stage or season of the cycle?

THE CHRONOLOGY OF A CYCLE

The economy is not homogeneous; it consists of a number of different components, each of which goes through its own cycle. It is really an aggregate term that describes a collection of individual cycles, all of which are in a different stage of development at any one point in time. In effect, each business cycle goes through a set chronological series of events ad infinitum.

I often think of a person standing on the platform of an imaginary station. Instead of a long straight track connecting it to other stations, this railroad track is circular. The journey taken by the train then becomes one continuous circle. Experience tells us that the train is arranged in a preset order. The engine is at the head, followed by the first-class carriages and the restaurant car. The tourist class carriages and caboose follow up in the rear. Anyone standing on the platform knows that once the engine has passed through the station the next thing to expect is the first-class section, and so forth. Once the caboose has gone through, it is time to expect a new cycle in the form of the reappearance of the engine. The train's line-up is always the same and because this one is always on time, it is an easy matter to predict when each section will pass through the station.

The economy is very similar because the business cycle also goes through a distinct set of chronological events, marked by the activity of various economic indicators. The principal difference between the train and the economy is that the "economic" carriages are of different lengths in each business cycle, and consequently leads and lags between the various economic events are rarely the same. Occasionally the economic train is arranged with some of the carriages in the wrong order, but if you keep your eye on the overall organization, it is still relatively easy to anticipate the next event. Figure 7.1 shows how the carriages of an imaginary economic train might be labeled. In a real economy there would be an infinite number of carriages; the present diagram greatly simplifies the process.

Why does the economy go through this cycle? How can the prevailing stage be identified? What are the implications for the various asset classes at each stage? These are issues that will be discussed in this and the next two chapters. Before examining the business cycle in more detail we should look at the concept of rate of change because it influences how individuals and institutions

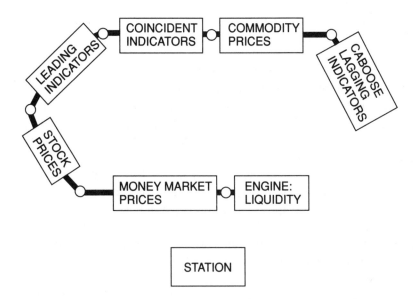

Figure 7.1 Train metaphor of the business cycle. (Source: *Pring Market Review*)

make decisions. This discussion will be expanded in Chapter 9 when we come to take a closer look at the price action of individual markets.

RATE OF CHANGE: AN INVALUABLE TOOL

Let's consider the example of a middle-aged woman who has unexpectedly lost her husband in a car crash. Her immediate response is one of shock and intense grief. She may never completely adjust to the tragedy, but as the months roll by she gradually comes to accept her misfortune and adjusts her life-style accordingly. The idea behind the concept of rate of change is that the accident causes an immediate and dramatic change in her outlook, but her emotions are brought back into balance bit-by-bit through the passage of time.

Important changes in economic decision making are also influenced by the rate of concept change. For example, a shopkeeper may have experienced expanding sales for several years, but his business has been held back because of space limitations. Eventually, he bites the bullet and doubles the size of his store. Chances are that he finances a part of this through increased cash flow, but the majority of the funds have to be borrowed from the bank, especially the additional inventory required to fill the new shelves. Before the expansion, he calculated borrowing costs at the prevailing 8 percent rate of interest, an expense that could be absorbed comfortably. Even if interest rates move up gradually, the anticipated expansion in sales will easily cover the additional carrying charges. However, within three months of taking out the loan, interest rates move up to 12 percent, much faster than even his worst case assumption. He may or may not be forced into bankruptcy, but at the very least he is compelled to severely cut back on his inventory. In this example it was the *speed of the rise* in interest rates, or their rate of change, that caused the problem, not the actual level. If he had known at the time of the planned store expansion that borrowing costs were going to be 14 percent and had he expected that he would still be able to make a profit at that level, all would have been fine; but as it turned out, it was the unexpectedly quick three-month jump from 8 percent to 12 percent that left him in an extremely vulnerable position.

Economists often take the pulse of the economy by expressing economic indicators on a rate of change basis. A rate of change is calculated by dividing an indicator by its level several periods earlier. An example is shown in Table 7.1. A popular time span is an annualized rate of change. Using the Commerce Department's *Leading Indicator Series* (the LEI) as an example, the January 1990 level would be divided by January 1989 and the result plotted as an oscillator that continually crosses above and below the zero level. A reading of zero would occur when the LEI was at the same level as it was in the previous year (see Figure 7.2). Annualized changes are popular because they compare identical calendar periods and avoid the need to make seasonal adjustments. More often than not, a rate of change oscillator appears on a chart as a fairly jagged, almost random series, so it is common practice to smooth the data with a

TABLE 7.1

Twelve-Month Rate of Change Calculation of Composite Index of
Leading Indicators

Date	(1) Leading Index	(2) Leading Index 12 Months Ago	(3) 12-Month Rate of Change (Col. 1/Col. 2)
Jan. 1989	146.0		
Feb.	145.6		
Mar.	144.7		
Apr.	145.8		
May	144.2		
June	144.0		
July	144.1		
Aug.	144.8		
Sept.	145.0		
Oct.	144.4		
Nov.	144.6		
Dec.	145.1		
Jan. 1990	145.4	146.0	0.9959
Feb.	144.1	145.6	0.9897
Mar.	145.4	144.7	1.0048
Apr.	145.2	145.8	0.9959
May	146.0	144.2	1.0125
June	146.2	144.0	1.0153
July	146.2	144.1	1.0146
Aug.	144.4	144.8	0.9972
Sept.	143.2	145.0	0.9876
Oct.	141.5	144.4	0.9799
Nov.	139.9	144.6	0.9675
Dec.	139.7	145.1	0.9628

moving average, which then allows a more accurate fix of the basic trend. (Moving averages are explained in Chapter 9.)

Rate of change is an important concept that influences economic activity, but when charted it also has three additional benefits. If you look closely at the LEI series itself, you can see that most of the time it is moving up slowly and only occasionally experiences a mild setback. In effect the raw data offer little feeling that the economy is experiencing an actual cycle. On the other hand, the smoothed rate

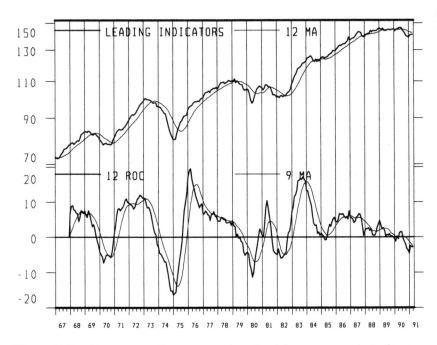

Figure 7.2 Commerce Department's coincident economic indicator and a 12-month rate of change. (Source: *Pring Market Review*)

of change indicator does encounter some worthwhile fluctuations, which gives us a better sense of the underlying cyclical rhythms.

The second benefit is that on most occasions the smoothed rate of change indicator *leads* the raw data. Remember the rate of change idea is really a statistical technique for measuring momentum or velocity. Think of someone throwing a ball in the air. At some point it loses its upward velocity, peaks, and starts to fall. If we could actually chart its momentum, we would have some idea that the ball was about to peak because the velocity would reach its maximum thrust well before. The same is true for economic indicators in that a smooth rate of change usually peaks ahead of the raw data.

A final advantage of this momentum approach is that the rate of change oscillator acts in a similar manner to the pendulum of a clock because it swings backward and forward between broadly prescribed limits. Once these limits have been reached, it is time to think about a reversal in the prevailing trend.

A TYPICAL CYCLE

Assume that business activity is weak and that the economy has been in recession for a couple of months. Eventually, the Federal Reserve responds to this and monetary policy is eased. These events coincide with a decline in the demand for credit as both businesses and consumers greatly curtail their borrowing demands. Because the potential supply of credit is increased through Central Bank easing, and demand is declining, the price of credit, namely interest rates, begins to fall. Declining rates are a necessary but not sufficient condition for an economic recovery to take place. It is important for declining rates to positively affect business activity. This almost always shows up first in the housing sector, which is the most interest sensitive part of the economy. Housing starts are consistently the most leading of all the economic (as opposed to financial) indicators, usually bottoming out during the recession. The term *economic indicator* usually refers to things you can actually see and touch. You can't really touch Money Supply or Net Free Reserves in the banking system, which are financial indicators. On the other hand, housing starts, auto sales, and industrial production are tangible items.

Since 1953, the average lead time between the low in housing starts and the onset of a recovery has been six months. Figure 7.3 shows the hypersensitivity of the housing industry to interest rates. Because most mortgages are fixed term, housing seems to be more sensitive to changes in long-term as opposed to short-term rates. The arrows on Figure 7.3 show quite clearly that the momentum of bond prices leads that of housing starts. Unfortunately, there does not appear to be any correlation between the intensity of momentum in the bond market and the housing market. Consequently, it is not true to say that a huge rally in bonds will translate into a booming housing industry and vice versa. However, this relationship does suggest strongly that we should not expect to see a rise in

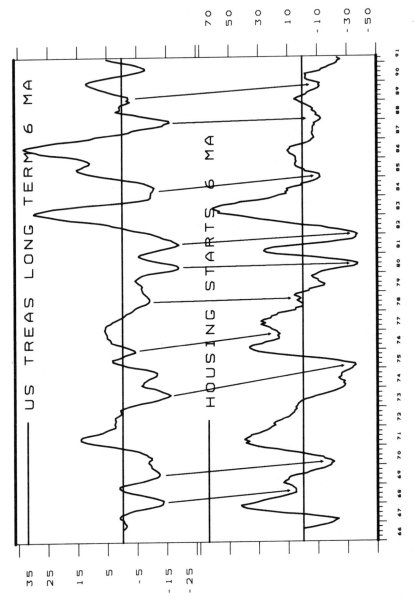

Figure 7.3 United States Treasury long-term government bond prices vs. housing starts momentum (six-month moving average of nine-month rate of change). Arrows show bond prices lead housing starts.
(Source: Pring Market Review)

the level of housing starts unless this is preceded by a bond market rally shown by a bottoming in bond price momentum.

Once housing starts and new home sales start to pick up, it means that consumers have begun to overcome their reluctance to spend for the first time since the recession began. This renewed optimism gradually spreads to other big ticket items normally purchased on borrowed money, such as automobiles. New homes have to be furnished. Hence, the spending trail naturally branches out to appliances, furniture, and other consumer durables. Eventually the recovery broadens to encompass other parts of the economy, such as the retail, wholesale, and manufacturing sectors. As spare manufacturing capacity is filled, profits escalate and businesses once again think about adding new plant and equipment. Capital spending and heavy machinery are typically the last areas of the economy to participate in the recovery. By that time, though, the conditions that brought about the expansion, namely growth in the money supply and falling interest rates, have reversed. The Federal Reserve is no longer worrying about the recession but has now become more concerned with fighting inflation because the tight labor and manufacturing situations have resulted in upward pressure on wages and prices.

While it has not yet reverted to an actual tight money policy, the Fed is certainly far less accommodating than it was earlier. Concurrent with the more stingy Central Bank policy, the resurgence in business activity translates into increased demand for credit. With supply tightening and demand increasing, the price of credit—interest rates—starts to move up. This begins as a slow, relatively subdued process, but as inflationary pressures continue to build, the Fed becomes far more stringent, eventually pushing interest rates up fairly dramatically, and a recession results.

AN INDICATOR FRAMEWORK

A starting point for ascertaining the prevailing stage of the business cycle is to arrange the three composite indicators published by the Commerce Department in chronological order. These are the Leading, Coincident, and Lagging series. Each indicator is constructed from individual economic indicators that have been categorized according to their historical turning points in the business cycle. *Vendors Reporting Slow Deliveries* is a series that typically turns ahead of the rest of the economy. Hence, it would be included in the Leading Indicator Composite, Expenditure on Plant and Equipment is a lagging indicator, and so forth. Table 7.2 summarizes the various components used in the construction of the three indicators.

Figure 7.4 presents the indicators themselves as a six-month average of an annualized rate of change. The objective of this figure

TABLE 7.2
Components of the Commerce Department Composite Indexes

The Leading Index

1. Average weekly hours, manufacturing.
2. Average weekly initial claims for unemployment.
3. New orders, consumer goods, and materials.
4. Vendor performance.
5. Contracts and orders for plant and equipment.
6. Building permits, new private housing units.
7. Change in unfilled orders, durable goods.
8. Change in sensitive materials prices.
9. Stock prices, 500 common stocks.
10. Money supply, M2.
11. Index of consumer expectations.

The Coincident Index

1. Employees on nonagricultural payrolls.
2. Personal income less transfer payments.
3. Industrial production.
4. Manufacturing and trade sales.

The Lagging Index

1. Average duration of unemployment (inverted).
2. Ratio of manufacturing and trade inventories to sales.
3. Change in labor cost per unit of output, manufacturing.
4. Average prime rate.
5. Commercial and industrial loans.
6. Ratio of consumer installment credit to personal income.
7. Change in CPI for services.

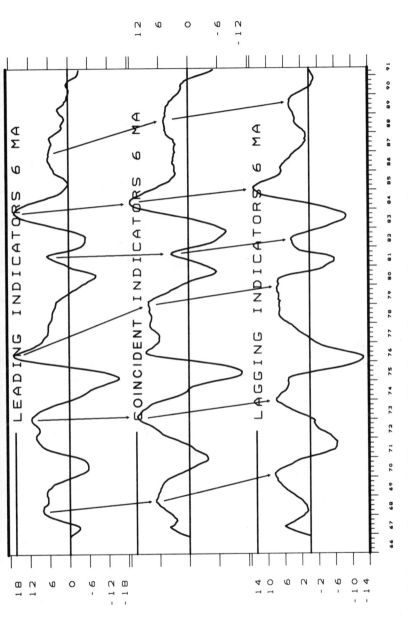

Figure 7.4 Leading, coincident, and lagging indicators (Commerce Department). Arrows join cyclical peaks to demonstrate the chronological sequence. (Source: *Pring Market Review*)

is to demonstrate the sequential progression of their cyclic rhythms. This arrangement is only the tip of the iceberg, as a complete business cycle comprises many more events than the six turning points illustrated by these three indicators. Figures 7.5 and 7.6 show a similar chronological arrangement, but this time expanding the number from three to seven.

Money market prices have been used as the reciprocal of short-term interest rates so that the direction of their movement corresponds to the other indicators. In these figures, each series has been expressed as a 12-month moving average of a two-year or 24-month rate of change. The two-year time span was chosen because it approximates half of an idealized cycle and, therefore, picks up the underlying business cycle fluctuation. The smoothing of the raw data by a 12-month moving average does delay the turning points, but reversals in its direction usually offer a reliable indication that the underlying cyclical trend has reversed. Final confirmation of a peak or trough occurs when the indicator crosses above or below its nine-month moving average.

The arrows connecting the cyclical peaks highlight the chronological sequence of events. The shaded areas represent recessions. It is also apparent that the troughs undergo a similar progression. Two elements stand out. First, the leads and lags are different in each succeeding cycle. For example, the peak in housing start momentum usually occurs well before that of the Leading Indicators, but in 1977 the LEI series actually led by a few months. Second, the magnitude of the movements of each indicator is different in succeeding cycles. In 1977–1980, for example, the decline in money market prices was particularly strong, yet the corresponding decline in the LEI was mercifully short.

It is also important to note that the cycle actually overlaps in the sense that the Real Money Supply series peaks before the Lagging Indicator Series and vice versa. In effect, the typical cycle would actually overlap the train of our earlier example. The arrows on the two charts join the cyclic peaks of each indicator. Most of the time the progression follows in the expected way, but occasionally one indicator reverses direction out of sequence. In such instances the

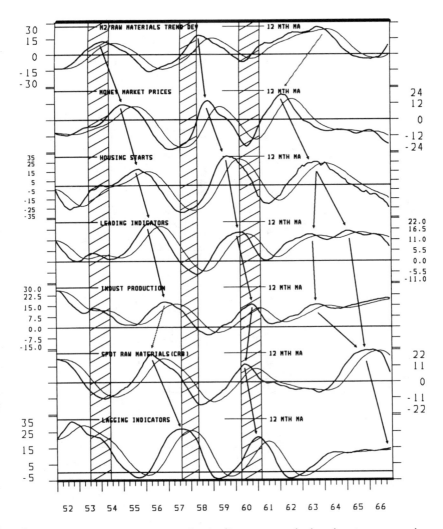

Figure 7.5 Seven economic indicators and the business cycle, 1952–1966. Shaded areas represent recessions. (Source: *Pring Market Review*)

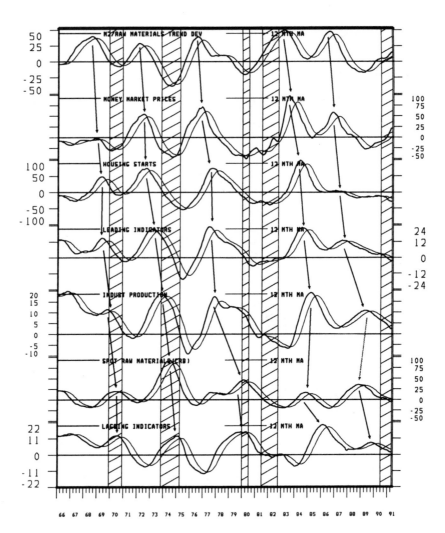

Figure 7.6 Seven economic indicators and the business cycle, 1966–1991. Shaded areas represent recessions. (Source: *Pring Market Review*)

location of the others can be used to verify the true position of the cycle.

The indicator approach is far from perfect, but it does demonstrate without doubt that there is a set sequence of events that play out in each cycle. By their very nature, these events influence the performance of the three markets.

8

Asset Allocation as the Cycle Unwinds

Chapter 6 established that there is a chronological sequence to the business cycle in which the bull and bear markets of bonds, stocks, and commodities are continually rotating. Because there are three markets, and each experiences a peak and a trough, it follows that there are six major turning points. These may be used to break the cycle down into six phases or stages. Each stage has a specific environmental characteristic, like the four seasons that occur in the calendar year.

Each season has different characteristics that are suitable for different businesses. Winter is obviously the best time to open a ski resort. Most *market* gardeners would agree that spring is a more suitable time for planting seeds and that summer and early fall are the best times to harvest the crop. On the other hand, summer provides the best environment for a beach resort, and so forth. All these businesses are potentially very profitable, but if they are opened at the wrong time of the year the results could be disastrous.

The six stages of the business cycle also have different characteristics that favor alternative asset allocation combinations. An entrepreneur would be unwise to open up and staff a ski resort in the summer. In a similar way, an investor would be advised to reduce his or her exposure to the equity market during certain phases of the business cycle.

UNDERSTANDING THE SIX STAGES

These six phases are illustrated in Figure 8.1. The cycle starts at Stage I, when bonds are positive and stocks and commodities are bearish, continuing through to Stage VI, when all three markets are in a primary bear trend. The diagram implies that each phase is of similar duration and that the six bull and bear markets are of equal magnitude. In the real world they are not. Sometimes two markets may reverse in the same month, so Stage I is actually bypassed. On other occasions, the interval between two market turning points can be quite lengthy. For instance, the bottom in equities occurred in August 1984, but the low in the commodity market did not occur until the final months of 1986, almost 2½ years later.

The magnitude of the percentage of increase on a total return basis also differs greatly. For example, the Stage I rally in bonds that began in 1974 was 5.8 percent, yet the Stage I rally of 23 percent that began in 1981 was of far greater proportion. The cycle stage indicates that the environment is favorable or unfavorable for a specific asset, but it does not give any clues to the magnitude or duration of a specific price trend.

It is also very important to remember that some markets occasionally fall out of sequence. This is a rare, but by no means unprecedented development. When this happens, it occasionally has great significance, although this is not apparent at the time. For instance, commodity prices peaked *ahead* of equities in 1929. In retrospect, this indicated a very deflationary environment because commodities were unable to maintain their normal strength into the appropriate part of the business cycle. In 1937 the opposite was true because commodities bottomed *ahead* of equities. This out-of-sequence rotation was an unusually bullish development for commodity prices that had begun a long-term upswing. Such exceptions are rare but serve to remind us that the sequential approach to

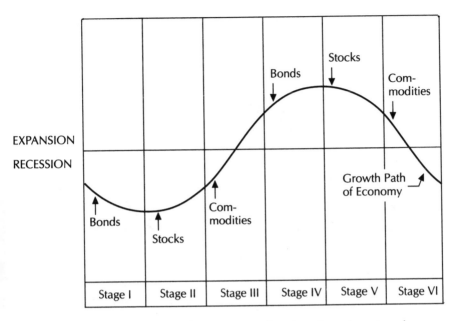

Figure 8.1 An idealized business cycle showing the six phases (stages) of the business cycle (down arrows indicate market peaks and up arrows indicate market troughs). The sine curve represents the growth path of the economy over the course of a business cycle. The arrows refer to the idealized peaks and troughs of the bond, stock, and commodity markets. In almost every business cycle since the beginning of the nineteenth century, this market sequence (bonds, stocks, and commodities) has repeated. Using these benchmarks, you can divide the business cycle into six stages. Correct identification of the prevailing stage results in a more profitable asset allocation. (Source: Pring-Turner Capital Group, Investment Advisors, Walnut Creek, CA)

financial market turning points is by no means automatic. It offers a framework and some useful guidelines, but should by no means become a substitute for independent thinking.

Figure 8.2 shows an idealized cycle for the three markets and how they interact. The lower portion represents a rough approximation of how the various asset classes might be allocated as the

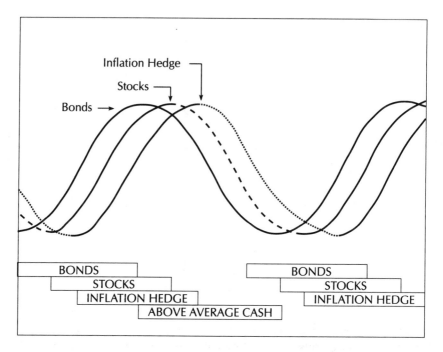

Figure 8.2 Asset exposure and the business cycle. Since bond, stock, and commodity prices reverse their trends at different points, each business cycle consists of three financial market subcycles. These are indicated above. The implications for asset allocation are represented by the boxes at the foot of the figure. (Source: Pring-Turner Capital Group, Investment Advisors, Walnut Creek, CA)

cycle progresses. The remainder of this chapter will elaborate on this process by describing the characteristics of each stage. It will go on to outline those assets to favor and those to underweight or avoid. Chapters 9 and 10 will pinpoint some of the methods and techniques that can help to identify these various stages more easily. Because the tolerance for risk bearing and the financial requirements for individual investors will differ, specific asset allocation recommendations are not made in this chapter. Instead this subject is covered in Chapter 12.

STAGE I (BONDS BULLISH; STOCKS AND COMMODITIES BEARISH)

Cash

Because two potential asset classes, stocks, and inflation hedge instruments, are in a bear market during Stage I, an overall defensive strategy is called for, and a substantial proportion of the portfolio should be allocated to cash. Cash is defined here as good quality debt instruments with a maturity of less than one year. This could include anything from money market funds to one-year Treasury Bills or CDs. The rationale is based on two factors. First, cash has a negative correlation with equities and inflation hedge instruments, and therefore serves as a stabilizing (capital preservation) influence. Second, during this phase cash is typically generating some of its highest returns for the cycle. As the new cycle unfolds, short-term interest rates decline and offer lower rates of return, but this enables the economy to enter a recovery phase, making stocks relatively more attractive.

Bonds

In a normal business cycle, Stage I occurs during the early part of a recession. In the case of a double cycle (discussed in Chapter 6), this phase usually begins just before the growth curve of the economy reaches the end of its downward trajectory, i.e., somewhere close to the zero reference line shown in Figure 6.6. This stage is characterized by weak economic activity, and a justified fear of the Federal Reserve of a recession. Sentiment in the bond market is usually quite bearish because prices have generally been falling for at least a year and occasionally as long as three years. Equally important is the fact that the previous bear market most probably was interrupted by at least one major rally, in which many participants positioned themselves in anticipation of a bull market. At the time of the actual low, many of them were either whipsawed one or two times or sat with a major paper loss. With this kind of experience, the last thing on the minds of most investors is the acquisition of more bonds, even though economic and financial conditions favor such action.

From an asset allocation point of view, this is clearly the optimal point in the cycle to take a very aggressive stance toward good quality long-term fixed income securities. Not only is this a stage when the allocation should be heavily weighted to long-term bonds, but it is also one in which the average maturity should be extended as far as possible.

Even though this is the low risk/high reward part of the cycle for bond owners, the optimal combination will depend on the asset toleration levels discussed in Chapter 12. The maximum bond allocation will, therefore, be a personal decision based on financial circumstances, age, and personality. Another factor that will affect the allocation decision will be the point when Stage I is actually identified. If bonds have already rallied 30 percent off their lows by the time you realize that Stage I is underway, the bull market will in all probability have realized a significant measure of its potential. In most instances it is better to play it safe by taking a far less aggressive position in both the total allocation to bonds and the average maturity than if you had been able to identify the rally at an earlier stage.

Another important consideration is the quality of the signal. For example, if you are following 10 different indicators, nine of which were positive, this would represent a far stronger signal than if only six, i.e., a barely bullish majority, had moved into positive territory. The probability of an explosive and long-lasting bull market would be much greater under the first scenario and would justify a far more aggressive investment posture.

Sometimes it is a good idea to try to qualify the various signals in a way similar to how the bond rating services categorize the credit rating of borrowers. In this way, AAA buy signals would indicate an aggressive allocation. On the other hand, a B signal would induce a much lower level of enthusiasm and support a lower allocation. For example, an AAA signal might occur where several reliable indicators give positive indications at a time when the market in question has only just started to rally.

Stage I is a favorable time to purchase good quality long-term instruments, but not poorer quality instruments. This is because the weak economic environment that is so positive for high quality paper increases the possibility for defaults in lower quality instruments. Whenever there is even a whisper of possible default, it is usually discounted by all bonds of a similar class. For example, in 1990 rumors of a default in just one or two junk bonds adversely affected the price of virtually all high yield issues, even though many of them continue to maintain interest payments to this day. From a risk management point of view, this is one area of the bond market that should be avoided at this stage in the cycle. Even with good quality issues, it is very important to make sure that the bonds purchased do not have an unfavorable call feature enabling the issuer to buy them back or redeem them once interest rates have sunk to a specific level. These kinds of features will foreclose on your ability to fully capitalize on the trend of falling interest rates implied by a Stage I environment.

Equities

The equity market as a whole is still in a primary bear phase, but it does not necessarily follow that all stocks are in a declining trend. Quite often it is possible to identify some that have already turned. In 1974 for example, Dow Jones bottomed in December, but certain interest sensitive sectors, such as utilities, had already bottomed in September. Figure 8.3 highlights the performance of the S&P Utility Index on both an absolute and relative basis to the S&P Composite during Stage I periods as defined by market peaks and troughs. The record is far from perfect, but the rising relative strength line in most of these instances indicates that utility stocks offer a better risk/reward than the overall market during a Stage I. Other defensive and, therefore, leading sectors such as financials and consumer staples, also have a tendency to put in a better performance than the overall market in Stage I, but this relationship is not as reliable as that of the utilities.

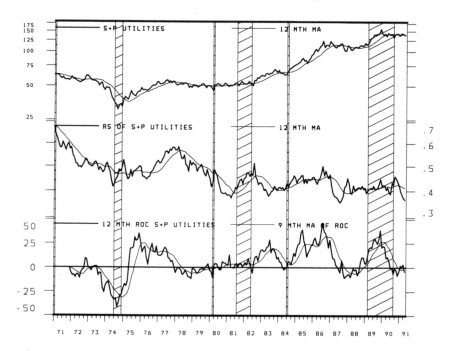

Figure 8.3 S&P Utility Index vs. S&P Composite, 1971–1991. Shaded periods indicate Stage I as defined by the markets. (Source: *Pring Market Review*)

STAGE II (BONDS AND STOCKS BULLISH; COMMODITIES BEARISH)

Cash

As Stage II unfolds, the advantage to be gained from holding short-term debt instruments diminishes. On an absolute basis the yield will gradually fall. There are usually at least two Discount Rate cuts during Stage II. Also, the stock market has now entered a bull phase, so the risk/reward for holding equities will have dramatically improved. In a relative sense, the opportunity cost of holding low yielding cash will have risen considerably. As soon as it is apparent that the cycle has progressed to Stage II, a significant portion of the cash allocation should be rotated immediately toward stocks. The actual amount of liquid reserves to be retained will be based on personal circumstances and the strength of the evidence that Stage II is, in fact, underway.

Bonds

Bonds are still experiencing a bull market during Stage II, but as it evolves the potential gain from holding long-term debt instruments progressively declines. There is still one more stage in which bonds are in a bull market, so a relatively high allocation is justified. Even so, a marginal rotation into stocks from bonds makes it appropriate at this stage because equities are in an earlier phase of their bull cycle and traditionally offer a *relatively* higher rate of return than bonds.

Equities

Stocks should be the natural beneficiary of any funds transferred from the cash or bond sections of the portfolio. The scale of the rotation will depend on a number of factors. These might include the quality of the buy signal, the amount that stocks have risen from their lows, etc. The first or second cut in the Discount Rate following an equity bear market has almost always given a reliable and powerful signal. However, if the market has already advanced 20 to 25 percent off its lows, it has clearly moved a long way toward discounting the good news. Under such circumstances, the risk/reward would not be as favorable as if it was only 5 to 10 percent from its low. Because bull markets are rarely one step affairs, it makes sense to wait for an intermediate-term correction to develop. When subsequent price weakness causes market sentiment to be less enthusiastic, stocks can once again be accumulated. This kind of delayed action is very difficult to put into practice because a sharp price run up in the order of 20 percent or so is very tempting.

Missing out on some of that appreciation involves strong discipline and much more patience than most investors have.

During Stage II, early market leaders continue to rally in an *absolute* sense, but at some point the *relative* trend of utilities and some other interest sensitive groups top out. In some cycles this is delayed until the closing phase of Stage III. For every loser in relative strength there must be a winner. In this case it often emerges from the manufacturing, retail, or auto areas. Each cycle differs so that it is not possible to lay down any hard and fast rules.

STAGE III (BONDS, STOCKS, AND COMMODITIES BULLISH)

Cash

This is the time in the cycle when all three markets are in a bullish phase; so cash should be held to a minimum. Another reason for maintaining a low cash reserve is because cash is giving its lowest return at this time.

Bonds

Stage III witnesses the terminal phase of the bull market in long-term debt instruments. As it progresses, bond exposure should be gradually reduced. Bond prices may continue to rally, but because other vehicles are in an earlier phase of development, the opportunity cost of holding bonds is growing.

There are three ways to reduce the impending danger from falling bond prices. The most obvious one is to pare back the bond allocation on a programmed basis. The second is to gradually reduce the average maturity of the bond allocation. Sometimes toward the end of Stage III, any zero coupon bonds with maturity dates in excess of five years and coupon bonds with a maturity greater than say five to seven years should be liquidated. Obviously it is not possible to time the end of this phase to the exact month, but if you gradually reduce your exposure as the danger signs discussed in Chapters 9 and 10 become apparent, you will be in a much stronger position to withstand the first intermediate-term price decline in the oncoming bear market. The big conflict at this stage is that money market instruments always offer significantly lower current yields than long-term bonds. The sale of bonds, therefore, means that you have to undergo some sacrifice in the form of a lower current income. This can be a particularly difficult decision for investors who rely heavily on their portfolio income for day-to-day expenses.

A partial solution to this dilemma is to examine the current position of the yield curve. Usually it rises or falls quite steeply in this part of the cycle. Once the curve has begun to flatten, there is little to be gained in the way of current yield, however long the maturity. In Figure 8.4 this point is reached at approximately the

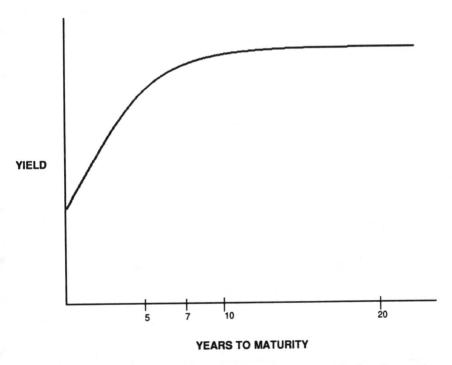

Figure 8.4   Bond yield over time. (Source: *Pring Market Review*)

seven-year mark. At seven years you are getting almost as much current income as from a 20-year bond, but the *capital risk is much smaller*. For example, assuming a coupon rate of 7 percent, a rise in yields from 7 percent to 8 percent would result in a 10 percent decline in the price of the 20-year bond, but only 4 percent in a five-year issue. (Various interest rate maturity scenarios and their effect on price are shown in Table 8.1.) In effect, by gradually reducing your maturity as the bull market comes to a close, you have maintained a similar reward but greatly reduced your risk.

The third way in which the risk/reward can be augmented is to rotate some of the portfolio allocated to Treasury securities to lower quality bonds. Obviously the quality should not be reduced to the extent of risking a default. However, it is appropriate to take on more risk because the economy is in the relatively early phase of a recovery. Consequently, the general risk of default is relatively low, and hence it is the appropriate time to go for the higher yield associated with these poorer quality securities. It is also worth noting that these bonds usually peak after Treasury securities! This is because other investors also want to lock in high yields and are unconcerned with quality problems.

TABLE 8.1
Price Fluctuations for Various Maturities (7% Coupon Rate)

Falling Securities Prices (Rising Interest Rates)			
Time to Maturity	Price at 7%	Price at 8%	Change (%)
6 months	100	99½	−0.50
1 year	100	99	−1.00
2 years	100	98⅛	−1.88
5 years	100	96	−4.00
10 years	100	93¼	−6.75
20 years	100	90	−10.00

Stocks

The arrival of Stage III means that commodity prices have started to firm. This means that you should keep a close eye open for the rotation process away from interest sensitive beneficiaries, such as utilities and financial issues. It is either already under way by this point or, more likely, it will start toward the end of Stage III. The timing will depend on the characteristics of the prevailing cycle. Once it is possible to identify that this process is underway, it makes sense to gradually switch these types of issues into equities whose businesses benefit from the upsurge in capital spending that occurs at the tail end of the business cycle. Specifically this would include technology, basic industry, energy, and mining groups. Any proceeds from a bond sale might also be used to augment the stock allocation in these areas.

This part of the cycle is one in which it is very difficult to lose money because all markets are in a rallying phase. Confidence starts to improve as investors forget the dark days of the recession and focus on the good times ahead. In many business cycles, stocks with a high beta are now coming into their own. Just as it makes good sense to undertake a responsible lowering of quality standards in the bond portfolio in Stage III, the same process can be applied to stocks. In this respect the equity allocation should now include more stocks with a beta greater than 1.0. This is not a carte blanche signal to go out and buy any stocks. Obviously care must be taken to invest in companies that satisfy your fundamental and technical criteria. However, because the market is often in a very positive mode at this stage, it is possible to go after more reward with less fear of downside risk.

Inflation Hedge

In Stage III commodity prices begin their bull market, which means that at some point commodity sensitive equities, such as energy or mining stocks, will be coming into their own. In some cycles they lead, and in others they slightly lag commodity prices. In either case, the new bull market has the effect of pulling up the share prices of companies that benefit from higher commodity prices. Gold and gold shares represent special cases because they usually *lead* major reversals in commodity prices. This and other aspects are discussed in Chapter 11. Essentially any additional equity money that is being switched from cash, bonds, or interest sensitive equities should now be rotated into earnings driven stocks, such as basic industry and inflation sensitive issues.

STAGE IV (STOCKS AND COMMODITIES BULLISH; BONDS BEARISH)

Cash

Stage IV begins as bond and money market prices peak and yields start to rally. As this stage progresses, cash investments will once again start to offer an increasingly attractive return. However, because interest rates usually form a saucer-like bottom as they trough out, it is some time before rising interest rates offer the kind of return that can successfully compete with a rapidly rising stock market. Cash allocation at this point should, therefore, be maintained at a relatively low level.

Bonds

Bond prices have now begun a bear market. It is seldom easy to spot exact turning points in markets, so you can never be entirely sure that a primary trend reversal has, in fact, taken place. Consequently the bond allocation should be gradually reduced as more and more evidence becomes available. Because the lower-quality issues tend to peak last and also offer the best returns, they should be maintained as a core position until sometime in Stage V when the potential for a declining economy will present a very real threat of default.

Stocks

Interest sensitive equities are usually in the process of peaking by the time Stage IV begins. These include utilities, banks, insurance companies, and stockbrokers. Even if these issues continue to work their way higher in an absolute sense, their performance *relative* to the overall market almost invariably starts to deteriorate. Either way, it is a wise policy to accelerate the rotation policy that began in Stage II in favor of earnings driven equities.

STAGE V (COMMODITIES BULLISH; BONDS AND STOCKS BEARISH)

Cash

Once Stage V has begun, only one market—commodities—is in a bull phase. For this reason, and because short-term interest rates have now become more competitive, any net proceeds from bond and equity sales should be moved into short-term fixed income securities.

Bonds

The move into a Stage V is usually caused by an accleration in the inflationary process as the commodity bull market picks up considerable upside momentum. The implication is that the relatively restrained bear market in bond prices might begin to increase momentum, but in this case the direction is down. The bond allocation and average maturity should be progressively reduced. As Stage V continues, those bonds that remain should be rotated into high-quality government issues where the threat of credit risk is minimal. It is important to make sure that the portfolio is securely constructed to withstand the financial shocks that will inevitably emerge in Stage VI, even if it means sacrificing some current income.

Stocks

Immediately after you are able to identify that Stage V has begun, steps should be taken to reduce the stock allocation. Not all equities will peak with the market averages; some will lead and others will lag. By this time, though, the majority will have already begun a bear move. In most cases the market averages will also have peaked, but in some cycles where the inflationary pressures are particularly strong, the weight of the inflation sensitive stocks will more than compensate for weakness in other areas so that the S&P Composite, for example, will go on to make a new high. Do not be fooled into confusing a higher market average with a positive environment for all equities. Indeed, the very fact that these market averages can reach new highs under such a selective background is a reflection of the weak underlying economy. Stage V is, therefore, one in which the stock allocation should be reduced and where equity exposure as a general rule should be limited to inflation sensitive and other earnings driven issues.

STAGE VI (BONDS, STOCKS, AND COMMODITIES BEARISH)

Cash

This is the time when none of the markets is in a bull phase; so cash is king. As Stage VI progresses, holding high-quality liquid investments becomes a more and more attractive proposition. This is because rates of return are at their cyclical peak, and all the other markets are falling, often precipitously. Mercifully, this phase of the cycle is almost always very brief, rarely lasting more than six months. If you are fortunate enough to anticipate these hard financial times and have built up a large cash hoard, it is certainly not a time for gloating and complacency. This is because some really outstanding investment opportunities lie just around the corner, and they almost always develop at a time when you least expect them.

Bonds

It is highly unlikely that you will be able to identify the bottom in the bond market until at least one to two months after the final low. Because bonds do offer a high current return at this point it is a good idea to begin a program of accumulation in anticipation of the bull market that is about to start. This could take the form of extending the average maturity in order to lock in the prevailing high yields or slowly expanding the bond allocation into price weakness. Either way, the high current return will help to cushion the value of your portfolio because you are likely to be early. Another possibility is to purchase bonds with a relatively short maturity of five years. This way the high yield can be locked in, but the risk of substantial capital depreciation in the event of rising rates will be minimized.

It goes without saying that risks of financial defaults are high during Stage VI. Therefore, any bond exposure or purchases should be limited to issues of the highest quality.

Stocks

Because stocks are usually outperformed by bonds during Stages I and VI, equity allocations should be kept to an absolute minimum. Inflation hedge equities should now be, or already have been, rotated into cash or very defensive stocks such as high-yielding electric utilities, convertibles, preferreds, bonds, etc.

SUMMARY

1. Stage I should emphasize cash and high-quality bonds.
2. In Stage II allocations to stocks should be increased, particularly those sensitive to interest rates. Rates of return are at their cyclical peak for both stocks and bonds, so cash holdings should be minimal.
3. Because all markets are in a rising phase during Stage III, cash should be at cycle lows.

4. Bond positions should be reduced in Stage IV, and the stock portion of the portfolio should be rotated toward earnings driven equities (e.g., basic industries, technology, and mining) and away from sectors that benefit from declining interest rates (e.g., utilities and financials). Stocks offer the best relative gains instead of cash or bonds in Stage IV.
5. The equity allocation should be reduced in Stage V.
6. Cash is king during Stage VI. Some bottom fishing in the bond market is desirable.
7. It will be difficult in most instances to identify the various stages until some time after they have begun. For this reason, alterations in the allocations should be made on a programmed basis.
8. Larger portfolio switches should be made only when you have a high degree of confidence that the environment has changed.
9. The actual allocations for each individual will be determined by personal financial objectives and risk aversion attitudes.

9
Tracking the Stages: Market Action

Risk management and diversification can greatly improve the performance of any allocation program, but that is only part of the story. The most important task is to correctly identify the prevailing stage of the cycle and promptly take suitable action in terms of the appropriate asset mix. This chapter is concerned with that identification process. Because every cycle has its own characteristics, the allocation procedure will always be a little different. It will also depend a great deal on a subjective assessment of each situation, which means that it is far from perfect. It would be wrong to start with the idea that it is possible to end up with the perfect mix every time. The chances are that you will rarely, if ever, obtain the ideal balance. The principal objective should be the rotation of the asset mix with the long-term objective of consistently beating the average risk free yield on money market instruments.

There are two strategies that should help in reaching this objective. The first is to avoid taking undue risk when conditions are confusing or unclear. The second is to be much more aggressive when you are confident that the indicators are unequivocally giving the all clear for a specific stage in the business cycle. For example, if the consensus of bond indicators is 55 percent favorable and 45 percent unfavorable it would be poor money management to go for an above average exposure. After all, it would only require a small swing of 10 percent by the indicators in the other direction to tip the balance into a negative mode again. Furthermore, a marginally bullish consensus implies marginal gains. Why take on more risk when the potential reward is so limited?

On the other hand, if 80 percent of the indicators are favorable, the odds of a large, low-risk gain are much higher. This is the kind of situation when a higher level of exposure makes sense, provided, of course, that the particular market in question is not overextended.

We also have to remember that each cycle has its own individual characteristics that can affect the magnitude of a price move for a specific asset. For example, the 1982–1984 cycle saw a huge move for stocks and a relatively small one for commodities. In 1970–1974 the situation was reversed as commodities rallied sharply and

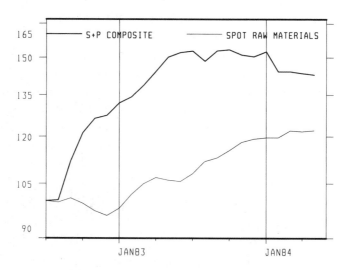

Figure 9.1   Stocks vs. commodities, 1982–1984. (Source: *Pring Market Review*)

stocks were able to put in only a modest performance. This is shown in Figures 9.1 and 9.2, which compare their respective performance in these two periods.

Assessing whether a small or unduly large bull or bear move is underway is not an easy matter. In Chapter 6, we briefly outlined the characteristics of the long, or Kondratieff, wave. Generally speaking, the magnitude of bull markets in bonds, and bear markets in commodities, is much smaller in the rising part of that cycle. During the transitional and downwave, the opposite is usually the case.

These inflationary and deflationary forces do not appear to influence the magnitude of general stock market rallies. However, the internal characteristics of each bull market are very strongly influenced by the prevailing stage of the long wave. For example, in the 1978–1980 period, right at the crest of the inflationary wave, inflation sensitive stocks experienced huge rallies and were strong

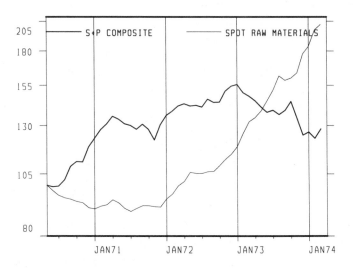

Figure 9.2   Stocks vs. commodities, 1970–1974. (Source: *Pring Market Review*)

relative performers. On the other hand, deflation sensitive stocks, such as foods and financials, put in a superb performance in the 1982–1990 period when deflationary forces had obtained the upper hand.

Generally speaking, the equity market as a whole appears to possess the greatest potential to rally the deeper and more prolonged the recession. For example, the mild 1966 *growth* recession was followed by a rally that took the S&P Composite up by 48 percent on a total return basis. On the other hand, the recessions of 1973–1974 and 1982 were much more severe and were followed by bull market advances on a total return basis of 69 percent and 64 percent, respectively. The principal reason for this tendency is because the weaker economic activity becomes, the greater incentive corporations have to streamline their activities. The alternative is usually bankruptcy. This means that when conditions eventually improve, increased revenues go straight to the bottom line. The faster profits can rise, the greater the potential for stock prices to advance.

This *recession* effect should be regarded as a tendency, rather than a hard and fast rule. Actual market performance will also depend on other factors, such as prevailing equity valuation, the speed of the decline in interest rates, market sentiment, and so forth. Normally these factors go hand-in-hand with a deep recession. If the economy is extremely weak, it almost invariably means that interest rates will fall sharply. This is because one of the key functions of the Federal Reserve is to do everything in its power to avoid a deep economic contraction. Consequently, if the Fed comes to the conclusion that things are worse than originally thought, it is likely to pursue a far more aggressive monetary policy. When the economy experiences extreme weakness, it inevitably translates into very pessimistic sentiment in the stock market. The result is that prices are beaten down to bargain basement levels. When the pendulum has swung so far in one direction, it usually swings in the other. In this sense, the depth of the recession sows the seed for the next major bull market because businesses become more efficient and stock valuations are very attractive.

CLASSIFYING THE SIX STAGES

The previous chapter described the six stages of the business cycle in some detail. We must now turn our attention to ways in which these business cycle phases can be identified. First, it should be strongly emphasized that while most business cycles experience the six stages, as defined by the chronological sequence of market peaks and troughs, some do not. You should not assume that it is always possible to extrapolate this progression mechanically because sometimes the actual peaks and troughs will not fit. For the most part, the business cycle is a fairly orderly process, and the financial markets respond in a predictable way. However, the normal order of business can be, and is, interrupted occasionally by special factors. We will consider these later, but first it is important to understand that there are really two ways in which the six stages may be classified. These are *environmental* and *actual*.

The term *environmental* refers to the monetary and economic background. For example, we already know that after a lag, contracting business conditions result in a reduction in the demand for credit as corporations and consumers retrench. At the same time, the supply of potential credit is increased as the Federal Reserve expands banking system reserves. This combination typically lowers interest rates and is favorable, first for bonds and later stocks, as equity market participants anticipate the next recovery. When the monetary and economic background is favorable for the bond and stock markets, they *typically* react in a positive manner, and vice versa. The word *typically* is emphasized because markets do not always respond in the way that they should. This is especially true of the equity market where prices are determined as much by psychological attitudes to the emerging fundamentals as the fundamentals themselves. In the next chapter the business cycle stages are identified with the help of some economic and financial indicators. An examination of the stages, as classified by the *actual* cyclical peaks and troughs of the markets, indicates that they often diverge for a time from the environment itself. You can be most confident that a specific phase in the cycle has been reached when the actual and environmental factors agree.

If each cycle repeated exactly in terms of chronological sequence, leads and lags, and magnitude of market moves, our task would be rudimentary, but the simple fact is that it does not. Because of these complications, it is important to rotate asset allocations in a slow and consistent manner. There are many times when the indicators offer clear-cut evidence that a specific stage has been reached, but more often than not, the market in question will already have moved a great deal before the evidence becomes this conclusive. This is why it is mandatory to rotate the asset mix gradually as more information becomes available and to be mentally prepared for the next step. Just when you think you have the situation under control and are convinced that you are on the right track, something new arises. Complacency can be an important enemy unless steps are taken to overcome it.

Anticipating the next market move is not unlike taking a long train journey. Say, for example, you plan on getting off at the next stop. If you are particularly anxious to meet someone important to you, chances are you will get out of your seat as you sense the train is approaching the station, grab hold of your luggage, and proceed to the door. You will not, of course, get out of the train until you know that it has actually come to a complete stop, but you have nevertheless prepared yourself both mentally and physically to get off immediately after the train arrives at your destination. The same should be true of the asset rotation process, except to say that it is usually a good idea to begin shifting a few assets when you have good grounds for suspecting that the cycle has started to move to the next stage. In some cases a partial rotation could be justified *ahead* of the markets, but it should never be done to the degree that your whole investment approach will be jeopardized in the event that you are wrong. Because the characteristics of each cycle are different, it makes sense to set an allocation range rather than a specific number for a particular stage (e.g., 30 to 50 percent for bonds in Stage I, rather than, say, 40 percent).

We have talked a lot about the *indicators* in a general sense, without describing them in detail. That is the subject of the remaining part of this chapter and the next one. I mentioned earlier that there are really two ways of categorizing the six stages: by the actual position of the markets, and by the background or environmental factors. Let's look at them in turn and see which benchmarks or pointers facilitate the six-stage identification process.

IDENTIFYING THE STAGES FROM THE ACTUAL POSITION OF THE MARKETS

The previous chapter described the chronological sequence between the turning points in the bond, stock, and commodity markets. We noted that it repeats consistently in the vast majority of cycles. Occasionally, one market or the other turns out of sequence, but the main difficulty in applying this approach is due to the varying leads and lags between markets in different cycles.

On the other hand, an understanding of this progression provides us with a useful framework that can help identify the current stage in the cycle. Once we know, for example, that bonds have peaked, the next turning point to anticipate would be that of stocks, and so forth. Not only can the knowledge of the sequence be used to anticipate turning points, but the action of the other two markets can also be used as a cross-reference. For example, if the analysis indicates that the bond market has bottomed, but commodities and stocks are still experiencing strong rallies, this would be inconsistent with the normal sequence. The likelihood of a bond market reversal taking place would be extremely low. On the other hand, if bonds rallied several months or more after stocks had begun a decline and at least six weeks after the commodity indexes had seen a peak, the odds of a cyclical reversal in bonds would be far greater.

Some Useful Trend Identification Techniques

Identifying major trend reversals in financial markets is rarely as easy as most of the pundits would have us believe. However, there are a few rudimentary techniques used by technical analysts that can point in the right direction. Technical analysis has been defined as "the study of data generated by the action of markets and by the behavior of market participants and observers. Such study is usually applied to estimating probabilities for the future course of prices for a market, investment or speculation by interpreting the data in the context of precedent."[1] Technical analysis is, therefore, the art of identifying a trend reversal at a relatively early stage and riding on that trend until the weight of the evidence proves that the trend has reversed.

Market analysis recognizes that there are many different trends, which can last from as little as a few hours to as long as 20 to 30 years. We are concerned here with the trend that revolves around the business cycle, known as the *primary* trend. When market participants refer to a bull or bear market they are talking about a primary trend with a one-to-three-year time span.

Moving Averages

If you study the price action of virtually any financial market, you will see that it is a very jagged affair, occasionally taking on an almost haphazard effect. When you think the trend is up, the price often retraces some of the previous advance, leaving you in some measure of doubt as to the trend's true direction. One of the most common techniques that technicians use to overcome this problem is the moving average (MA). As the name implies, it is a statistical procedure that attempts to smooth out these period-to-period fluctuations, leaving you with a clearer picture of the underlying trend.

Moving averages can be figured in a number of different ways, but the most widely used is the simple or mean average. It is calculated by adding up a series of observations and dividing the total by the number of observations. The average *moves* when data for the next period are available (because this is added to the total)

---

[1] Market Technicians Association Board of Directors; subject to the approval of members.

and the data for the first period are deleted. A calculation for a 12-month moving average is shown in Table 9.1. Various illustrations in this chapter show that the moving average is much smoother than the raw data and reflects the underlying trend better. The most reliable signals of a trend reversal come when the moving average reverses direction. When this occurs close to the ultimate high or low, it provides a wonderfully timely and reliable signal, such as the ones for the bottom of the 1973–1974 bear market and the top of the 1966–1968 bull market. Unfortunately, while most of these moving average reversal signals are pretty reliable, too often they are triggered after the market itself has already moved a long way. In most instances, moving average reversals provide confirmation of something we already know, and occur too late to be of much practical use.

Because of this drawback, technicians use moving average *crossovers* rather than *reversals* to signal when a trend has re-

TABLE 9.1
12-Month Moving Average Calculation

Date	Index	12-Month Total	Moving Average
Jan. 1990	101		
Feb.	100		
Mar.	103		
Apr.	99		
May	96		
June	99		
July	95		
Aug.	91		
Sept.	93		
Oct.	89		
Nov.	90		
Dec.	95	115.1	95.92
Jan. 1991	103	115.3	96.08
Feb.	105	115.8	96.5
Mar.	101	116.0	96.67
Apr.	100	115.7	96.42
May	102	116.3	96.92
June	103	116.7	97.25

versed. Moving average crossovers offer more timely signals than reversals, but because they occur with greater frequency, they are less reliable. This conflict between timeliness and sensitivity is a constant dilemma for any trend following approach. On balance, though, their superior timeliness more than compensates for a few false signals.

Moving average crossovers might provide us with an objective method for determining when a specific market has reversed, but we still need to determine the appropriate time span on which to base the calculation. Longer time spans, such as 36 or 48 months, result in moving averages that generate fewer whipsaws, but because they reflect longer trends, crossovers tend to develop well after the turning point. They are, therefore, of relatively little practical use. On the other hand, a six-month moving average will provide much more timely signals, but because this average is more sensitive, it will also trigger a far greater number of false or whipsaw signals. Because we are interested in trends that last between one and two years, a moving average that falls between these extremes is more appropriate. Figure 9.3 shows the CRB Composite plotted against two moving averages calculated from different time spans.

No time span is perfect, but 12 months is one of the most consistently reliable because it eliminates seasonal distortions. Figure 9.4 demonstrates how this might work in the marketplace. We can see from the figure that the late summer of 1982 was a Stage II because bonds and stocks were in the early phase of a bull market and commodities were in a bear trend. This is very easy to sort out with the benefit of hindsight, but how could we have known at the time that the July bottom was the final one for the equity market? There is no way to know for sure, but a quick review of the relationship between the markets and their 12-month moving averages would have helped. For example, Stage I actually began in the fall of 1981 when the bond market bottomed and was signaled in the early part of 1982 when the Bond Index crossed above its moving average. At this juncture, the action of the other markets was consistent with a Stage I because both the S&P Composite and the Commodity Index were below their averages. Stage II began in August 1982 when the stock market reached its low but was not actually signaled until

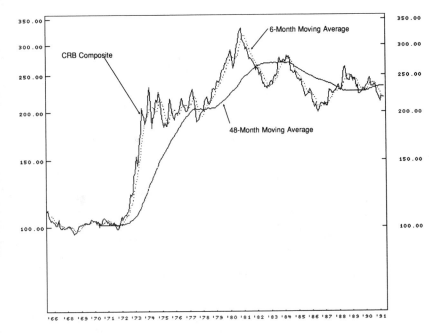

Figure 9.3 CRB Composite and two moving averages. (Source: *Pring Market Review*)

September when the S&P crossed above its moving average. Bonds remained above their average and the commodity series was below its average; therefore, all three markets were consistent with a Stage II in September of 1982. Stage III began in November but was not signaled until February 1983.

The ensuing three bear markets unfolded in the normal sequence, as bonds, stocks, and commodities all peaked and crossed below their moving averages in the expected order. These negative trends for bonds and stocks were relatively brief because the economy was experiencing the slowdown phase of a double cycle (described in Chapter 6), rather than a full fledged recession. The surprise came when they reversed to the bullish side. Equities bottomed slightly behind bonds but crossed above their moving average *ahead* of the Bond Index. This is not an unprecedented action, but certainly

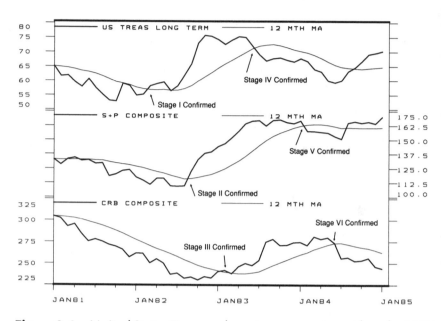

Figure 9.4　United States Treasury long-term government bonds, S&P Composite, and CRB Composite. (Source: *Pring Market Review*)

unusual. Quite often, when a market moves ahead of its normal position in the cycle, it indicates some degree of urgency to get going. From a practical point of view, this often means that the new trend is going to be a big one. In this instance the stock market experienced a magnificent bull run. One of the most classic examples of this phenomenon occurred in 1929 when commodities peaked *ahead* of stocks. In effect, the commodity market was in such a hurry to turn down that it was warning of the deflationary period that lay ahead.

Rate of Change

The second technique that can provide us with clues of an impending trend reversal is a rate of change (ROC) Indicator mentioned in the next chapter, which measures the momentum or velocity of a price move. If we light a fire, we know from experience that the moment of maximum intensity, when the fire is burning at its most furious rate, occurs early. The fire itself does not stop burning immediately when the flames die down, but continues to burn more slowly. An ROC indicator operates in a similar manner because it usually reaches its point of maximum (minimum) intensity well before the final peak (trough) in the actual price. In effect, the ROC gives us some advance warning of a potential trend reversal.

A 24-month ROC for the three markets is shown in Figure 9.5. The very nature of the ROC calculations enable this indicator to emphasize the cyclical swings of the underlying market. This offers two advantages. First, careful review of these relationships indicates that the momentum turning points usually follow the typical bond, stock, and commodity sequence. Momentum reversals are

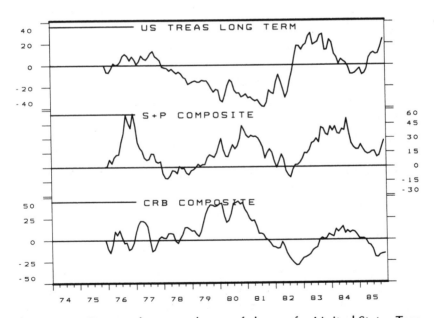

Figure 9.5 Twenty-four month rate of change for United States Treasury long-term government bonds, equities, and commodities, 1974–1986. (Source: *Pring Market Review*)

usually easier to spot from a cursory examination than turning points in the price itself.

In some cases momentum analysis indicates that the cycle for a specific market actually skips a beat. This can be very instructive. For example, the down cycle in commodities during the 1977–1978 period was almost nonexistent, yet for bonds it was very pronounced. This indicates that the economy was undergoing a secular or very long-term inflationary purge.

The opposite was true once the Long Wave had turned over. In this respect 1980–1981 was the watershed period. Note how the unusually strong upwave in bonds was accompanied by an almost nonexistent one in commodities. The fact that commodity momentum did not experience a rally in either of these periods emphasized the deflationary character of the economy. Before 1980, bull markets in bonds and bear markets in commodities were relatively brief, but since that time the reverse has been true.

Second, because an ROC indicator has a tendency to oscillate around the zero equilibrium level, it gives an indication as to whether a market is overextended. Its position can, therefore, provide important information about the maturity of a move. For example, Figure 9.6 shows that by the time the ROC of the S&P Composite reaches the +40 percent or −25 percent level, the bull cycle in stocks is approaching a terminal phase. Sometimes this indicator continues to move much higher, as it did in 1986 and 1987. In most instances, though, once the indicator peaks from a reading in excess of 40 percent the probabilities favor a high risk/low reward environment. If an overbought momentum reading for the equity market is preceded by a clear-cut peak in bond momentum, and the Bond Index itself has already crossed its 12-month moving average, the odds of an impending stock market peak will be even higher. However, this would not actually be confirmed until the S&P crossed below its 12-month moving average.

The ROC indicator is, therefore, used as a guide to tell us how overextended a specific market may be, but it does not signal a trend reversal and the beginning of a new stage. Nevertheless, when a specific ROC indicator is overextended in either direction, consistent with the position of the other two markets, there is a strong

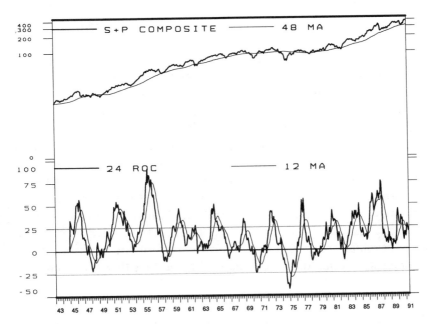

Figure 9.6 S&P Composite and 24-month rate of change. (Source: *Pring Market Review*)

possibility that a new stage is about to begin. Only the passage of time will tell for sure. Because our investment tactics involve the gradual rotation of assets as more information becomes available, there is no reason why momentum reversals from extreme levels cannot be used as a benchmark for making some small changes. If this move turns out to be premature, damage to the portfolio will be limited. On the other hand, considering that such reversals usually occur fairly close to the end of a trend, these rotations will likely be made at advantageous prices. Some cushion is then built in if the moving average crossover is unduly late, and the very fact that small shifts are being made greatly reduces the number of times when sudden market action forces us to make difficult decisions about major changes.

A good example of how this type of approach might work in practice occurred in the 1986–1987 period. During the summer of

1987, the position of the markets in relation to their 12-month moving averages indicated a Stage IV because bonds were bearish (i.e., below their average) and stocks and commodities were bullish (i.e., above their average). The bond ROC had peaked in mid-1986 and was in a sharp downtrend for most of 1987. The Bond Index itself (Figure 9.7) actually crossed below its 12-month moving average in early 1987. By the early fall of 1987 stock market momentum (see Figure 9.6) was extremely overextended. This would not have told us *when* the stock market was going to peak, but the combination of a falling bond ROC and an overbought equity velocity warned that, under normal circumstances, the top was probably not far away. At the time, the dividend yield on stocks of just over 1 percent was historically low, so the market was also at an extreme of overvaluation. A prudent interpretation of the position of the momentum indicators, combined with the fact that the cycle had

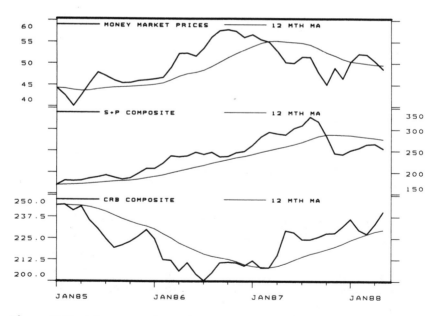

Figure 9.7 Money market prices, equities, and commodities, 1985– 1988. (Source: *Pring Market Review*)

already been in a Stage IV for some time, would indicate a shift away from stocks. This combination of indicators would not have told us to get out of equities altogether, because the trend was still up; it merely established that the risks were escalating. When risk rises to an intolerable level, it makes sense to cut back on the exposure. In this particular instance, the 12-month moving average crossover would have been totally useless because all the damage had already been done by the end of October when it was finally penetrated. This combination of an instantaneous reversal being contained within a two-month time span is unprecedented. Quite frankly, the indicators described here are not designed to cope with this type of situation. Nevertheless, the principles of diversification, outlined in Chapter 1, combined with the process of a slow but gradual rotation described above, do limit the risk in a situation of this nature.

A variation of the momentum approach is to smooth the 24-month ROC with a moving average, as in Figures 9.8 and 9.9. In this example we have used a nine-month time frame. In most instances a reversal in the primary trend of momentum is signaled when this indicator reverses direction. The arrows on these two figures join the peaks and troughs, respectively. This approach greatly simplifies the recognition of major turning points because once an indicator reverses direction, this new trend normally perpetuates. In a powerful inflationary environment the bond velocity can *miss a beat* as it did in 1978–1979 by completely failing to reverse to the upside. In an opposite vein, commodity momentum did not experience a cyclical rally along with stocks and bonds in 1990.

Sector Rotation in the Equity Market

We have already established that the business cycle can, in general terms, be divided into inflationary and deflationary parts. We also know that the stock market consists of companies involved in all phases of economic activity. Some areas, such as housing, benefit from falling interest rates, which are a deflationary event. Others, such as oil companies, thrive on rising energy prices, which tends to

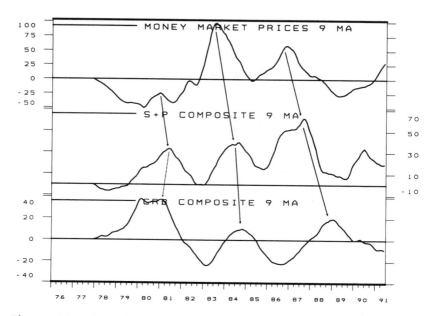

Figure 9.8 Three financial markets (peaks) and a smoothed rate of change. (Source: *Pring Market Review*)

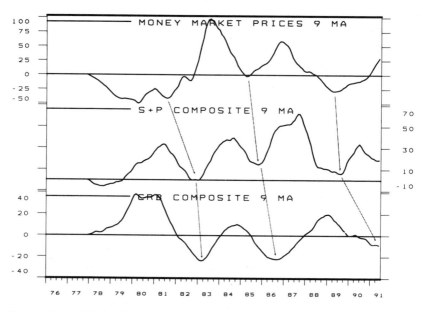

Figure 9.9 Three financial markets (troughs) and a smoothed rate of change. (Source: *Pring Market Review*)

occur in the inflationary or terminal phase of the cycle. This is a great simplification because not all areas of the market can be conveniently categorized in this way. However, it is true to say that certain sectors normally put in their best relative performance in the late stages of a bear market and the early phase of an equity bull market. A prime example is the electric utility group, which is relatively recession proof. These companies benefit greatly from falling interest rates. Not only do borrowing costs represent a high proportion of their total expenses, but they also pay generous yields; therefore, for investors current income becomes an important factor in total return. When interest rates fall, these dividends become more valuable, and the price of the stocks advances.

At the other end of the economic spectrum, mining stocks are very cyclical because their profits are sensitive to the prices of the commodities in which they deal. High prices also reflect a tight capacity situation. Both phenomena are experienced at the tail end of the business cycle, consequently, these companies put in their best relative performance toward the middle and end of an equity bull market and in the early phases of a bear market.

Relative Strength

This inflation vs. deflation analysis can be taken a step further by comparing the performance between two diametrically opposed market sectors. Before we proceed with this discussion, a few words on the concept of *relative strength* are in order.

Relative strength (RS) is calculated by dividing the price of one series (the numerator) by another (the denominator) and plotting the result as a continuous series. Usually the first item is a stock or industry group and the second is a measure of the overall market, such as the S&P Composite. It is normal to plot the relative line underneath the price of the item being measured so that its *absolute* and *relative* performance can easily be compared. When the relative line is rising, it means that item A (usually a stock) is outperforming item B (usually the market) and vice versa. Relative strength does not tell us anything about the absolute price, only about the relative performance between the two series. For example, if the stock falls by 10 percent and the market by 20 percent, both series have lost ground in an absolute sense. However, because the stock declined less than the market, the relative line will rise. Even in a down market, it is important to purchase stocks with a rising relative strength line. In our asset allocation approach, the portfolio will always contain some stocks because the allocation is never reduced to zero. Therefore, it is important, even when the allocation is low, to ensure that the equity portion contains stocks that are acting better than the market as a whole.

There are several important principles involved in the interpretation of relative strength between an item, such as a stock or industry group, and a market average.

1. Relative strength moves in trends just like the price itself.
2. When both the price and relative strength are rising, they are said to be *in gear*. When the RS line fails to confirm a new high in the security being monitored, it means that it is no longer outperforming the market. Because the RS line often leads the absolute price trend, this relative weakness also warns of a more general underlying technical deficiency in the security itself (see Figures 9.10 and 9.11). The opposite set of circum-

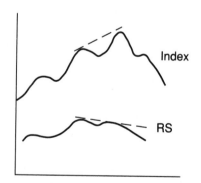

Figure 9.10   Relative strength (RS) vs. Index. (Source: Adapted from Martin J. Pring, *Technical Analysis Explained,* McGraw-Hill, NY, 1991, pg. 195)

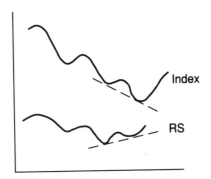

Figure 9.11   Relative strength (RS) vs. Index. (Source: Adapted from Martin J. Pring, *Technical Analysis Explained*, McGraw-Hill, NY, 1991, pg. 195)

stances holds true in a declining market where an improvement in RS ahead of price is regarded as a positive sign. Quite often bear market lows in the equity market are preceded by an improvement in interest sensitive stocks such as utilities because they are early leaders when a new bull market begins.
3. It is often possible to construct a trendline joining a series of peaks or troughs for both the absolute and relative series. When they are jointly crossed, a reversal in trend is indicated. Generally speaking, the longer the lines, the greater the significance of the breaks (Figure 9.12).

If we roughly categorize deflationary periods as those when bond momentum is rising, we find that this is usually a time when the relative and absolute performance of electric utility stocks is favorable. In Figure 9.13 the shaded areas represent periods when the bond momentum (a six-month MA of an annualized rate of change) is above its 12-month moving average. The approach is far from perfect, but it is certainly true to say that this type of environment captures most of the big *relative* moves in this period.

The shaded periods in Figure 9.14 represent inflationary conditions, i.e., when commodity momentum is rising. These figures demonstrate quite clearly that by and large, oil stocks should be

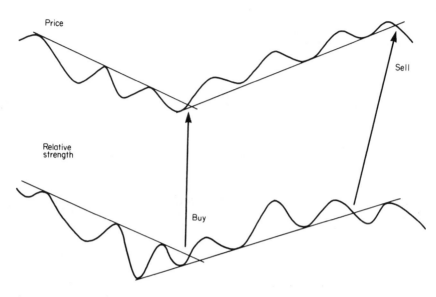

Figure 9.12   Relative strength trendline violations. (Source: Martin J. Pring, *Technical Analysis Explained*, McGraw-Hill, NY, 1991, pg. 195)

avoided in deflationary times and electric utilities should be under-weighted in a portfolio when inflationary pressures are strong.

In addition to pointing us in the direction of the better performing sector, this procedure also provides a vital clue as to the current position of the cycle. It does not pinpoint the exact stage but, by flagging inflationary and deflationary conditions, it at least provides corroborating evidence as to whether the cycle is in an early or terminal phase.

Relative Strength and the Inflation/Deflation Conflict

It is possible to construct a relative strength indicator from two stock market sectors that reflect the conflicting deflationary and inflationary pressures described above. The direction of the trend of

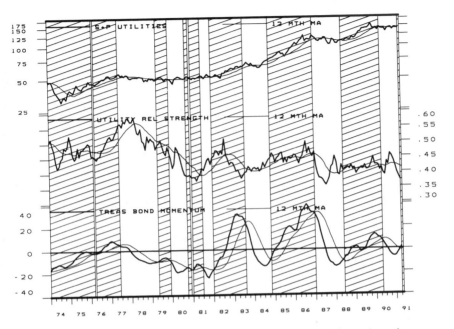

Figure 9.13 Electric utilities showing periods when bond momentum is rising. Shaded areas show when bond momentum is above its 12-month moving average. (Source: *Pring Market Review*)

this series will then provide a valuable clue to which sector has the upper hand. We also know that each bull market is born out of a recession when deflationary pressures are greatest and aborted at the end of the cycle when interest rate and inflationary pressures are strongest. Therefore, this relationship also gives us a valuable clue to the prevailing stage of the business and stock cycles. Ideally, we would construct two indexes composed of a wide selection of deflation and inflation sensitive equities. This would be a fairly complicated process, but there is a short cut.

The bottom series in Figure 9.15 shows the relative strength between the Dow Jones financial and energy sectors. (Data for the raw series are published daily in the *Wall Street Journal* and weekly

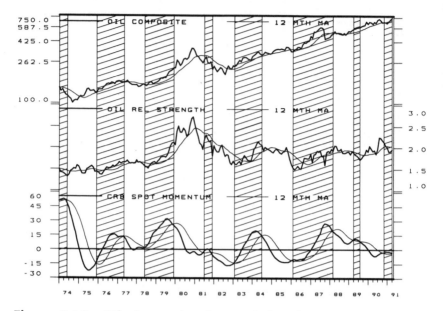

Figure 9.14 Oil shares showing periods when commodity momentum is rising. Shaded areas show when CRB momentum is above its 12-month moving average. (Source: *Pring Market Review*)

in *Barron's*. The calculation is made by dividing the financial index by the energy series.) A rising line is bullish for financial stocks relative to energy. If these two sectors experience a similar price performance, the RS index would be plotted as a horizontal line. However, this relative series is almost always in a state of flux because the elements reflect differing economic forces.

Major reversals in the direction of this relationship are consistently signaled at a relatively early stage when it crosses above and below its 12-month moving average. These crossovers confirm that the character of the market has changed, or is about to change, from one favoring inflation to one more supportive of deflationary stocks. This can be quite revealing in a more general sense because an early

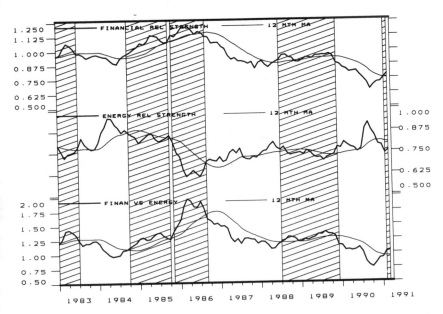

Figure 9.15   Relative strength between the Dow Jones financial and energy indexes. Shaded areas show when the financial/energy ratio is above its moving average. (Source: *Pring Market Review*)

warning of an emerging bull market in stocks occurs when this financial/energy series bottoms, and vice versa.

It can also be used to orient a portfolio toward inflationary or deflationary stocks. In Figure 9.15 the shaded areas represent favorable periods for the financial index. These have been defined by the position of the financial/energy ratio relative to its 12-month moving average. When it is above the average, this is positive in a relative sense for financial issues.

Finally, the two series shown in Figure 9.16 represent the momentum (nine-month smoothing of a nine-month rate of change) of the relative strength of the financial and energy indexes to the S&P Composite. Note how they are continually moving in opposite di-

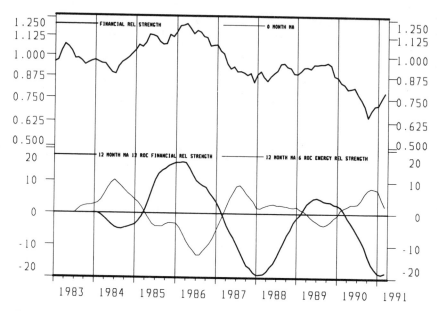

Figure 9.16 Momentum of the relative strength of the Dow Jones financial and energy sectors. (Source: *Pring Market Review*)

rections as first one sector and then the other outperforms the market. When they reverse direction, a change in the internal character of the market is indicated. This can be quite revealing in itself because confirming evidence of an emerging bull market in stocks occurs when the relative strength momentum of financial stocks bottoms.

10

Tracking the Stages: Business Cycle Benchmarks

In the last chapter we discovered that there are two ways of looking at the six stages. The first involves the position of the markets themselves, and the second relates to the economic and financial environment. This chapter is concerned with the second part of this approach, namely an examination of the economic and monetary background, and how this shapes the background for the three markets. Unfortunately, these background factors cannot be categorized easily and reduced to one or two indicators considering that the economy itself is a fairly complicated entity. It is quite possible to find one indicator that works very well in signaling major turning points for a specific market over a number of different cycles, yet it fails at the very time we need it most. This is because the secular or very long-term forces of inflation and deflation are constantly shifting, and because of institutional changes as well. For example, 200 years ago the predominant sector of the economy was agriculture, later it was manufacturing and basic industries, and in the last couple of decades the service industries and technology have gained in significance.

This chapter can be divided into two sections. The first is concerned with an examination of a group of indicators that have been combined into one consensus indicator, or barometer, to monitor the economic and monetary environment for a specific market. This process is worth going through for two reasons. First, it will demonstrate in a practical way that the business cycle does experience different seasons or environments. Second, we will be able to gain a better insight as to the kind of economic and financial environment favored by each particular asset class. A detailed description of the various components from which these barometers are constructed is presented in Appendix A at the back of the book. The barometers are also updated each month in the *Pring Market Review* (P.O. Box 329, Washington Depot, CT 06794).

The second part of this chapter will describe some indicators and concepts that also provide us with clues as to the prevailing stage of the cycle. These will be of a more practical nature that you will be able to follow without too much effort. The integration of these ideas with the technical discussion in the previous chapter, and the risk control concepts outlined at the end of Chapter 4, will put you in a good position to assess the prevailing stage of the cycle.

BUSINESS CYCLE BAROMETERS

No one indicator can be expected to consistently and accurately signal every turning point for a specific market because each business cycle has its own characteristics and idiosyncracies. However, it is possible to construct a model or barometer that contains a number of economic, financial, and technical indicators that *on average* have worked reasonably well. The concept involves establishing 10 to 15 indicators that have had an above average record at identifying bull and bear markets for specific asset classes over the last 40 years or so. Bullish and bearish benchmarks are then set for each one. As an example, we may find that a Discount Rate cut is bullish for the stock market, or a rally in a particular commodity index bearish for bonds, etc. These indicators are then combined into one overall consensus indicator, the barometer. A positive environment for a specific market is signaled when the majority or consensus of the barometer's components is in a bullish mode.

If we introduce a number of different rules and conditions, it is possible to construct a barometer that has consistently called every market turn over the last 40 or so years within a month of the cyclical top or bottom. Such an approach looks good on paper but defeats the object of the exercise. We are interested in devising a barometer that will work well in the future, precisely because it *accurately* identifies periods in which the economic and monetary background is favorable for a specific market. Making up special rules just to fit the data means that the model will give *a lot more* false signals in the future than we would like. The phrase *a lot more* is highlighted deliberately because no barometer, however well researched, will operate perfectly in the marketplace. After all, we know that markets do not always respond to the emerging fundamentals as they *ought to* because they are as much a reflection of crowd emotions as of crowd logic. They often overshoot on both the upside and downside. This means that even the best designed barometer is bound to fail from time to time.

Each of the barometers discussed below contains a number of different components. A specific indicator is included in the barometer's overall reading when it reaches an empirically derived benchmark. When more than 50 percent of the components are in a positive mode, the barometer indicates a favorable background for that specific market and vice versa.

By constructing a barometer for bonds, stocks, and commodities, it is possible to arrive at an objective identification for a stage in the cycle. Figure 10.1, for example, shows the various stages between 1979 and 1991 as defined by the barometers. Note how the chronological sequence fits the expected pattern, but occasionally, as in late 1984, the barometer arrangement skips a stage or even two stages as in late 1989 when it moved directly from Stage V to Stage II of the next cycle.

Often the stage identified by the barometers will differ from that indicated by the markets relative to their 12-month moving averages, i.e., the concept described in the previous chapter. This is to be expected because markets usually lead but sometimes lag the emerging economic conditions, and the barometers themselves may not always accurately reflect the environment. When both agree, we can have greater confidence that a particular stage is in opera-

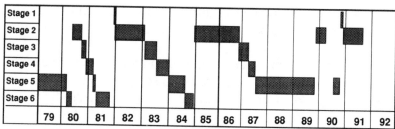

Stage 1 - Bonds Bullish Stocks/Inflation Bearish
Stage 2 - Bonds/Stocks Bullish Inflation Bearish
Stage 3 - All Bullish

Stage 4 - Bonds Bearish Stocks/Inflation Bullish
Stage 5 - Stocks/Bonds Bearish Inflation Bullish
Stage 6 - All Bearish

Figure 10.1 Barometer signals and the six stages of the business cycle. (Source: *Pring Market Review*)

tion. This means that portfolio strategy can be more aggressive. When the two diverge, a more cautious policy is appropriate. Remember, investments should not be regarded as black and white or *buy* and *sell*, but rather in shades of gray. If you approach the problem in this way it will be easier to make allocation changes when the indicators conflict.

The Bond Barometer

The Bond Barometer is shown in Figures 10.2 and 10.3. It consists of 12 indicators. When all of them are bullish, the barometer moves to a 100 percent reading. Shaded areas indicate those periods when the barometer is bearish, i.e., 50 percent or less.

Bull markets in bonds typically begin several months after the economy has started to contract, and the Federal Reserve has begun to ease monetary policy. For this reason, the Bond Barometer contains several components of the economy that are closely correlated to interest rates. These include capacity utilization (manufacturing), help wanted advertising (labor), and commodity prices (inflation). When these economic indicators slip below predetermined benchmarks, it indicates that the economy is weak enough to be consistent with rising bond prices. Commodity prices also serve

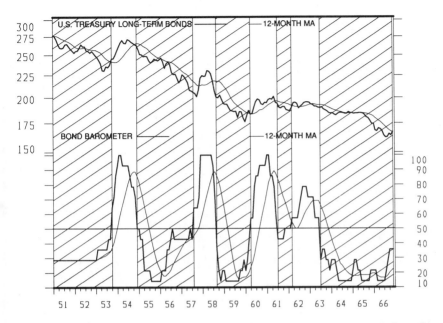

Figure 10.2 United States Treasury long-term government bonds and Bond Barometer, 1951–1966. Shaded areas represent periods when the barometer is bearish for bond prices, i.e., at or above 50. (Source: *Pring Market Review*)

what might be termed a sequence function. Because commodity prices follow bond prices in the cycle, it is important to establish that they have already reversed their cyclical trend before a bond market turning point is identified. For example, since commodity price peaks precede bond market bottoms, the commodity component of the Bond Barometer only turns bullish for bonds when the Commodity Index itself crosses below its 12-month moving average and vice versa.

The Federal Reserve influences the barometer through changes in the level of the Discount Rate. Lowering the rate is bullish for bonds and raising it is bearish.

Finally, a few of the Bond Barometer's components are derived from the relationship between the yield on corporate AAA bond

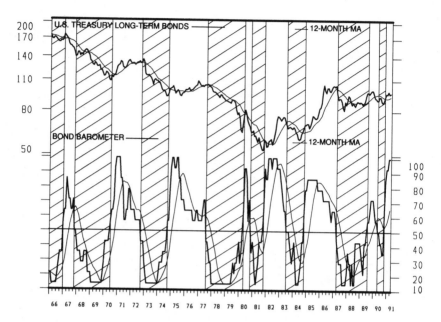

Figure 10.3 United States Treasury long-term government bonds and Bond Barometer, 1966–1991. Shaded areas represent periods when the barometer is bearish for bond prices, i.e., at or above 50. (Source: *Pring Market Review*)

yields and their 12- and 9-month moving averages. The inclusion of technical components enables the barometer to be more sensitive to market conditions.

By and large its performance has been satisfactory. It indicated a negative environment for most of the postwar secular bear markets, and it captured most of the bull moves since the secular low in 1981.

However, no indicator is infallible, and the barometer failed completely during 1967–1968 decline. There is no way around this because the indicators were correctly flagging a weak economy and easy money for most of this period. This period represents a classic case in which market action diverged from what *ought* to have happened.

Another failure occurred in 1980 when the barometer's signals were unduly late. In this period the Federal Reserve reversed its monetary policy, literally on a dime. Since the barometers assume that economic and monetary changes are normally gradual, their slow moving components were unable to pick up these unexpectedly sharp swings on a timely basis.

The Stock Barometer

The Stock Barometer is shown in Figures 10.4 and 10.5 Its components fall into three categories: financial, economic, and technical. Because the injection and draining of liquidity (cash) from the system always precede changes in economic activity, and because

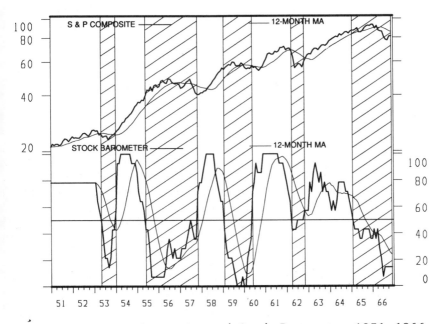

Figure 10.4 S&P Composite and Stock Barometer, 1951–1966. Shaded areas indicate bearish periods, i.e., when the barometer is at or below 50 percent. (Source: *Pring Market Review*)

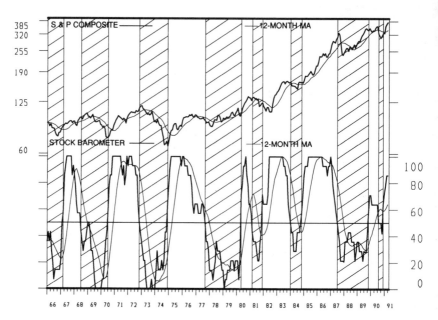

Figure 10.5 S&P Composite and Stock Barometer, 1966–1991. Shaded areas indicate bearish periods, i.e., when the barometer is at or below 50 percent. (Source: *Pring Market Review*)

the stock market anticipates or discounts economic events ahead of time, the monetary components represent the greatest weighting. These include money supply (M2) deflated by commodity prices, and a rate of change of the relationship between the yield curve and money supply. Movements in short-term interest rates and changes in the Discount Rate are also factored in. Technical indicators measuring the price trend of the S&P Composite, and the percentage of a basket of industry group indexes in positive trends are also included. One component looks at a basket of leading economic indicators and measures how many there are in an improving trend. Because this diffusion indicator turns well ahead of the economy, it gives a reliable confirmation that stock market price moves are based on preliminary evidence that the economy is reversing. In effect it identifies when the stock market is discounting a nonexistent recovery or slowdown. Another economically derived component, the Torque Index, is discussed later.

The performance of this barometer since 1948 has been generally acceptable. It is important to remember, though, that the majority of this accomplishment was achieved with back-tested data, and the actual market place record began only in 1988. Several periods are worth discussing.

First, it is important to remember that the function of the barometer is to indicate phases when the environment is bullish or bearish for equities *in general*. In the 1978–1980 period the barometer was in a negative mode, and yet the S&P Composite gained about 25 percent on a total return basis. At first sight this would seem to be a complete failure. However, this particular rally was extremely selective. Interest sensitive issues mostly declined and the market averages were propelled by inflation-driven sectors, such as energy. This period was not one in which all issues participated, and a significant number did not. The barometer, therefore, correctly failed to give a green light. Moreover, *the comparative total return on risk free cash was approximately the same.*

The 1988–1989 rally was also a special case because the market was fueled by a record number of stock retirements, due to buy-backs and merger related activity. The supply of equities was reduced in record amounts and potential demand artificially stimulated from the cash payouts from the buy-back and merger activity. Consequently, the market rallied in a manner that was inconsistent with the bearish environment suggested by the barometer. This situation was very unusual, and it is doubtful whether it will ever develop again in the same way. However, this example shows that factors outside the realm of the normal business cycle can and do develop from time to time.

The Inflation Barometer

The Inflation Barometer is shown in Figures 10.6 and 10.7. It has been designed with the objective of flagging positive and negative periods for raw industrial commodity prices. Most of the time,

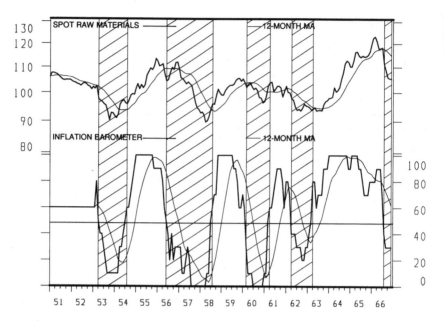

Figure 10.6   Spot Raw Materials and Inflation Barometer, 1951–1966. Shaded areas indicate bearish periods, i.e., when the barometer is at or below 50 percent. (Source: *Pring Market Review*)

industrial commodity prices move in tandem with those in the agricultural sector, but occasionally the latter are affected by weather related developments. Industrial commodity prices, therefore, represent a *purer* reflection of business conditions and fit more consistently into the business cycle framework.

Commodity prices gain their maximum thrust at the tail end of the business cycle when capacity is at its tightest in both the manufacturing and labor markets. The barometer, therefore, includes several indicators that monitor these economic sectors. The trend of the stock market is also included. Equities themselves do not reflect inflationary or deflationary pressures, but if the cycle is progressing in the expected way, we would expect to see the stock market turn ahead of the commodity market. If commodities rally ahead of stocks, the chances are that the advance will be short lived and vice

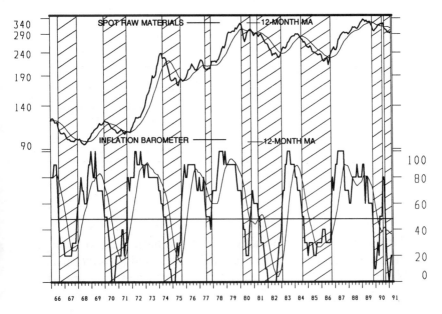

Figure 10.7 Spot Raw Materials and Inflation Barometer, 1966–1991. Shaded areas indicate bearish periods, i.e., when the barometer is at or below 50 percent. (Source: *Pring Market Review*)

versa. The stock market looks ahead, and if it is unable to see an economic expansion, it is doubtful whether one is going to materialize. Under such conditions it is highly unlikely that inflationary pressures will build.

Because a commodity index may be influenced by an exceptionally strong movement in one or two specific commodities, a broader measure of commodity strength or weakness is also included as a component. This is a diffusion indicator that measures the percentage of a basket of commodity prices that are in a positive trend. If a majority of them is, this component is considered bullish.

Long-term trends in industrial raw materials prices are less influenced by psychological factors and are more influenced by the economy than either bonds or stocks. This probably accounts for

TABLE 10.1
Average Annualized Monthly Return for the Six Stages,
1953–1991*

	Stage					
	I	II	III	IV	V	VI
Bonds	26.5	14.9	7.2	−6.2	−4.8	0.7
Stocks	−2.8	25.6	23.3	15.3	4.28	−12.4
Cash	4.7	9.1	7.4	4.8	7.9	7.3

* As defined by the barometers.

the better relative performance of the Inflation Barometer than either of its counterparts on both an *ex ante* and *ex post* basis.

All the barometers are described in more detail in Appendix A, together with appropriate figures of the principal components.

Table 10.1 shows a summary of the performance of stocks, bonds, and cash during the six stages as defined by the barometers. This material covers the 1968–1991 period and includes reinvested dividends and interest.

SOME USEFUL SIGNPOSTS FOR BUSINESS CYCLE STAGE IDENTIFICATION

Following and updating the kinds of models we have just described is a tedious task for most investors. Thus, it makes sense to describe a few straightforward benchmarks and ideas that have consistently been helpful in identifying the prevailing trend of a specific market and the current stage in the overall cycle. The process is really one of sifting out a number of technical, economic, and monetary clues and trying to put them into a recognizable pattern. When all the ducks, so to speak, are favorably in line, that is the time when the risk is lowest and exposure to that particular asset category should be above average. On the other hand, if the evidence is in total conflict, a more cautious approach is called for.

The Federal Reserve

The Federal Reserve signals its intentions in a number of different ways, but its most widely publicized action comes from changes in the Discount Rate. Alterations in the level of this key interest rate are not made lightly, especially at cyclical turning points. Very rarely does the Fed quickly reverse policy once a new one has been established. For example, if the Fed follows a series of Discount Rate hikes over the period of a year or more with a cut, it signifies two things. First, that the Central Bank now recognizes that the economy is more in danger of contracting than of an inflationary overheating. Second, that it has taken action to back up this conclusion. It is true that the Fed cannot force people to go out and buy houses and cars, but by lowering interest rates it can certainly bring down financing costs. This action may persuade people at the decision making margin to do so. Figure 10.8 shows the relationship between bond yields and the Discount Rate. We can see that once the rate has been lowered for the first time after a series of hikes, this rising trend generally continues and vice versa. The chart also indicates that movements in the Discount Rate tend to correlate reasonably well with changes in bond yields. The magnitude of these movements differs, but their direction is usually the same. This provides us with our first stage-determining benchmark: *When the Discount Rate is lowered after a series of hikes, it is usually a reliable signal that bond prices have already or may soon bottom out.* In effect, the first Discount Rate cut indicates that the market cycle is probably in Stage I. If it occurs after bond prices have just crossed above their 12-month moving average, then the odds that a new bull market in bonds has just begun are that much higher. The next signpost would be a stock market bottom. Occasionally the Discount Rate is lowered after the stock market has also crossed above its 12-month moving average. In this case the rate cut would actually confirm that Stage II had been reached. The timing of the cut in terms of the stages usually depends on the depth of the recession. For example, the 1981–1982 recession was quite sharp, and the first rate cut in late 1981 did not have much immediate effect on the stock market, which bottomed in August 1982. It is interest-

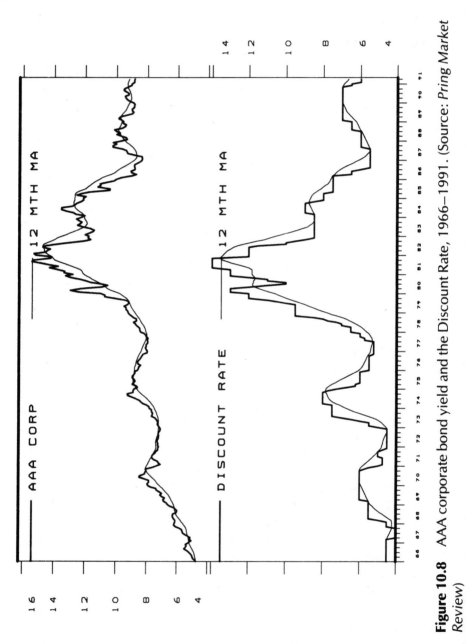

Figure 10.8 AAA corporate bond yield and the Discount Rate, 1966–1991. (Source: *Pring Market Review*)

ing to note, though, that many interest sensitive issues actually bottomed in 1981. In most cycles it is the *second* cut in the rate that signals Stage II. However, if either the first or the second cut is associated with the S&P Composite being in a positive position vis-à-vis its 12-month moving average, treat it as a Stage II environment.

At the other end of the spectrum, fears by the Federal Reserve of a resurgence of inflationary pressures are usually signaled by a Discount Rate hike after a series of cuts. Figure 10.8 shows that the interval between the last cut and the first hike is often quite long. Cyclical interest rate troughs look more like saucer formations as the economy gradually picks up steam, compared to interest rate peaks which are closer in shape to an inverted V formation. The first Discount Rate hike usually occurs close to a bond market top, sometimes before and sometimes just after. This means that the first hike either develops at the very end of Stage III or at the beginning of Stage IV. The best way to find out is to compare the Bond and Commodity indexes to their 12-month moving averages. If the Bond Index is below and the Commodity Index is above the respective averages, then you can be reasonably sure that Stage IV has begun. On the other hand, if bonds and commodities are still in bullish trends, the cycle is still in Stage III. Even so, the rate hike is a warning that this stage is in a terminal phase. In all probability bonds are about to peak. Therefore, look at the rate hike as a signal to begin paring back bond positions.

In Chapter 5 the relationship between the stock market and the Discount Rate was discussed. The so-called *three step and stumble* rule points out that after the third Discount Rate hike has taken place, the stock market usually runs into trouble. In terms of the six stages, the third hike usually comes toward the end of Stage V and sometimes in Stage VI. When the inflationary background is particularly strong, as was the case in the late 1970s, the third hike can come as early as Stage IV, but this is very unusual. Figure 10.9 flags these periods and indicates the prevailing stage (as defined by the markets) at the time of the third hike. The prevailing stage at the time of the first cut is also shown.

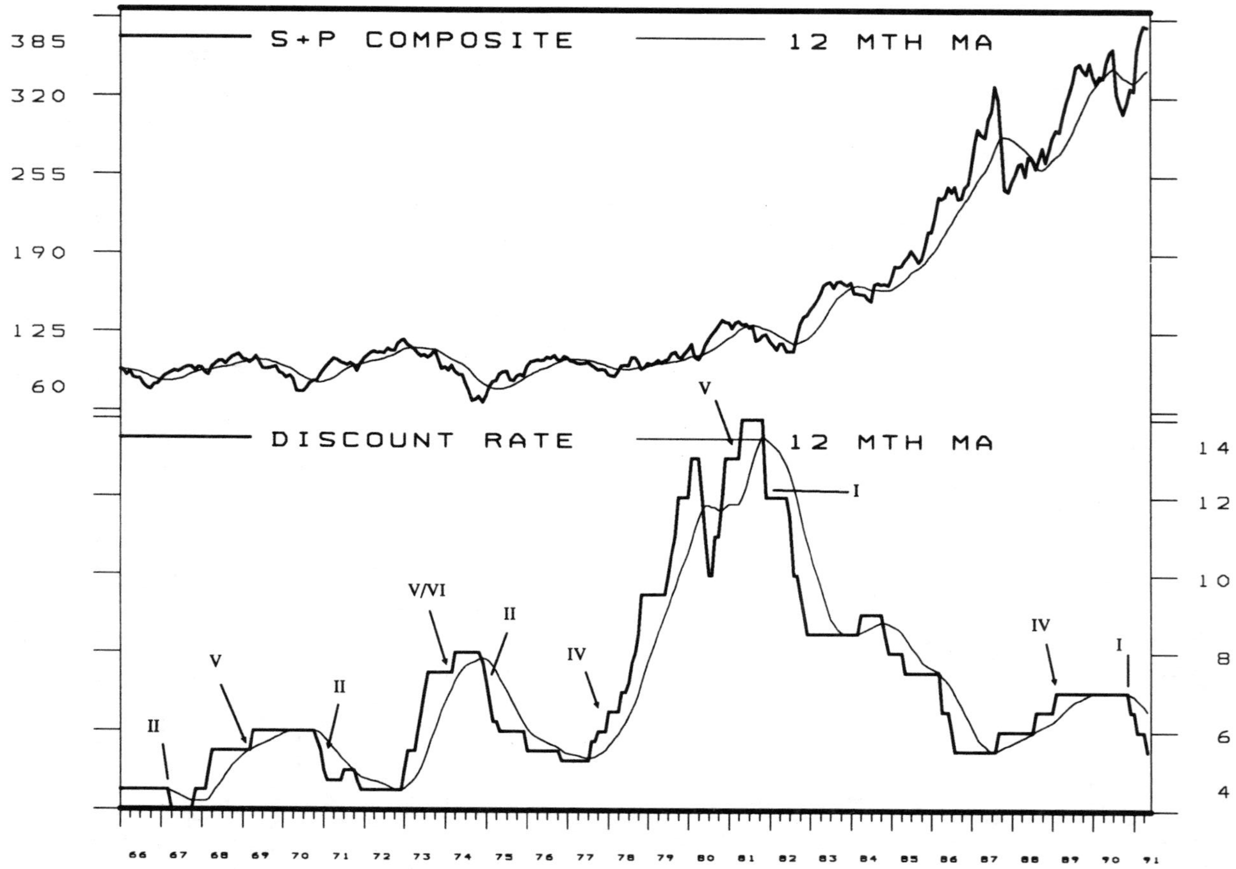

Figure 10.9 Stock prices and the Discount Rate 1966–1991. (Source: *Pring Market Review*)

The Yield Curve

Another pointer to the direction of monetary policy comes from the yield curve. It is the ratio between an interest rate at the short end of the yield spectrum with one at the long end. Sometimes economists relate the yield on three-month T-Bills to that of 20-year government bonds (the government yield curve). More often it takes the form of a ratio of three-month commercial paper to AAA quality corporate yields. This is known as the corporate yield curve. My preference is for the latter because the government yield curve is occasionally subject to distortion as foreign central banks buy and sell Treasury Bills as a by-product of their currency support operations. The commercial paper/AAA ratio is one that more closely reflects business conditions and is therefore better suited to business cycle analysis. Data for both series are regularly published in *Barron's* and the *Wall Street Journal.*

The normal relationship is for the yield on short-term instruments to be below that of bonds. This is because the longer the duration of the maturity, the greater a lender's risk. As a reward for this risk, a higher return is expected. A normal yield curve is reflected by a ratio that is less than 1.00. The lower the reading, the wider the spread and the easier monetary policy is assumed to be.

When short rates are above long rates, i.e., a reading in excess of 1.00, the curve is said to be *inverted*. This kind of situation usually indicates that liquidity is being drained from the system as a result of Central Bank stinginess. Inversions typically occur at the tail end of the business cycle when inflationary pressures are greatest. Figures 10.10 and 10.11 show that *most* recessions have been preceded by a yield curve inversion. An inversion is therefore a normal, but not necessary, condition for a period of economic contraction. It is also true to say that every inversion has been followed either by a full-fledged recession or a *growth* recession. When the yield curve crosses above the 1.00 threshold, it represents an important business cycle signpost.

There are really two types of inversion, those that barely cross above the 1.00 level and fail to remain there for any degree of time, and those that are deep and long. Obviously, there is no way of

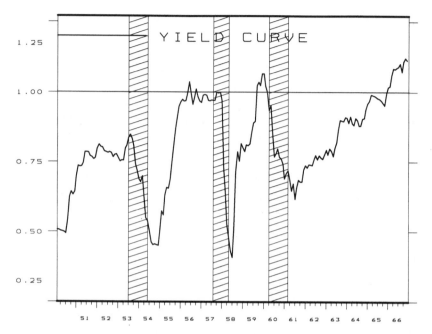

Figure 10.10   Yield curve vs. recessionary periods, 1950–1966. Shaded areas represent recessions. (Source: *Pring Market Review*)

knowing how long the curve will invert, but generally speaking, if the inversion moves above the 1.125 level, it tends to remain there for at least six months. In such situations, it is usually safe to conclude that bonds are in a bear market. When the yield curve subsequently reverts to a *normal* reading below 1.00 this usually represents a fairly reliable signal that the cycle has moved to Stage I (sometimes even as far as Stage II). Unfortunately, there are no reliable market timing conclusions that can be drawn from a mild inversion for either the equity or bond markets.

The equity market is usually in the process of topping out as the curve starts to invert. Sometimes the inversion occurs just after the final peak, as in 1963 and 1973, or sometimes right at the peak, as in 1966 and 1981. The 1978 inversion failed to affect the major averages adversely. However, it was difficult in this period to make money in the equity market because the advance was highly selec-

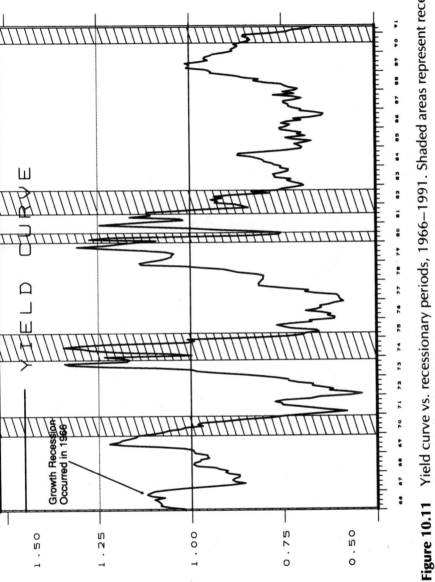

Figure 10.11 Yield curve vs. recessionary periods, 1966–1991. Shaded areas represent recessions. (Source: *Pring Market Review*)

tive, and the return on cash balances between 1978 and 1980 was approximately the same as that for equities. Nevertheless, it is fairly safe to conclude that when a deep yield curve inversion begins, the cycle is in the early phase of a Stage IV. The S&P may still have farther to run on the upside, but the potential reward relative to the risk is low. This event gives a pretty strong signal that it is time for a downward readjustment in the portion of the portfolio allocated to equities.

USING THE CYCLE TO INVEST IN EQUITIES

The first signs that a new recovery is in the cards come from the monetary and financial indicators, as the momentum of real money supply bottoms and interest rates start their descent. After a lag, the stimulatory effect of falling interest rates is initially felt in the *real* economy in the form of a rising number of housing starts. Because a considerable portion of housing costs are eaten up by mortgage payments, it is natural that housing should be extremely sensitive to changes in the level of mortgage interest rates. Housing starts data sometimes bottom before and sometimes after the stock market, but they are not much help by themselves as a bottom picking device. However, when housing starts are related to another leading economic indicator with less of a lead time, reliable advance warnings of equity bear market bottoms are given. I have termed this indicator the *Torque Index. Torque converter* is defined in the Oxford American dictionary as "a device to transmit the correct torque from engine to axle in a motor vehicle," and that is precisely what appears to happen in the economy once the Torque Index bottoms. It is calculated by dividing the monthly reported number on housing starts by that of vendors reporting slow deliveries.

Vendor performance is a statistic that is derived from a survey of manufacturers that are reporting slower deliveries. The greater the number of slow deliveries being reported, the tighter the economy. The significance of relating these two indicators is that if the economic sequence is proceeding according to plan, an advance warning of a reversal in the downward trend of housing starts should occur as they begin to fall less rapidly than vendor performance data. The actual Torque Index is calculated as a 6-month moving average of a 12-month rate of change of the ratio itself. Figure 10.12 shows that the Torque almost invariably bottoms out and has either crossed or is just about to cross above zero at the time the stock market reaches its bear market low. A zero crossing normally represents a pretty reliable signal that Stage II has begun.

Unfortunately, the record of this indicator at market tops has not been sufficiently consistent to signal when equities are about to face an imminent decline. Almost every bull market peak in equities has been preceded by a decline into negative territory by the Torque Index, but the lead time has been so long that such signals have been misleading. Even though the relationship between the Torque and the market averages has been inconsistent, zero crossovers since 1966 have almost always indicated a narrowing of the market advance. From an investment point of view a negative Torque signal, when combined with other evidence of potential market weakness, indicates that the equity allocation should be adjusted downward or, in some cases, reoriented away from leading industries such as financials and utilities to lagging or inflation sensitive sectors. This collateral evidence might include rising interest rates, high valuations, etc. The statistical record of the two components, their ratio, and their momentum are reproduced in Appendix B for anyone wishing to follow the Torque in the future.[1]

The News Background

The relationship of the news background, and the response of the various markets to it, can provide some useful anecdotal evidence of the direction of the primary trend. Generally speaking, markets can be expected to rally on good news and decline in the face of bad news. Because they look ahead and anticipate or discount future

[1] A one time update of this material can also be obtained by sending a self-addressed, stamped envelope to the International Institute for Economic Research, P.O. Box 329, Washington Depot, CT 06794.

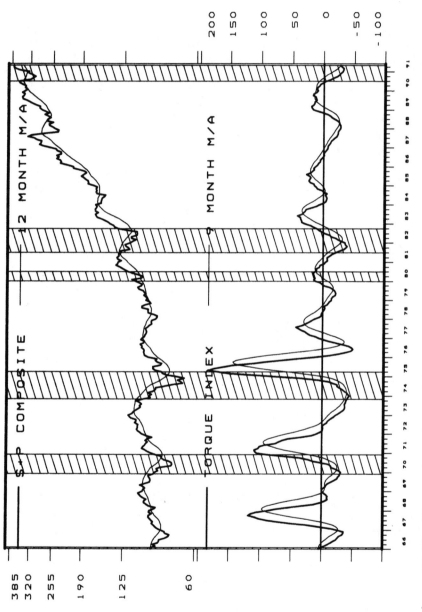

Figure 10.12 The stock market and the Torque Index. Shaded areas represent recessions. (Source: *Pring Market Review*)

events, markets often react in a way that at first may seem irrational. A classic example occurred in January of 1991. We are taught to believe that investors rush into gold as a safe haven in times of trouble, but on the day when war finally broke out against Iraq, the gold price declined by $30. The reason was that risks of war had *already* been factored into the price. Investors had several months' warning that war was likely to erupt. When hostilities finally commenced, there was nothing on the horizon to worry about, and the price collapsed. War is neither a typical nor a predictable business cycle event, but there are some important news events that have a tendency to recur. These developments, and the markets' response, can be used with the indicators already described to pinpoint the prevailing stage in the cycle.

In formulating these judgments, it is important to imagine the kind of business conditions that might prevail and how one would expect the market to respond. If it responds in an apparently irrational way, this is indicative of a major turning point. The stock market, because it is relatively more influenced by psychology than the other markets, usually gives the easiest and most reliable clues. For example, equities bottom in the middle of a recession and rise in anticipation of a recovery. If after a prolonged decline, the market suddenly reverses direction and rallies on very heavy volume, this is often a good tip-off that a bear market low has been seen. Valuable confirmation can often be found in the news background. If it is positive, this is not a recession based rally. What is really required is a very discouraging economic report or a string of some highly publicized layoffs. Bad news is almost a prerequisite for a new bull market and without it, a rally from a long-term oversold condition is highly suspect. It also helps if the rally is accompanied by general disbelief and is described by experts as "technical" or the result of "bargain hunting." A sharp rally that develops "despite the end of the world" should normally be trusted because it means that investors have already taken this into consideration and are now beginning to focus on the recovery.

Market tops take longer to form and are more subtle. They usually develop under an extremely favorable news background. Economic experts are typically forecasting a rosy economy for as far as the eye can see. Analysts will be revising their forecasts upward to levels previously deemed ridiculous but that are now taken seriously. The dividend yield on the Dow Jones might be less than 3 percent, and discounts on many closed-end stock funds will be turning into rich premiums. There is a well-known saying on Wall Street that "a bull market argument known is a bull market argument understood." It could also apply to bear market arguments. The wisdom behind the statement refers to the fact that whenever a bullish factor has become widely publicized, it has already been factored into the price. In late 1980, for example, a very bullish article on the oil stocks appeared in the "Heard on The Street" column in the *Wall Street Journal*. It seemed obvious from the article that there were many good reasons why the stocks should go much higher. The problem was that the good news had already been discounted. The article was written only after prices had run up, and the author had been bombarded with bullish reports from the street. By the time the article was published *everyone* had had the opportunity to understand the bullish argument. There was no one left to buy. Needless to say, December 1980 levels were not reached by the oil sector for several years.

One classic indication of crowd psychology for any market is the emergence of a financial book into the top ten best-seller list. For equities, what better timing than Edgar Lawrence Smith's best selling book in the late 1920s *Common Stocks as Long-Term Investments* or Adam Smith's *Money Game* at the top of the 1968 speculative bubble. William Donaghue's book on money markets was brilliantly timed for the secular peak in interest rates in the early 1980s. Ravi Batra's prediction of a depression in 1987 flew into the bestseller list just after the crash, but the market later went on to make a new high. Finally, Charles J. Givens's *Wealth Without Risk,* which reached the list in 1990–1991, indicated that the public was completely absorbed with the S&L and banking crisis, and that this had been fully discounted. It was during this period that smaller-company (higher-risk) stocks ended their eight-year bear market relative to the blue chips.

These types of observation cannot easily be categorized into the stages environment because they do not occur with regularity, are

TABLE 10.2

Expected Events During the Six Stages

	Federal Reserve Policy	Yield Curve	Economic Indicators	Events	Others
Stage I	First Discount Rate cut Reserve requirements eased	Yield curve peaks or has already peaked on its way back below 1.0	Capacity utilization below 82%	Doom and gloom book in best-seller lists Substantial layoffs Brokerage firms announce layoffs	Deflation sensitive equities usually bottom on an absolute and almost always relative basis
Stage II	Second Discount Rate cut	Should be below 1.0	Torque Index above 0 LEI crosses above 12-month MA Housing starts bottom or have bottomed	Substantial layoffs Auto promoting, airline discounts	Stocks rise "mysteriously" on bad news
Stage III		Sometimes bottoms	LEI crosses above 12-month MA Industrial production and coincident indicators cross above their 12-month MAs		Relative strength of inflation sensitive equities vs. deflation sensitive equities begins to favor inflation

(continued)

TABLE 10.2 (*Continued*)

	Federal Reserve Policy	Yield Curve	Economic Indicators	Events	Others
Stage IV		Sometimes bottoms	Torque Index falls below 0 Housing starts peak Capacity utilization above 82%		Commodity rally picking up steam
Stage V	Discount Rate raised for third time, sometimes more	May start to invert	Torque Index usually below 0	Stock market book makes the best-seller list Excellent earnings reports Brokerage firms move to larger offices	Deflation sensitive equities noticeably weaker on either an absolute or relative basis (usually both)
Stage VI		Often inverts, i.e., above 0 Ted Spread (the ratio between yields on three-month Treasury Bills and three-month Eurodollars) widens sharply		Congress/media complain about high interest rates Financial crisis	

228

often subtle in their message, and take a long time to result in market action. They serve instead as a supplement to the more precise events described earlier.

SUMMARY

Table 10.2 offers a brief synopsis of the important events, both internal and exogenous, that provide some clues to the prevailing stage in the cycle. Clearly this is not a fail-safe method because each cycle will have its own idiosyncracies. Some events will be repeated and others will not. However, the guide can be used as a cross-check that will be reliable in most cases.

11

Gold and the Business Cycle

Gold has been freely traded only since 1968, and consequently its history in relation to the business cycle is relatively short. The price was fixed at $35 per ounce for most of the postwar period. Thus, during the first ten years in which it was allowed to float, the price was undergoing an adjustment as it regained its purchasing power, relative to commodities and goods and services. It is important to note that other commodities had been in a long-term uptrend since 1932. Also, it was illegal for United States citizens to own gold until 1975. This fact further compounds the difficulty of establishing where the price of gold fits into the cycle. In effect, the price appears to have formed a relationship with other financial markets only since 1980.

GOLD INVESTMENT VEHICLES

The principal gold investment vehicles include gold itself, gold shares, and gold share mutual funds. Gold coins represent another alternative but are not covered here. The price of the metal and North American gold shares have traditionally experienced a very close relationship. This is also true of South African shares, but political events have occasionally distorted their relationship with the gold price. Even though the shares and metal prices move very closely, their relative performance can differ considerably as shown in Figure 11.1. The relative strength line drawn in the second panel is constructed by dividing the monthly average of Friday P.M. fixes by the Toronto Stock Exchange Gold and Silver Share Index (adjusted for United States dollars). When the line is rising, it indicates that the metal is outperforming the Share Index and vice versa. Historically, the ratio has moved from the 0.12 to 0.15 extreme, favoring the shares to the 0.03 to 0.08 zone favoring the metal. This ratio is best incorporated into an investment strategy at the time when a decision is being made to invest in some form of gold asset. If the line is crossing below the 0.12 area on its way down, it favors

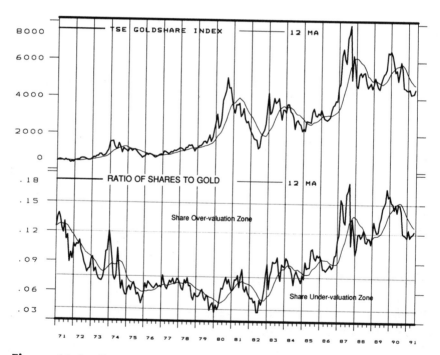

Figure 11.1 Toronto Stock Exchange Gold Share Index vs. gold. (Source: *Pring Market Review*)

the shares. On the other hand, a rally through 0.08 indicates that bullion has a higher probability of being the superior performer. When the evidence is unclear, the shares would be preferred because most mines usually pay small dividends. Figure 11.2 shows a similar relationship, but this time with the Dow Jones Precious Metal Share Index (published in the *Wall Street Journal* and *Barron's*). Unfortunately, the history of this index is not so long, but in this case the benchmarks appear to be 0.0078 and 0.0058. No-load gold mutual funds represent an even better alternative because they are diversified. Gold mining shares can differ in their performance, and the funds offer the additional advantage of professional management.

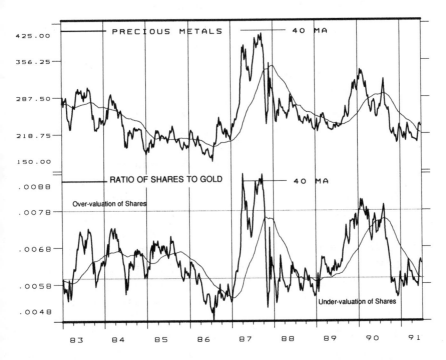

Figure 11.2 Dow Jones Precious Metal Index vs. the gold price. (Source: *Pring Market Review*)

CAUSES OF MAJOR SWINGS IN THE PRICE OF GOLD

Many views have been put forward on the principal causes of major swings in the price. The media often link price movements of financial markets to some kind of news event. After all, it seems only logical that market participants make buying and selling decisions based on some type of news. In the case of gold, it is always assumed that the fear factor is at work. The outbreak of hostilities, an assassination attempt, or a similar event appear to be rational justifications for a rally. They often are for a day or so but not on a sustainable basis. The net effect usually depends on whether the price is in a primary bull or bear market. For example, Russia's invasion of Afghanistan in 1979 was considered to be a major stimulatory influence on the price; but at the time gold was in a primary bull market, and the war scare was really the "icing on the cake" so far as the bulls were concerned. In effect, the invasion exacerbated a trend that was already in force.

On the other hand, the Iran–Iraq war, which broke out in 1981, should, in theory, have been an even more positive factor for gold in view of its potential for pushing up oil prices, but it was not because the gold price was in a primary bear market at the time. The rallies that took place in response to this event turned out to be temporary interruptions in an overall declining trend. Other events, such as the assassination of Anwar Sadat and the 1981 military crackdown in Poland also occurred in a bear market environment and had only a temporary upward effect on the price. The only time that the fear factor can have a long lasting "beneficial" effect on the price arises when gold becomes the currency of last resort. A prime example occurred in the mid-1970s in Vietnam just after the United States pullout. Monetary order had broken down, and refugees used gold to buy their way out of the country because it was the only medium of exchange that was trusted by everyone. It is this question of trust that is the driving force of bull and bear markets. More specifically, it is changes in the level of confidence of individuals and institutions in the integrity of the purchasing power of money. This swing factor in the psychology of investors toward gold seems to have a much greater effect on the price than the day-to-day fundamental demand for jewelry and industrial uses and the supply (mine production) relationship. Obviously, if the fundamentals and the investment trends are moving in the same direction, their joint impact will be that much more influential. Often they are because anticipation of price inflation and a more robust economy normally occur simultaneously and vice versa.

Gold is quite simply an inflation hedge. There are some who argue that gold is also a deflation hedge, i.e., insurance against the integrity of the banking system. These arguments are largely based on the fact that the price of gold held up very well during the Great Depression. The problem with that argument is that commodity prices also held up very well during this period. In fact, they bottomed in 1932 and spent most of the rest of that decade in a rising trend. It seems more likely that gold is useful as a deflation hedge only if it is considerably undervalued *relative* to other commodities and real estate as the deflation begins. If the gold price remains unchanged or even declines slightly in the face of a sharply falling commodity market, its purchasing value has actually been enhanced. We cannot say that gold has been an inflation hedge in this type of environment, but the effect has basically been the same in that an ounce of gold has maintained its purchasing power. In a truly rational world we should expect to see the price advance at the same rate as the Consumer Price Index. In reality, though, the price is continually diverging from what might be called this fair market level, as investors overshoot in both directions. Gold pays no interest, and hence it is unlikely to outperform cash over the long haul. Therefore, investments in the yellow metal make sense only when it is well below fair value. It is very difficult to come up with a reasonable valuation because of the limited price history since 1980. On the other hand, experience since then indicates that cyclical turning points in the price do appear to fit into the chronological sequence experienced by bonds, stocks, and commodities. The interaction of business cycle and technical indicators can, therefore, give us a good indication of when gold assets are a timely investment and when they are not.

THE BUSINESS CYCLE AND MAJOR TURNING POINTS IN THE GOLD PRICE

Gold Shares Versus Stock and Commodity Prices

The gold price has established a consistent relationship with the business cycle only since 1980. However, gold shares possess a much longer history of trading experience. Because these equities and the price of gold itself have a very close relationship, we can use them to give us a greater degree of confidence that the events since 1980 represent the rule rather than an exception. Figures 11.3 and 11.4, for instance, show the chronological sequence of peaks and troughs for stocks and the Toronto Stock Exchange Gold and Silver Share Index (adjusted for United States dollars) and the CRB Spot

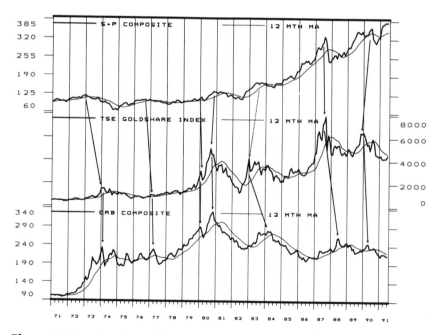

Figure 11.3   Stocks, gold shares, and commodities, showing chronological sequence (peaks). (Source: *Pring Market Review*)

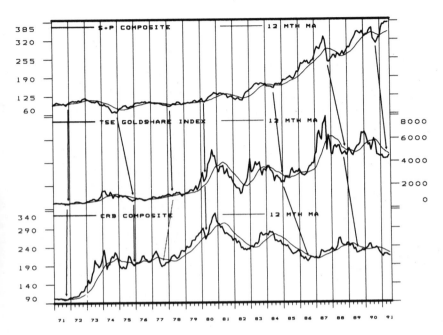

Figure 11.4   Stocks, gold shares, and commodities showing chrono-logical sequence (troughs). (Source: *Pring Market Review*)

Raw Materials Price Index between 1971 and 1991. In virtually every cycle the turning point in the Gold Share Index falls between that of equities and commodity prices. The leads and lags vary quite a bit in a similar way to the other relationships. The sequence is not perfect considering that commodities bottomed ahead of the gold shares in 1977, and the gold shares peaked ahead of the stock market in 1990.

Gold Versus Commodity Prices

Between 1980 and 1991 the price of gold bullion itself established a leading relationship against commodity prices. In this respect Figures 11.5 and 11.6 compare the gold price to the CRB Spot Raw

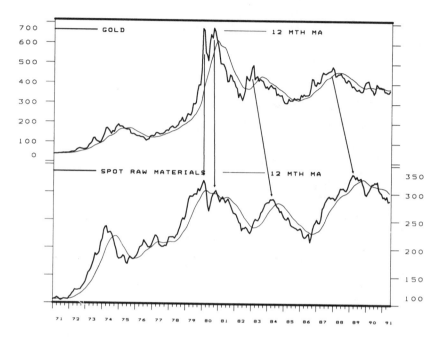

Figure 11.5   Gold vs. the CRB Spot Raw Materials Index (peaks). (Source: *Pring Market Review*)

Materials Index. The arrows in Figure 11.5 connect the tops and those in Figure 11.6 link the bottoms. The 11-year history between 1980 and 1991 is too brief to conclude that this is a long-term relationship. However, when this evidence is linked to the relationship between the same one for the shares, there are sufficient grounds to expect that the gold price will normally discount future inflation.

Gold Versus Bond Yields

Because bond yields and commodity prices are closely interlinked, it follows that trends in the gold price should have some predictive

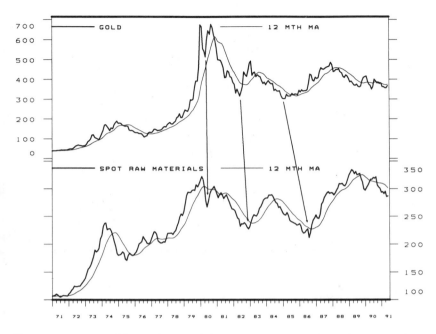

Figure 11.6   Gold vs. the CRB Spot Raw Materials Index (troughs). (Source: *Pring Market Review*)

qualities concerning interest rates. Figures 11.7 and 11.8 show that this is normally the case. The peaks and troughs have been linked by arrows, as in the gold/commodity comparisons. Again the gold price fits nicely into the cycle because it has a *tendency* to lead bond yields.

When gold is introduced into the equation, the sequence appears to be gold, commodities, and then bond prices. As long as the gold price is in a falling trend and bond prices have bottomed, it is usually safe to hold bonds. It is only after gold has started to rise that bond prices peak. Even then, the lags can be considerable. For example, gold bottomed in February 1985, but bonds continued in a strong bull phase until the spring of 1986.

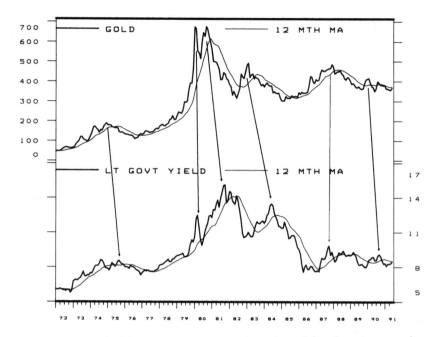

Figure 11.7 Gold vs. government bond yields showing peaks. (Source: *Pring Market Review*)

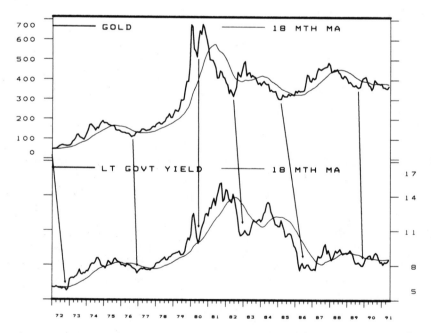

Figure 11.8 Gold vs. government bond yields showing troughs. (Source: *Pring Market Review*)

BACKGROUND FACTORS IN GOLD PRICES

I have been unable to find any economic indicator that can be used for the purposes of forecasting the gold price. Two important background indicators that do influence it are the United States dollar and commodity prices. Because gold has a tendency to lead commodity prices, they are obviously of little help in forecasting reversals in the trend of the gold price. However, the most dynamic stages of gold bull markets seem to occur when the gold prices and commodity prices are rising simultaneously.

The dollar also has its drawbacks. For example, between mid-1979 and 1980 the gold price more than doubled in a period when the dollar was essentially unchanged. Moreover, the gold price moved

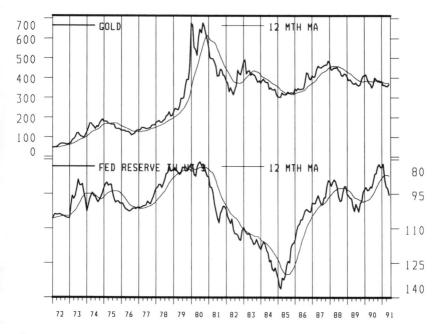

Figure 11.9 The gold price vs. the Dollar Index (plotted inversely). (Source: *Pring Market Review*)

sideways between 1988 and 1990 while the dollar fell. These relationships are shown in Figure 11.9. Note that the Trade Weighted
Dollar has been plotted inversely so that both series move in sympathy with each other.

The best approach is to try to assess where we are in the business
cycle by fitting the gold price between a measure of the stock market
and commodity prices because this is the normal sequence of events
as shown in Figure 11.10. This figure represents the three markets
in momentum format (six-month moving average of a 12-month rate
of change). The cyclical peaks have been joined in order to demonstrate the expected sequence. In Figure 11.11 the actual series
themselves are represented, but this time the lines join the cyclical
bottoms as defined by the momentum reversals in Figure 11.10. We

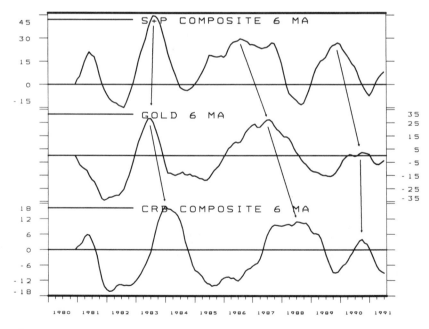

Figure 11.10 Stock, gold, and commodity momentum compared.
(Source: *Pring Market Review*)

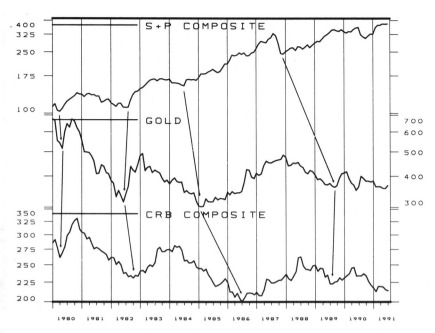

Figure 11.11 S&P Composite, gold, and CRB Composite. (Source: *Pring Market Review*)

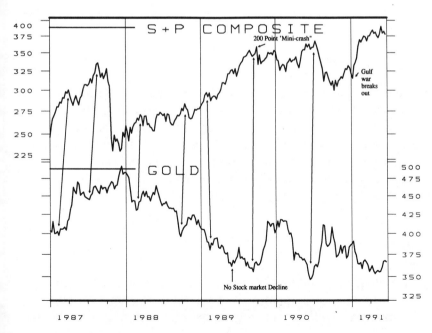

Figure 11.12 S&P Composite (peaks) vs. the gold price (troughs). (Source: *Pring Market Review*)

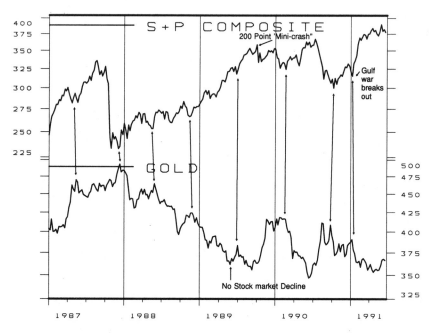

Figure 11.13 S&P Composite (troughs) vs. the gold price (peaks). (Source: *Pring Market Review*)

noted earlier the leading relationship between stocks and gold over the course of the business cycle. However, in the 1987–1991 period, the two markets began to move in opposite directions for virtually the whole time instead of just part of the time. This trend is shown in Figures 11.12 and 11.13; important turning points for each market are connected by arrows. It would appear as if a new factor, fear, has been creeping into the gold market.

SUMMARY

1. Primary bull moves in the gold price are fueled by investors' fears of future inflation. These fears fluctuate through the business cycle from being almost nonexistent during the mid-

dle stages of a recession to extreme levels in the tail end of the recovery.
2. Since 1980, turning points in the gold price have typically followed the stock market but led those of commodity prices. The relatively short history of this relationship indicates that this link should be treated with some caution.
3. Because of this tentative association and the fact that gold does not pay any dividends or interest, it has not been included in our allocation models but is treated more as an ancillary asset.

12

Allocating Assets for Your Personal Investment Objectives

The principles of asset allocation outlined earlier apply to everyone. However, because each person has unique investment objectives, the emphasis placed on specific assets at each stage of the cycle will be different. This chapter outlines the nature of these objectives for broad categories of investors and how they can be implemented. A description of this kind has to be general in nature because it is not possible to cover all situations. This discussion should therefore be used as a rough guideline or starting point for your own circumstances. In the first place, your own position is unique. Factors such as temperament, stage of life, financial resources, financial requirements, and so forth will each have a bearing on how you decide to balance your investment objectives. Also, the character of each cycle is different, which means that the allocations will never be identical from one cycle to another.

There are three investment objectives that are more or less shared by everyone: liquidity, income, and growth. The term *liquidity* refers to the portion of a portfolio that can easily be turned into cash to meet unexpected demands. It is true that we can always sell stocks or bonds and realize cash in fairly short order, so in a sense these items are in fact liquid. This is very different from real estate, which normally takes several months to dispose of. Even so, equities and long-term debt fluctuate in price, and you may need to sell them at an inconvenient moment when their value is temporarily depressed. These assets might be liquid, but they cannot be counted on to realize a specific price at the time of an emergency. A prudent investor, therefore, needs to balance his portfolio so that enough liquid resources are always available for emergencies without placing the overall investment plan in jeopardy.

It therefore makes sense for all investors to allocate part of their portfolio to some form of liquid asset, such as a money market fund or a bank CD. Precisely what proportion will depend on the overall financial objective of the investor and the specific stage of the business cycle. Liquidity need not mean that an asset has to mature within a year. You may decide that you will need money for your child's education in two years. The safest thing to do might be to place the money in a money market fund so that you can be sure that it will be there when needed; but suppose money market funds are only paying 5 percent and two-year CDs are yielding 8 percent. Because you have already decided that the money will not be needed for two years, you would clearly be better off investing in the higher yielding CD. Liquidity would not be sacrificed, and the return on the investment would be substantially greater.

Not all of the portfolio should be managed in such a targeted way, but there are clearly some situations when it makes eminent sense to do so. When the time horizon under consideration is much longer, such as a planned retirement in 20 years, such a policy would not be appropriate. This is because the investor would be sacrificing a considerable amount of potential growth purely for the sake of liquidity. If this 20-year period experienced a significant amount of inflation, the portfolio would lose a considerable amount of its purchasing power. The provision of liquidity for an unexpected demand or even for an expected one is a good thing, but if taken too far, it can adversely affect the overall long-term performance.

The second investment objective is income. The amount of income that should be produced from a portfolio depends a great deal on the circumstances of the individual concerned. For example, if you are in the middle of your career and have more than sufficient salary to meet day-to-day expenses, then income from your investments will not be a significant requirement. On the other hand, if you have just started up a new business and cannot quite make ends meet, income and safety of principal will be the overwhelming considerations in your investment policy. The requirement of a retired couple for portfolio income is self-evident. In their case, they must first determine their income requirement and work backward from that point.

The third and final investment objective is growth. Generally speaking, the more substantial the potential growth, the greater will be the risk and uncertainty. It follows that younger people with smaller financial responsibilities are in a better position to invest for growth than older people who rely on their investments for current income. Younger people are also in a superior position to rebound from a financial disaster than those at a later stage in life. Even so, retired people need to preserve the purchasing value of their capital; otherwise their standard of living will be threatened. At a later stage of life it appears that the growth objective changes its purpose from wealth accumulation to wealth preservation. In this respect, it makes sense for even the most risk averse investor to sacrifice a small amount of current income in favor of some type of growth. This need not be an insurmountable burden to bear. It is usually possible to obtain a current yield on a utility stock that is only marginally below that of a good quality long-term bond. While the interest payment on the bond will always be the same, the dividend of a carefully selected utility will most probably rise periodically. At some point this would also reflect positively on the price of the stock itself.

DESIGNING YOUR PORTFOLIO

Recognizing that liquidity is a relatively small factor, the principal investment decision comes down to achieving a balance between stocks and bonds. The optimal balance for a specific individual will depend on three factors: temperament, financial responsibilities, and stage of life. Investment is always a constant battle between fear and greed. When things are going well, most of us are tempted to go for a little more reward and find ourselves in the frame of mind that makes the decision to take on more risk that much easier. Unfortunately, this type of situation almost always arises after the market has experienced a healthy advance. The problem is that this is not usually a good moment to take such action. At the other end of the spectrum, when the value of our portfolio has been shrinking for several months, there is the temptation to throw in the towel and liquidate those growth securities. This attitude is also likely to be wrong because that's exactly what everyone else is doing. This is why it is very important to establish a plan and then to *stick to the plan*. Unfortunately, this is not a simple case of investing say, 70 percent in bonds during Stage I, rotating into 80 percent stocks in Stage II, and so forth. This is because everyone has a unique set of financial circumstances, responsibilities, temperament, etc. Let's briefly consider the important aspect of temperament before moving on to the other factors.

Temperamental Factors

It is a relatively easy matter for all investors to decide on their own financial responsibilities, income needs, and so on, but temperament is another matter. Unfortunately, it is probably the most important factor of all. If you think that you have a good understanding of the allocation process as described here and can identify the various business cycle stages with some degree of confidence, the chances are that you will be quite successful at this endeavor.

Unfortunately, something very important happens as soon as you put the book down and call a broker or mutual fund company to execute your strategy. A new ingredient, emotion, enters into the picture. As long as you were looking at the asset allocation process from a theoretical point of view it was possible to take an objective stance, but as soon as your own money is on the line, objectivity turns into subjectivity. It is actually not that difficult to beat the market, but it is beating yourself that is the hard part. The ability to overcome personal biases and to admit that you can be, and often are, wrong, is just as important in the investment process as actually coming up with the correct analysis. It is also useful to have some idea of your tolerance for risk taking. Occasionally, we find a situation in which everything seems to fall into place, and we are unable to overcome the temptation of expanding a position to a far higher level than that called for by our allocation plan. This type of move is often rationalized as "just for this one time only." The market will often move in the anticipated direction for a while, but inevitably there is a setback. If our tolerance for risk taking has been overstretched, chances are that we will be psyched out by this unexpected turn of events. As the paper loss grows, doubts and contradictions arise, and we ask ourselves questions along the following lines: "Well, just suppose I am wrong, can I afford to take any more losses? The indicators are pointing to higher prices, but the market is not acting the way it should—perhaps it's going to be different this time? I'll buy the argument that my analysis is correct, and I know the price will go up, but why not sell now and buy in at a lower price later on? Surely this makes a lot more sense than riding through what could be a pretty nasty correction?"

Once the paper loss has thrown us psychologically off balance, the natural tendency is to run for cover and liquidate the whole position. Several weeks later we find out that our original analysis was quite correct, but by that time we are so unbalanced from a psychological point of view that we find ourselves unwilling to reallocate any money to that market again. These are the kinds of questions and self-doubts that permeate the minds of all investors at one time or another. Anyone who is overexposed relative to their personal risk tolerance is far more vulnerable to these mental snares and delusions, and therefore more likely to make a mistake. The one thing that can always be counted on is the market's ability to continually probe and test for every weakness. The solution is to quantify your tolerance for risk taking at the outset. A position taken more in line with this assessment greatly reduces the odds of being mentally "stopped-out" of a position at the wrong time.

Another potential problem comes from pride of opinion, which often stands in the way of sound decision making. It is common practice to make an investment based on a sound and logical analysis of the market situation, only to find later that conditions have changed. Typically, this realization occurs at a time when the position is under water, and the investor is unwilling to liquidate the asset. This lack of action is usually justified on the hope that it will "come back and I can break even." Such an attitude stems from the fact that investors are reluctant to recognize the change in condition that has taken place—in effect, pride stands in the way of a logical decision. Now that the investment is no longer linked to economic conditions, there is no rational or logical event that can alter the decision. A useful way around this problem is to establish at the outset the kind of event that would change your opinion about the suitability of the investment in question. If you do go ahead and purchase the asset, and the event materializes, you have already established a benchmark for liquidation.

Another trap that many investors fall into is trying to anticipate changes in the indicators before they actually occur. This can lead to an incorrect allocation and open up the possibility of significant losses. A typical error occurs when people speculate about a change in monetary policy that is not backed up by the indicators. When investment decisions are based on this kind of hope and rumor-mongering, they are rarely correct.

In some instances it does make sense to anticipate a signal from a specific indicator. For example, a smoothed momentum of a critical economic indicator might be close to its threshold level of zero. These types of indicators very rarely change direction until after they are approaching an overbought or oversold extreme. It is therefore reasonable to project that an indicator that is fast approaching a zero reading will soon move through it. This is a more sensible way of anticipating change because it is very unlikely that the economy, which is very slow to turn, will generate a whipsaw signal.

SUGGESTED ALLOCATIONS FOR INDIVIDUAL SITUATIONS

If it is assumed that each individual or institution has a unique combination of investment objectives and risk aversion, then it is apparent that it is not possible to develop one allocation program that is suitable for everyone. The remainder of this chapter will suggest allocation possibilities for several broad investor categories. Because these possibilities are general in nature, they are presented as starting points only. You will need to customize your own guidelines based on personal circumstances and temperament.

It is also important to bear in mind that each stage in each cycle will be signaled in a distinctive way and with a different degree of certainty. If you have a high degree of confidence that a specific stage has begun, but, by the same token, the market has already realized a great deal of its potential, a smaller allocation would be more appropriate than if the signal had been given after a modest price move.

Please note that the statistics measuring the return for each stage represent the stages as defined by the barometers. The data cover the period between 1953 and 1991 and are expressed in the form of an average total return monthly gain, which has been annualized.

Strategic Versus Tactical Asset Allocation

The allocation guidelines discussed below fall into two parts, strategic and tactical. Tactical decisions are the ones with which this book has mostly been concerned. They involve the rotation of assets during the course of the business cycle, depending on your assessment of the economic, financial, and technical environment. On the other hand, strategic allocation decisions are based on the circumstances and investment objectives of the individual or institution in question. Strategic decisions set the guidelines or limits for specific assets at each stage in the cycle. For example, a retired couple would give a much higher priority to capital preservation and current income in their investment planning than a newly married, younger couple. Their allocation decisions, at all stages of the cycle, would have a much lower target for growth oriented investments than those producing a high degree of current income. The retired couple would still make tactical decisions as the cycle unfolded, but the guidelines under which they operated would be much more conservative. They would add to their equity position in Stage I, but their maximum position, under the most favorable of circumstances, would always be far less than the younger family's.

AN ALLOCATION MODEL

This example is given as a neutral or base model from which subsequent ones will diverge, depending on individual investment objectives. It is a purely tactical model and does not take any strategic assumptions into consideration. This model, like all the others, assumes what we might call an average aversion to risk. If you feel that you are above or below average, you should adjust your allocation accordingly.

It is important that changes in the allocations should be made on a gradual basis and not all at once. The various figures give the impression that the allocation process is static and remains in force until the next stage emerges. This is not so because the guidelines are meant as a rough target. For example, the portfolio might enter Stage VI with, say, a 20 percent bond allocation, but this would gradually be increased as additional evidence indicated that Stage I was just about to begin. The same sort of tactics would be employed as the cycle emerges from Stage III, i.e., the terminal phase of the bond bull market. This time the process would be reversed as the bond allocation is slowly reduced in anticipation of a bear market in long-term debt instruments.

Stage I

Stage I experiences the initial phase of the bull market in bonds. Therefore, long-term fixed income instruments should form the backbone of the portfolio. The basic suggestion is for a 50 percent allocation because this period represents the time of greatest potential for bonds (see Figure 12.1). A 50 percent allocation to bonds can have many different implications depending on the average maturity and quality of the issues held in the portfolio. In Stage I, the allocation should steer clear of poorer quality bonds, i.e., anything rated below A. Federal government obligations are the preferred vehicle due to their unquestionable quality and liquidity. If you are betting on a substantial decline in rates, it is also important to make sure that the bonds do not have a feature enabling the issuer to call them away in the event that rates do decline sharply. Because Stage I represents the initial stage of the bull market, the average maturity should be extended out to the maximum, consistent with your investment objectives and risk aversion. In our example, an average maturity of 25 years has been assumed.

Stocks are also represented, for although the bear market is still in force, some leading equities, such as utilities and financial issues, are probably in the process of bottoming. For example, the October 1974 low was preceded by a bottom in utility stocks, as was the low in August 1982. The lead time in 1982 was much longer, and a considerable number of issues bottomed ahead of the S&P. The initial thrust off the final bear market low can be a pretty dynamic affair. Therefore, maintaining a small allocation to equities means that the portfolio will participate, even if the indicators are somewhat belated in triggering a Stage II signal. This exposure and the good experience accompanying it create greater confidence to make a larger allocation. This is an important factor because the news background is normally quite discouraging at this stage, and the last thing most investors want to do is accumulate stocks.

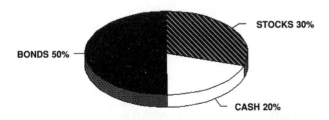

Figure 12.1   Stage I allocation. (Source: *Pring Market Review*)

The recommended 30 percent equity exposure in Stage I should principally be limited to early bull market leaders, such as interest sensitive sectors, for two reasons. First, these stocks would normally begin their bear markets well ahead of the general market and, therefore, would be in a better position to start a new bull market. Second, these more defensive issues usually offer a higher yield than the average stock. Thus, if the equity bear market does have further to run, they are likely to suffer minor damage compared to the averages. In any event, their relatively generous dividends will offer some compensation for seeing the capital value erode. Statistically the barometer models indicate that the average annualized monthly decline for stocks in Stage I since the 1950s is -2.84 percent. In five of the seven cycles equities actually advanced. Since Stage I is usually quite short, it makes sense to add to equities so that the increased allocation for Stage II is not too sudden an adjustment.

Cash makes up the balance of the portfolio with a 20 percent allocation. This may seem overly cautious, considering that a better return could be achieved in the bond market. However, it is appropriate to maintain some liquid balances in order to preserve the diversification feature. Also Stage I is normally quite brief, and it is likely that the final allocation to bonds would be almost instantaneously rolled into equities as Stage II is signaled. This quick rotation would have the effect of disrupting the sense of psychological balance that is so important to a successful investment program. In those rare periods when Stage I has lasted a long time, market action has often been quite volatile. A classic example occurred in the 1981–1982 period, when bond prices gyrated in a very wide, disruptive trading range. In such an environment, it is very difficult to hold on to a large and exposed bond position without getting psyched out. If you have a greater feeling of comfort from holding a substantial cash reserve, you are more likely to force yourself to add to the stock allocation when Stage II is finally signaled.

Stage II

Stage II probably offers the best consistent potential for quick stock market gains as the equity market literally explodes off its bear

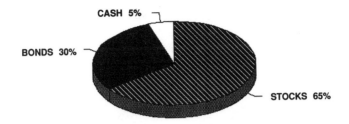

Figure 12.2 Stage II allocation. (Source: *Pring Market Review*)

market low. Even though bonds also rise (average 15 percent), the total return for stocks is usually greater (25 percent). Equities are now given a much larger allocation, as they move from 30 percent to 65 percent, while bonds slip from 50 percent to 30 percent (see Figure 12.2). This may appear to be an unusually large rotation of assets, and indeed it is. However, it is important to remember that this switch would normally be made on a fairly gradual basis. It would start toward the middle to end of Stage I, gradually increasing as evidence of a stock market bottom became conclusive.

The cash position is reduced to 5 percent, the smallest of any of the business cycle phases. It is always a good idea to have some cash in reserve in case some potentially good stock purchase candidates appear, but because this is often the most dynamic part of the cycle, liquidity should always be maintained at a relatively low level. At this stage, it would not be imprudent to extend some of the cash instruments out for one to two years in order to lock in a higher yield.

Stage III

This is also a bullish phase, but as it draws to a close bond prices undergo a distribution phase prior to the beginning of their bear market. Their average annualized monthly gain now slips to 7 percent. This means that the allocation should be further rotated in favor of equities. The bond position is therefore reduced from 30 percent to 20 percent (see Figure 12.3). It is also appropriate to

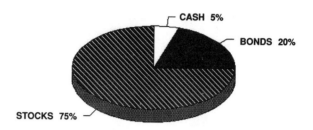

Figure 12.3   Stage III allocation. (Source: *Pring Market Review*)

shorten the average maturity, toward the 7- to 10-year area, reducing the quality somewhat in order to obtain a higher current return. Because the economy is quite healthy at this point, the danger of default is not normally a threat.

The 10 percent addition to stocks, which now stand at 75 percent, should be invested in inflation beneficiaries, which have either begun or are about to start a period of superior relative performance. During Stage III stocks have averaged an annualized monthly gain of 23 percent.

Stage IV

The beginning of Stage IV signals the beginning of the bear market in bond prices. This means that exposure should be pared back a little more. If it has not already happened, the average maturity should also be shortened. Stocks remain at 75 percent and bonds are reduced to 15 percent, the 10 percent balance being held in cash (see Figure 12.4). It may, at first sight, appear inappropriate to increase the equity position to its maximum, just as the stock market is in its last few months of a bull run, but there are three factors that should be taken into consideration. First, there are no reasonable alternatives because bonds are in a bear market, and money market yields are still quite low. If the yield on one- to three-year money is significantly higher than money market rates, it may make sense to allocate some assets into that category, which would mean a lower

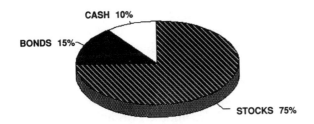

Figure 12.4 Stage IV allocation. (Source: *Pring Market Review*)

than 75 percent allocation to equities. Second, the market averages often make their actual high well after Stage V has been signaled by the economic and financial indicators. A good example of this occurred following the mid-1977 sell signal from the Bond Barometer. The final peak in the equity market was not seen until February 1980, nearly three years later. Third, the opportunities in the inflation hedge sectors are usually still plentiful, and in some cycles it is the ability to position assets against an unusually inflationary background that can best preserve the purchasing value of a portfolio. In Stage IV stocks still average 15 percent whereas bonds have lost 6 percent.

Stage V

Even so, it is still important to rotate a great deal of the stock portion of the portfolio into cash as Stage V begins (see Figure 12.5).

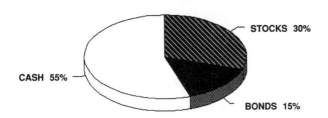

Figure 12.5 Stage V allocation. (Source: *Pring Market Review*)

By this time the return on money market instruments has started to improve, and many defensive equity groups such as utilities, which are well into their bear market, have now been joined by many others. In some cycles the S&P Composite continues to work its way to marginal new highs, but in others it merely succeeds in holding in the lower part of a large distributional trading band that began sometime toward the middle of Stage IV. During this part of the cycle the market is experiencing a kind of civil war. Early leaders are trying to drag the averages down, but the basic industry and inflation sectors are still in a bull market and are trying to push them up. The verdict on whether the market does make new highs or not depends on whether weakness in the defensive groups is sufficiently offset by strength in the lagging sectors.

From an investment point of view there are three important things on which to focus. First, even though the averages may not have given up much ground, maintaining the aura of well-being, the overall environment is quite risky. Second, any additional gains in the averages will be very narrowly based, making it much more difficult to select good performing stocks. Third, equity exposure should be concentrated on those groups that generally benefit from end of the cycle economic pressures, such as mines, energy, etc.

At this stage it seems appropriate to reduce the stock allocation down to the 30 percent level. The actual allocation to bonds remains the same, but since the risk of credit defaults will escalate as Stage VI approaches, it makes sense to gradually weed out the lower quality issues in favor of government and AAA corporate paper. The average maturity of the bond portfolio should also be brought in to the 5- to 7-year area at this stage.

Because Stage V offers very little in the way of opportunities but presents lots of risks, the cash portion of the portfolio is raised to 55 percent. Another factor in favor of liquid assets is that their yield has now begun to rise to a respectable level.

Stage VI

Cash is still king in Stage VI (see Figure 12.6), but as it becomes more evident that commodity prices have peaked, we know that the

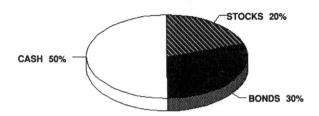

Figure 12.6   Stage VI allocation. (Source: *Pring Market Review*)

clock has started to tick for the demise of the bear market in bonds. Exposure to the bond market should, therefore, be increased. Not only is the bottom at hand, but bonds can now be purchased with sufficient current income to offer partial compensation for what will ultimately prove to be a temporary loss of market value. Our barometer models actually show bonds eking out a small gain, so an increase in the allocation can be justified on these grounds alone. An alternative way of increasing exposure is to maintain the existing allocation but to sharply extend its average maturity from say 5 to 25 or even 30 years. However, this step should only be taken when evidence of a weakening economy and a bear market in commodities starts to materialize.

The suggested allocations at this stage of the cycle are 20 percent stocks, 30 percent bonds, and 50 percent cash. A very high cash reserve is appropriate not only because the other markets often decline sharply in Stage VI, but also because the return on money market instruments is now at its highest for the cycle.

The Outer Ranges

The preceding comments apply to a theoretical target allocation that assumes that signals of the various stages were neither timely nor untimely and also were not indicating an extreme economic condition, such as a strongly inflationary or deflationary environment. On the other hand, the actual range could be substantially different, depending on the quality of the signal and its timeliness. For example, a range of 40 to 70 percent for bond exposure might be appropriate in Stage I. The lower end of the band at 40 percent might be employed as an investment tactic if the bond market had already rallied by a significant amount from its bottom before it was realized that a new bull market had begun. A quick review of the longer-term charts of bond prices shows that the initial thrust off the bottom often accounts for a significant proportion of a bull move, so it would not make a lot of sense to risk as substantial a portion of capital as if the bull market was in an earlier stage. On the other hand, an emerging new stage can sometimes be very obvious. In this type of situation, it will be prudent to make an above average allocation immediately. For example, if stocks are yielding over 6 percent, the market explodes on record volume from an oversold condition and rallies above its 12-month moving average, which is within 5 percent of the monthly bear market low; then we have some very powerful fundamental and technical signals. If the Torque Index is above zero and the yield on three-month commercial paper is below its 12-month moving average, this indicates that the monetary and economic backgrounds are also favorable. It would be handy if the Discount Rate had been lowered, but this might be too much to hope for at such an early stage. In any case the appearance of the other factors would be sufficient to justify a well above average stock allocation.

Very few tops and bottoms are that obvious, but when they do occur and can be identified, they represent unusually clear-cut signals. Most of the time, though, signals for an allocation rotation will be given one at a time. Thus, a bullish or bearish case is gradually built up over an extended period. This is why a gradual shade of gray approach is preferred over the instantaneous black and white one. For example, history tells us that the third hike in the Discount Rate following a series of cuts is a danger signal for the stock market. Unfortunately, the time between this hike and the eventual market high has varied considerably. It was as little as one month and 1.8 percent from the high in July 1956, to as much as 10 months and 19 percent in December 1989. All that we can say with any degree of certainty is that the third Discount Rate hike is a sign of an impending top, comparable to the snow line on a mountain that warns us that we are closing in on the peak. In this instance we do not know how far the snow will continue before we reach the top, merely that we have reached the last and final part of the climb and that we should be prepared for the summit to appear. In a market sense, the hike in the Discount Rate offers a similar warning, but it is not a signal to sell everything. It is more of a benchmark that tells us to lower the equity allocation in view of the increased risk.

ASSET ALLOCATION FOR THE CONSERVATIVE (INCOME-CONSCIOUS) INVESTOR

The principles of the allocation rotation are similar in nature to those described earlier, but this explanation assumes that the investor's objectives are more targeted to achieving a good income stream and preservation of purchasing value. Risk taking is therefore kept to an absolute minimum, and growth becomes a lower priority, except as it relates to beating inflation. The typical profile of such investors would include retirees who have reached a stage in life when they rely almost totally on the income generated from their investments and are not generally in a position to take substantial risks with their capital. Not all retirees will fit exactly into this category, and the category itself is not necessarily limited to more mature investors.

For example, a retired executive may have accumulated a significant portfolio through a judicious exercise of stock options, which has now been converted to a more diversified portfolio. The chances are that this person continues to receive a generous pension from his company; hence, reliance on income from the portfolio will be much less than for someone who supplements social security benefits with investment income.

At the other extreme, a widow of a retired executive may find his former pension cut substantially on his death and is now forced to rely to a much greater degree on investment income for survival.

A younger person who is no longer able to work and has received a lump sum disability payment will, in effect, have an almost identical investment objective as a recently retired older person. Neither one is in a position to take substantial risks, and both have a requirement for current income.

All fo these individuals have similar, but not identical, investment objectives that are skewed toward safety and income. These differences mean that the allocation suggestions represented in Figures 12.3 and 12.4 should be used only as guidelines for an average investor falling into this category.

Stage I

Bonds continue to represent a considerable portion of the portfolio, but a somewhat less risky position is appropriate. A new category, "Intermediate-Term Debt Securities," has been added in these examples (see Figure 12.7). Intermediate securities are generally categorized as those with a maturity of five years or less. They should represent an important part of a conservative investor's portfolio because they will appreciate in price from the Stage I decline in interest rates. At the same time, if rates do move up, there is less risk of a price decline. The principal advantage of these securities is that they enable investors to lock in the high yields that prevail at this stage of the cycle for very little risk. Because most cycles do not last much longer than five years, if the timing is right, these securities can be rolled over at high rates at a similar point in the succeeding cycle.

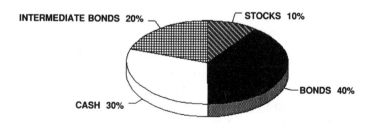

Figure 12.7   Stage I allocation. (Source: *Pring Market Review*)

The other important change that can be seen in comparison to the previous example is that the stock allocation has been reduced to 10 percent from 30 percent.

Stage II

This is also apparent in Stage II (see Figure 12.8). Here the stock allocation is less than half of that in the earlier pro forma example (i.e., Figure 12.2). The composition of these equity portfolios would also be different because the conservative portfolio would be limited to stocks that are rated A quality or higher. Higher-quality ratings are given to companies with a consistent record of maintaining profits and whose balance sheets and profit and loss statements successfully meet various financial tests. The share prices of such companies are, therefore, far less volatile than the rest of the market and are normally much more liquid. The stock portion of a conservative investor should be liberally spiced with near-bond equivalents, such as electric utilities. Price movements of these securities are similar to the bond market, but the potential for some small profit growth combined with the rising stream of dividend payments offers a good hedge against the declining purchasing power of fixed income securities.

Convertible preferred shares and convertible bonds are another vehicle for obtaining a good income stream while still achieving

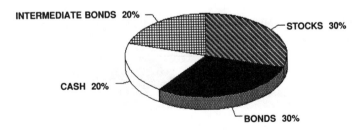

Figure 12.8   Stage II allocation. (Source: *Pring Market Review*)

some growth. (These securities were discussed briefly in Chapter 2.) Even though convertibles afford a higher degree of protection than straight equity issues, it is still of paramount importance to check out the financial strength of the company in question. Remember, high and tempting yields are usually available because the market is factoring in the possibility of a default. When in doubt, conservative investors are better advised to go for a lower yield and safety.

Stage III

The allocation is self-evident from Figure 12.9. The principles of safety expressed in the previous discussion on Stage II continue to apply.

Stage IV

Stage IV often heralds the beginning of a more dynamic stage in the inflationary part of the business cycle. This presents a dilemma for the conservative investor who is trying to simultaneously maintain a high current return and the real purchasing value of his portfolio. This is because an effective inflation hedge usually involves the sacrifice of some safety and income. One compromise is to allocate some funds to convertible bonds or preferred shares of equities that

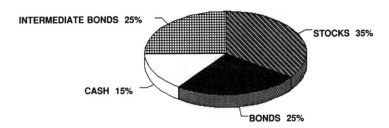

Figure 12.9 Stage III allocation. (Source: *Pring Market Review*)

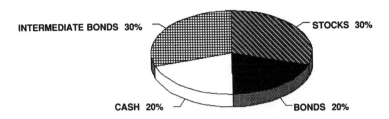

Figure 12.10   Stage IV allocation. (Source: *Pring Market Review*)

benefit from inflation. Another alternative is common shares of major oil or natural gas companies. Such issues typically offer some exposure to energy prices; yet the day-to-day activities of refining and marketing activities also produce a stable flow of earnings that are paid in dividends. Because this phase of the cycle also implies that bond prices are in a bear market, exposure to bonds is reduced both in an aggregate sense and through a reduction in the average maturity of the bond portfolio. This is also an appropriate time to lower the quality of the bond portfolio a little because these issues offer a higher current return and because there is little risk of default at this stage in the cycle (see Figure 12.10).

Stage V

Equities are once again reduced as Stage V approaches and are now downgraded to a 10 percent allocation (see Figure 12.11). Some-

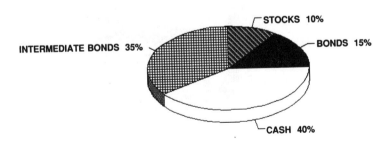

Figure 12.11   Stage V allocation. (Source: *Pring Market Review*)

times this phase of the cycle can last quite a while, but it is not a time for the conservative investor to be taking undue risks. Only if the threat of inflation was particularly pronounced would an allocation above 10 percent be appropriate. Cash, with a 40 percent allocation, is now king. The 35 percent allocation to intermediate-term bonds would average two to three years, depending on where the most efficient yield could be achieved. For example, if two- and three-year monies were both yielding the same, the shorter-term maturity would be appropriate. On the other hand, if two-year money offered a 6 percent return, but a three-year maturity brought 7 percent, it would make more sense to go out three years. There is, of course, some additional risk associated with this longer maturity, but if yields went up substantially, they could still be cashed in at close to par for some longer-term paper, once Stage I gets under way. In effect, a two- or three-year maturity is almost a cash equivalent, but usually offers a far more generous yield.

Stage VI

Stage VI is an environment when interest rates are rising, and stock prices are falling. The actual recommended allocation for conservative, income conscious investors is the same as in the previous stage, but the content is slightly different (see Figure 12.12). The stock allocation should now be purged of any inflation hedge issues

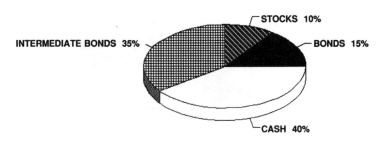

Figure 12.12   Stage VI allocation. (Source: *Pring Market Review*)

in favor of early market leaders that will benefit from falling interest rates. Electric utilities, securities brokers, and insurance stocks are a few that come to mind. If yields move up substantially, it would also make sense to lengthen the maturity of the intermediate-term bond allocation to five or even seven years.

This outline is intended as a rough guideline that indicates the main business cycle pointers and is not meant to be followed chapter and verse. Each cycle will have its own idiosyncrasies, and each investor his own psychological makeup, financial responsibilities, and resources.

AN AGGRESSIVE ASSET ALLOCATION POLICY

This description assumes that our hypothetical investor is in the early years of a career and that several more decades of earning power lie ahead. It is assumed that this investor is not only interested in more growth but also has the ability to shoulder the greater risk associated with such a policy. A younger investor may also be more likely to act quickly and handle a faster rotation of assets.

Stage I

A more aggressive stance is signaled in Stage I, with a relatively high 35 percent allocation to stocks and a small 5 percent cash reserve. Bonds are given a 60 percent quota as noted in Figure 12.13. Because the risk of default is always high at this stage of the

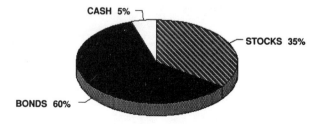

Figure 12.13   Stage I allocation. (Source: *Pring Market Review*)

business cycle, quality should not be sacrificed. The bond portfolio average maturity should be extended to 25 to 30 years. This is more than the "normal" portfolio and is justified not because the investor is younger and, therefore, more likely to be around at maturity, but because longer maturities offer greater potential for capital gains when interest rates decline. If the Stage I signal was particularly strong and timely, an allocation to zero coupon bonds, with their substantially greater leverage, would be appropriate.

Stage II

Equities usually perform better than bonds as this phase gets under way, so the equity portion of the portfolio is increased substantially to a 70 percent allocation (see Figure 12.14). Sectors that usually do well at this stage in the cycle include utilities and financials. Because this is a more aggressive portfolio, it makes sense to include securities brokers and mutual fund companies. These securities generally have a much higher beta than electric utilities or insurance companies.

Stage III

Bonds are reduced by a further 10 percent, and stocks are increased accordingly, as shown in Figure 12.15. This new money may well

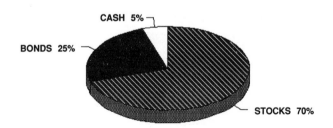

Figure 12.14   Stage II allocation. (Source: *Pring Market Review*)

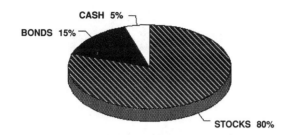

Figure 12.15 Stage III allocation. (Source: *Pring Market Review*)

find its way into economically sensitive issues, such as papers or steels, which are often improving in terms of relative strength as commodity prices start to pick up. If the relative strength of junior issues is in an uptrend they should also be included in the portfolio's makeup.

Stage IV

Bond prices have now peaked for the cycle, so their representation falls to a cycle low of 10 percent (see Figure 12.16). This money is now rotated into equities, especially into inflation sensitive issues, such as energy and mines. Interest sensitive stocks often peak in an absolute sense at this point and almost certainly in relative terms. Therefore, they should be significantly reduced in favor of economi-

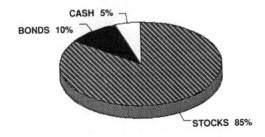

Figure 12.16 Stage IV allocation. (Source: *Pring Market Review*)

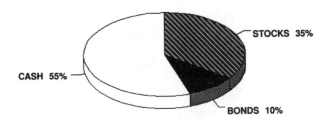

Figure 12.17   Stage V allocation. (Source: *Pring Market Review*)

cally sensitive sectors. Technology is an industry that often starts to come into its own in Stage IV.

Stage V

The stock market is now officially in a bear market. Even if the averages work their way marginally higher, the environment for most stocks has now turned hostile, and hence it makes sense to dramatically curtail the equity allocation. A reduction to 35 percent is recommended. Cash is the principal recipient of these funds, and the cash portion of the portfolio expands to 55 percent. Bonds remain at 10 percent (see Figure 12.17).

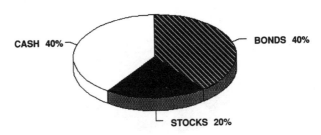

Figure 12.18   Stage VI allocation. (Source: *Pring Market Review*)

Stage VI

The equity bear market is now under way with a vengeance, and stocks are reduced to 20 percent, as noted in Figure 12.18. The proceeds are put into bonds as a preparation for the new bull market. Cash is also reduced to help achieve the bond objective.

Conclusion

As long as human nature remains more or less constant, the business cycle is likely to repeat. On the other hand, institutional changes and people's ability to learn from their most recent mistakes guarantee that the process will not repeat exactly. This does not mean that the principles of asset allocation described here will no longer operate, but that the character of each cycle will be different; so, too, will be the execution.

Gradualism is the key word when altering the composition of a portfolio. The day does not begin with bright sunlight, but develops bit by bit as the sun emerges from the predawn light and slowly works its way above the horizon. The investment process is similar because the evidence of a new bull market in any asset class emerges in a piecemeal manner as well. Some indicators give us advance warning of an emerging bull trend while the bear is in its final death throes. Prices may continue to plunge sharply lower, but careful analysis can often reveal subtle indications of an impending reversal. This is the time to prepare yourself psychologically for a change in the environment and to consider taking on a new position.

Gradualism is important from several aspects. First, sound investment decisions are always based on an assessment of probabilities. The odds of being right increase with more abundant evidence.

If a particular investment case is not well supported by the facts, the chances of success are low, and the allocation should also be low. When the evidence is more compelling and the market is not over-extended, go for a more substantial exposure. Because the evidence usually emerges in a somewhat slow and frustrating manner, the allocation process should follow a similar pattern.

Second, the most important investment objective is maintenance of principal. In this respect, it is important to remember that you need a larger percentage gain to overcome a loss. For example, a $10,000 portfolio that experiences a 50 percent loss requires a gain of 100 percent just to break even. Gradual changes in a portfolio help to protect the investor from gross miscalculations that could lead to major losses.

One of the most important impediments to investment success is human nature. We are all tempted to buy after the market has risen, when the news is good. This is much more comfortable for us psychologically than making a purchase when the outlook is gloomy and there seems no end in sight to the bad news. Unfortunately, that is precisely the wrong time to take risks because this favorable environment will already have been factored into the price. The term "good" news does not necessarily refer to the economy but indicates "good" news for a particular asset. Thus bad economic news is actually "good" news for high-quality bonds when the threat of default is not a problem. On the other hand, "good" economic news, after a point, becomes bad news for bonds because a stronger economy has the effect of pushing up interest rates and depressing bond prices.

There is always the temptation to become enamored of a particular asset and overweight it from time to time. This is usually a subtle form of greed that is invariably punished by the market. The gradualist approach helps to minimize both the temptation to buy at the top and to place too much emphasis on a particular asset. It helps the investor to gain a sense of perspective and psychological balance. The movement of funds into an asset in a slow, deliberate way will lead to far less disappointment in the event of a mistake. If the market moves temporarily against your position but the indicators are pointing to higher prices, it will be much easier to add to the asset because your state of mind will be more objective. After all, if you are sitting with a large position that has gone against you, it is far less likely that you can bring yourself around to adding to it. Also, the very fact that you already have a substantial exposure means that fewer resources are available. Any additional changes will result in an even more overbalanced portfolio.

A correct and timely recognition of the six stages is by no means an easy task, but if you follow the pointers described in earlier chapters, the odds of investment success will be greater. It is extremely unlikely that you will be able to rotate your assets perfectly every time. Indeed, if you do manage to sell at the top and buy at the bottom in any circumstance, this is more likely to be a function of chance than any other factor. Perfect or even near-perfect rotation is an impossibility. A more reasonable objective is to increase the value of your portfolio in a slow and gradual way, rarely if ever trying to hit the home run. *Success is achieved at the margin.* A little gain here and a little one there is not a very spectacular path to wealth accumulation, but a far more effective one.

Try to let your assets compound slowly over a long period. Do not be led astray by the latest investment fashion or by excessive economic forecasts in either direction. Examine the indicators that you have chosen to follow and see what they are telling you. Their message will be far more reliable than the latest media hype being followed by a gullible crowd. In this way the All-Seasons Investment Approach is one of safety first, taking on risk only when the road is clear.

The investment process is not a static process but very much a dynamic one. Each cycle presents us with the same characters, and the plot concludes in more or less the same way. However, the actors and their interpretation of their parts is always different, and the plot does vary sufficiently each time to cause some degree of uncertainty and confusion. It always seems easy when we look back, but the reality of the present is quite a different phenomenon, with so many quoted experts and commentators providing us with ready-made answers along the way. We also have to do battle with our own human frailties; the fear, the greed, and the uncertainty. This is why it is important to keep things as simple as possible. Keep your eye on the ball and avoid the temptation of being deflected in your interpretation of the indicators by those around you. Remember how the business cycle operates: recession, Federal Reserve injection of liquidity, Discount Rate cuts, bond rally, stock rally, economic pickup, rallying commodities. Then the rise in interest rates, the good news associated with a stock market peak, perhaps a third or fourth Discount Rate hike, a commodity peak, recession, and the beginning of a new cycle.

Obviously, the economic data is the most important area to monitor, but watching too many indicators can lead to confusion and is, for the most part, beyond the resources of the average investor. The simplest and most clear-cut signals are provided by the Fed: not every single squiggle in the Fed Funds Rate, but the major implications of a reversal in the prevailing *trend* in the Discount Rate.

The second area that almost anyone can monitor is the media. Doing so can provide a basis for forming a contrary opinion. Monitoring the media is by no means a simple matter, but there are times when a major theme becomes apparent from both the electronic and print media. It is not the function of journalists to make accurate forecasts but to report what is going on. This means publishing the most newsworthy forecasts. If the consensus is overwhelmingly bullish or bearish, it will almost certainly be reflected in the media. To make matters more difficult, the arguments are always compelling, especially when they are supported by the prevailing price trend. When a theme is spotted, view it with suspicion—especially if you find yourself in total agreement. Then go back to the indicators to see what they are saying. The crowd is rarely correct in its collective judgment. After all, if everyone is bullish, who is left to buy? If the indicators and the consensus are in opposing camps, you can be sure that the indicators will prove to be correct.

Obtaining an approximate identification of the prevailing stage of the business cycle is not a particularly difficult assignment. The task that defeats most investors is putting this knowledge into practice by overcoming the human frailties that we all possess. The All-Seasons Investment Approach can be of tremendous help in this direction if executed with gradualism and supplemented with generous doses of patience and discipline.

APPENDIXES

A

The Bond Barometer

The objective of the Bond Barometer is to develop an indicator that identifies major swings in bond prices associated with the business cycle. There are three major objectives. The first is to preserve capital and enable bond investors to avoid the significant loss of principal that can result from bear markets. The postwar period (1945–1981) of secular declining bond prices indicates how devastating the buy and hold approach can be. The second objective is to identify cyclical turning points (i.e., those associated with the business cycle) within a few months, working on the assumption that once a trend has begun it will continue for well over a year. The third objective is to devise an indicator in which misleading whipsaw signals are kept to a minimum so that investors can take comfort in knowing that once a signal is generated, it is unlikely to reverse for a considerable period of time.

The economy, monetary policy, and technical factors are complex forces affecting bond prices, and no single indicator can identify all major turns on a timely basis. For this reason, the Bond Barometer consists of a number of different indicators measuring economic, technical, and monetary conditions, each of which has experienced the taste of failure from time to time. With this combination, the barometer is not adversely affected when individual indicators fail.

Monetary indicators show their bullishness for bond prices by reflecting an easy-money policy; economic indicators show it through economic weakness; and technical indicators through a positive trend in prices. As monetary policy eases, the economy weakens and technical trends improve, so each indicator is added to the barometer. A reading greater than 50 percent has usually identified a good environment for bond prices. Conversely, a reading of 50 percent or less indicates bear market conditions.

ECONOMIC INDICATORS

Over the long haul, the rate of inflation is an important factor in determining the level and trend of bond yields. Two indicators measuring inflationary pressure are included in the barometer. The first is the Leading Inflation Index, published by the Columbia business school. It is constructed from price surveys, commodity indexes, employment, growth, and changes in the level of outstanding debt. It is plotted in Figure A.1 together with an annual rate of change of the Consumer Price Index (CPI), and shows in a rhythmic sense that it has led most turning points in the CPI. The magnitude of its movements has not always translated into an equivalent movement in the CPI. The Inflation Indicator subtracts points from the barometer whenever it is above its nine-month moving average, and points are added when it crosses above this benchmark.

The other inflation indicator is derived from the trend of the CRB Spot Raw Materials Index. This is a better indicator than commodity indexes incorporating agricultural products because the prices of industrial raw materials are very sensitive to economic conditions and, therefore, better reflect its underlying trends. It can be seen in Figure C.3.

Points are subtracted from the barometer whenever the CRB Spot Raw Materials Index rises 10 percent above its 12-month moving average. Subtraction stops when the index falls below or is at this same benchmark. Since commodity prices invariably peak

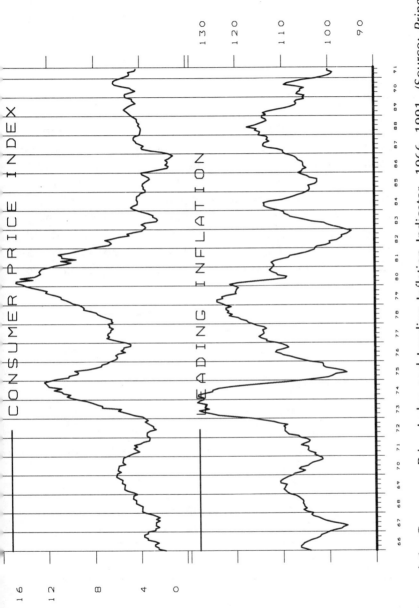

Figure A.1 Consumer Price Index and Leading Inflation Indicator, 1966–1991. (Source: *Pring Market Review*)

283

and trough ahead of bond prices within a relatively short time, the trend in commodity prices can be a valuable guide to identifying major peaks and troughs in bond prices.

Manufacturing Capacity

The level of capacity utilization and percentage of vendors reporting slow deliveries are both good indicators of tightness in the manufacturing area. These series could be considered separately, but we have discovered that combining them achieves a more reliable method for identifying major bond market turning points. One point is subtracted from the barometer whenever a six-month moving average of a nine-month rate of change crosses above its 12-month moving average. This relationship is expressed as an oscillator in Figure A.2, so whenever it crosses below the reference line,

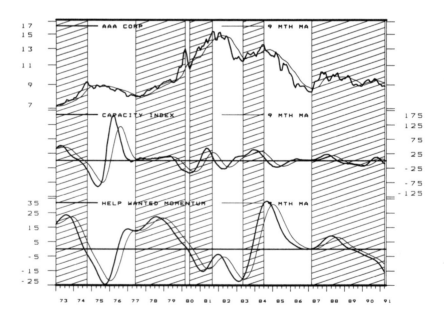

Figure A.2 Selected Bond Barometer indicators—economic. Shaded areas represent rising bond yields. (Source: *Pring Market Review*)

economic weakness, resulting in an improved reading in the barometer, is signaled.

Help Wanted Advertising

Help wanted advertising is a reliable measure of the demand for labor. It is expressed as an index (1967 = 100) of classified help wanted advertising lines in over 50 newspapers nationally. A rising quantity of help wanted advertising indicates an expanding economy of rising rates.

Help wanted advertising is also expressed in the barometer as an oscillator. Figure A.2 shows that the series is very smooth and does not change direction often. Points are subtracted from the barometer whenever the Help Wanted Advertising Index crosses above its zero reference line.

Coincident Indicators

The Composite Coincident Indicator is published by the Commerce Department. It monitors several economic sectors, such as industrial production, that move coincidentally with the economy. It is incorporated in the barometer as a deviation from a 12-month moving average, Figure A.3. It is considered positive for prices whenever it falls below the average, and vice versa.

The Growth Indicator

The Growth Indicator is constructed from a rate of change of several equally weighted indicators monitoring different sectors of the economy. Whenever it crosses below its zero reference line, it signals that the economy has weakened sufficiently to be consistent with an interest rate peak. This indicator has been particularly timely in identifying peaks since its lead time has been very short. It has not been quite so helpful at interest rate troughs since the lead time has varied and tends to be longer.

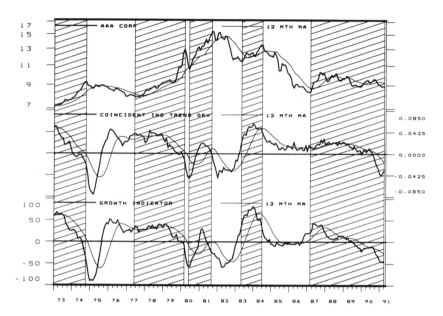

Figure A.3 Selected Bond Barometer indicators—economic. Shaded areas represent rising bond yields. (Source: *Pring Market Review*)

We view it as our most reliable and timely individual indicator for identifying interest rate peaks.

MONETARY INDICATORS

The Discount Rate

The Discount Rate is a very important indicator since it reflects major changes in monetary policy. Other things being equal, a hike in the Discount Rate is bearish for bond prices and a cut is bullish. Occasionally the Federal Reserve raises or lowers the Discount Rate and then reverses itself within two or three months. These actions are rare but point out the wisdom of using the Discount Rate in connection with a 12-month moving average crossover. In most cases these minor policy changes are filtered out by the moving average rule, and yet it still captures the bulk of the interest rate trend influenced by major policy changes.

In view of its importance, the Discount Rate is given a double weighting in the barometer. Whenever the rate is above its 12-month moving average, it acts as a bearish barometer component. When it falls below the average, it becomes a positive force in its own right, and also cancels the bearish influence of one other indicator. (If the barometer is already at 100 percent, this rule has no effect.) This canceling effect stays in force for 10 months after each Discount Rate cut. For example, if the rate is lowered in August while the coincident indicator is bearish, the lowering of the rate cancels the negative influence of the coincident indicator for 10 months, or until it goes bullish. If the rate is then lowered once more in December, the 10-month countdown begins again in December. The holding period is canceled if the Discount Rate rises or if the barometer has already reached 100 percent.

Real M2 and Money Market Prices (Monetary Squeeze)

The second monetary indicator is constructed from the relationship of Real Money Supply (defined as M2 adjusted for commodity prices) to money market prices. If Real Money Supply is falling, it normally indicates tight money, which is initially bearish for bond prices. However, the declining effect of Real Money Supply sooner or later adversely affects the level of economic activity, which then becomes bullish for bond prices. By relating Real Money Supply to money market prices (which usually lead bonds), this indicator helps to identify the point at which the decline in real money balances become a favorable bond market factor, and vice versa.

This indicator is expressed in the barometer as a smoothed rate of change and is considered a bearish factor for bond prices whenever it is below its zero reference line. While a positive zero crossover is required for Bond Barometer purposes, it is worth noting that a bottoming out action in this indicator often coincides with interest rate peaks. It is shown in Figure A.4.

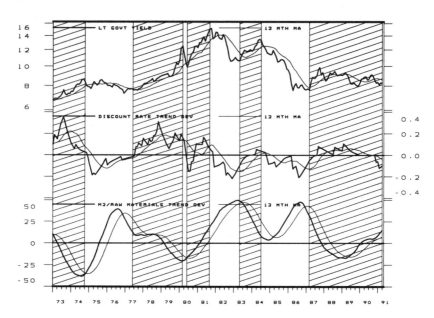

Figure A.4   Selected Bond Barometer indicators—monetary. Shaded areas represent rising bond yields. (Source: *Pring Market Review*)

TECHNICAL INDICATORS

The final two indicators included as components are technical in nature. They are represented by two moving average crossovers in Moody's AAA Corporate Yield series. The first has a 12-month span and the second has a nine-month span. Points to the barometer are subtracted whenever the deviation from a nine-month MA crosses 0.5 percent above its moving average. Points to the barometer are also subtracted whenever the deviation from a 12-month MA crosses above its moving average.

The technical indicators are not given a large weight in the barometer, but they do serve to tip barometer readings at the margin and result in reasonably accurate signals.

B
The Stock Barometer

The interaction of technical, economic, and financial forces with equity prices is a highly complex process, changing from cycle to cycle. A barometer approach, which incorporates a consensus of several consistently accurate indicators, is more reliable than any single indicator. Drawing on past relationships to project future trends is valid provided that the following are true:

1. The data are researched back over a long period covering a variety of business cycle environments.
2. The sensitivity of equity prices to any of the indicators used in the barometer has not changed materially.
3. The barometer is not dominated by one particular indicator whose failure would jeopardize its future performance.
4. The rules are as simple and few as possible. It is always possible to "fix" a barometer with many different rules, several of which apply only to specific periods. If a barometer needs such artificial constructions in order to work, it would be of little use in identifying future bullish and bearish environments.

A major investment goal is to identify changes in the long-term environment for equities, so it is important for strategic reasons to construct a barometer which keeps misleading (whipsaw) signals to an absolute minimum. Once a signal has been triggered, it should stay in force for a considerable length of time. This consideration was a predominant one in the construction of the Stock Market Barometer. As a result, the barometer's performance has, to some extent, been sacrificed in order to avoid whipsaw signals.

Market tops tend to be rolling affairs in which equities undergo a distribution process over a relatively long period of time, so if the barometer can lead the peak in equity prices by several months, exposure can be gradually adjusted. Market bottoms, on the other hand, are often preceded by a sharp final downleg, and the barometer is specifically designed to identify bullish periods for stock prices after the market has reached its final lows.

The barometer has been given a conservative bias because the first rule in an investment policy should be to maintain principal and avoid undue risk. As a result, the barometer would have kept investors out of major bear market periods such as 1960–1970, 1970–1974, and the crash of 1987.

Since the barometer includes several economic series that are published with a one-month lag, they have been adjusted accordingly. For example, housing starts for November are not posted until December, which is the reporting month.

It should also be noted that the barometer contains revised economic data, which is not necessarily the data actually published at the time. Because every indicator subject to revision is smoothed at least once, marginal revisions do not materially distort the results. The barometer consists of 11 economic, financial, and technical indicators. It starts off with 100 percent of its components in a bullish mode. As a specific indicator goes negative its contribution is removed. Readings of 50 percent or lower signal periods of risk.

ECONOMIC INDICATORS

The indicators can be categorized into three sectors: economic, financial, and technical.

The Torque Index

The business cycle is the underlying driving force that determines the level and momentum of corporate profits, a major ingredient in stock prices. The stock market discounts profits and is, therefore, a leading indicator of business activity. Most economic indicators are of little use in forecasting because they lag the stock market.

One indicator that typically leads important peaks and troughs in the equity markets is the ratio of housing starts to vendor performance, which we call the *Torque Index*. Vendor performance measures the percentage of sellers reporting slower deliveries. A low reading points up slackness in the economy since few vendors are experiencing supply difficulties. This relationship is useful because it measures the ratio of an interest sensitive sector indicator to a manufacturing one.

The Torque Index identifies the point when (or just before) housing starts begin to improve, which gives an advance signal that the recovery is just about to take hold. It also offers an early warning when the recovery is narrowing, a sign that is normally digested by the equity market before it peaks. This ratio is plotted as a smoothed rate of change and is removed from the barometer when below its zero reference line. It makes a positive contribution when it recrosses back above zero.

The Torque Index has been a very reliable lead indicator of stock market peaks and troughs, especially in recent years. Apart from its false optimism in 1977, its major failures occurred in the 1950s and mid-1960s when it was prematurely bullish, and in 1991 when it failed to signal a major rally.

Commodity Prices

Commodity prices normally begin their ascent during the early stage in a business cycle. This phenomenon is almost always associated with an advancing stock market, but eventually upside momentum accelerates, forcing interest rates to move sharply higher, which ultimately causes a capitulation in equity prices. Because the lead time between commodity price lows and the ultimate high in stock prices is unduly long, signals derived from positive commodity trends lag for nine months before this indicator is removed from the barometer. In this case the signal is a 12-month moving average crossover by the CRB Spot Raw Materials Index.

The lead time of commodity price peaks to stock market lows is much shorter than at stock market peaks, so the point is removed immediately after the Commodity Index crosses below its 12-month MA.

After considering a number of different commodity indexes, we chose the CRB Spot Index because it resembles swings in econommic activity more closely than most others. This is not to be confused with the CRB Futures Composite, which includes prices of a large number of food items that are more influenced by weather conditions than economic activity.

The Leading Economic Indicator Diffusion Index

This indicator is calculated from a basket of ten leading economic indicators that are above their 12-month moving averages. Because the resulting data is very volatile, it is in turn smoothed by a six-month MA (the nonsagged line in Figure B.1). The actual data fall between zero (when all the indicators are below their 12-month MA) and 100 (when they are all above), but we have deducted 50 from the total. In this way, readings in excess of 50 show that a majority of the indicators are above their 12-month MAs, i.e., expanding, and vice versa.

The correlation between this indicator and the stock market is reasonably close, as a comparison of the two series shows. Since it leads stock market peaks by a considerable period of time, there is a delay of seven months between the actual moving average crossover and the time when it affects the barometer. A more coincident relationship occurs at stock market bottoms, so a lag of only one month to allow for the delay in reported data is needed. Typically, a late-stage cycle rally in the economy is positive for basic industry and inflation hedge stocks.

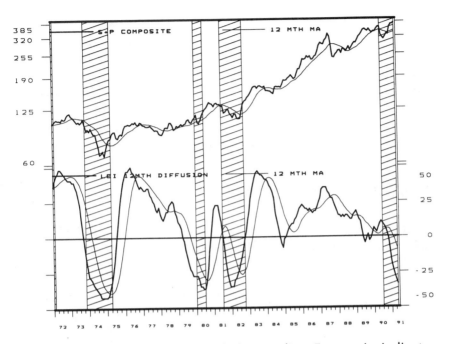

Figure B.1 S&P Composite and the Leading Economic Indicator Diffusion Index. (Source: *Pring Market Review*)

FINANCIAL INDICATORS

M2 Adjusted by the CRB Spot Raw Materials Index (CM2)

This indicator adjusts M2 by changes in the CRB Spot Raw Materials Index. Adjusting M2 by commodity prices rather than the CPI (i.e., Real M2) has three benefits. First, commodity prices lead the CPI, so the adjusted M2 indicator results in a longer lead time vis-à-vis the equity market. Second, commodity prices are subject to more volatile swings than the CPI, so it is easier to identify cyclical movements. Finally, commodity prices are available on a much more timely basis than CPI data. In almost every instance, it has led stock market peaks by a wide margin. Even at troughs the lead time has usually been sufficient to prepare for a major upswing.

Since 1953, no business cycle-associated stock market bottom has occurred when CM2 has been below its moving average.

Points are removed from the barometer whenever the CM2 is below its 24-month MA. It peaked a year ahead of the S&P in 1986 and then experienced a sharp downtrend for the next 12 months. A positive reading in CM2 is pretty well a prerequisite for a (business cycle) stock market bottom, so weak action indicates a high degree of equity market vulnerability. It is plotted in Figure B.2.

The Inverted Yield Curve and M2

When the Inverted Yield Curve is plotted on a smoothed ROC basis against the stock market, it is found to have unduly long

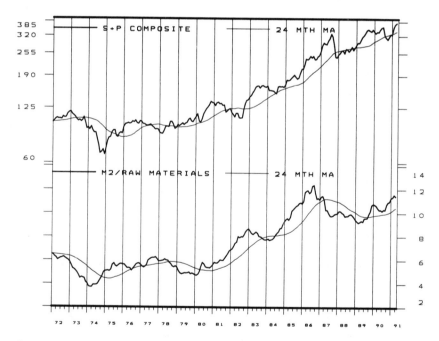

Figure B.2   S&P Composite and M2 adjusted by the CRB Spot Raw Materials Index. (Source: *Pring Market Review*)

leading characteristics. On the other hand, a similar momentum reading for M2 demonstrates a more coincident, but sometimes less reliable relationship. However, if both these indicators are combined with a special weighting for Real M2, it gives a much more timely indication of major equity peaks and troughs. Two versions of this relationship are used in the construction of the barometer.

The first is a smoothed 18-month ROC. The level of the barometer is lowered whenever the 18-month ROC is below its nine-month MA. Note that since 1953, this indicator has correctly predicted a recession whenever it has fallen below its zero reference line.

The second way in which this data is used is on a smoothed nine-month ROC basis. The level of the barometer is reduced as long as it is below its zero reference line. The nine-month ROC is plotted in Figure B.3.

The Trend of Short-Term Interest Rates

The trend of short-term interest rates influences the barometer in two ways. First, a simple 12-month MA crossover by the 4 to 6-month Commercial Paper Yield lowers the level of the barometer.

The Money Flow Indicator

The second way in which the Commercial Paper Yield affects the barometer is through the Money Flow Indicator, which is calculated by dividing the S&P Composite by the yield on the 4 to 6-month Commercial Paper rate. The data is then plotted on a smoothed ROC basis against the S&P Composite itself. When the Money Flow Indicator rises above the smoothed ROC of the S&P, it gives a bullish signal. Negative crossovers usually signal a bearish environment for equities and are responsible for lowering the overall level of the barometer. Its record is shown in Figure B.4. Shaded areas represent periods when it was in a bearish mode for equities.

The Money Flow Indicator is really trying to measure whether stock prices are rising because of support from falling interest rates,

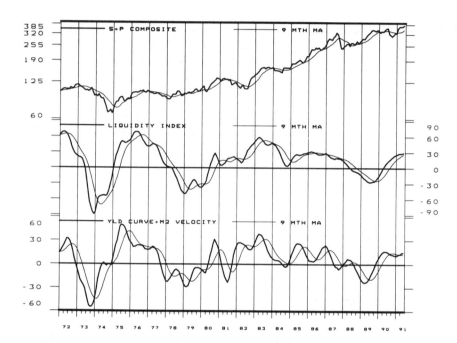

Figure B.3 S&P Composite, liquidity index, and yield curve/M2 velocity. (Source: *Pring Market Review*)

or whether they are advancing for some other reason. Apart from a few whipsaws, this indicator has generally had an extremely good record in calling major turns in stock prices over the last 35 years.

Its major error occurred in the period between 1962 and 1966, when gently rising short-term interest rates maintained it in an unduly conservative mode for five years. It also failed in the 1988–1989 period. This particularly poor performance further underlines the need to use a number of different indicators to insolate major reversals in equity trends.

The Discount Rate

The Discount Rate has long been used as a tool for identifying positive and negative environments for stock prices. It typically lags short-term interest rates determined by market forces, so its

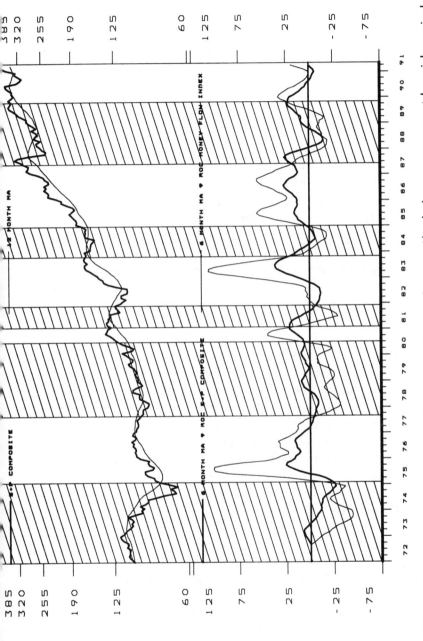

Figure B.4 S&P Composite and the Money Flow Indicator. Shaded areas represent bearish periods. (Source: *Pring Market Review*)

importance lies in the fact that it represents a policy signal by the Central Bank. Decisions to alter the level of the Discount Rate are not taken lightly, and a reversal in the trend of a series of hikes or cuts is usually very significant. Since these changes almost invariably indicate a major reversal in monetary policy, Discount Rate movements are given a significant weight in the barometer. The rules are as follows.

1. The overall level of the barometer is increased by a double weighting on the first decline following a series of hikes. (All other barometer components have an equal weighting except for the Leading Indicator Diffusion Index.)
2. This weighting is reduced by half after the first rise.
3. At the time of the second rise, the Discount Rate is in a neutral mode, neither improving nor depressing the barometer.
4. If a third rise occurs (an indication that the Fed is very serious about tightening monetary policy), the barometer reading is lowered by a double weighting.
5. Since the Discount Rate tends to be a lagging indicator, its negative weighting, resulting from the third hike, is halved whenever the 4 to 6 month Commercial Paper Yield is below its 12-month MA. If this proves to be a temporary phenomenon, the double negative weighting is replaced when it recrosses its moving average. As long as the Commercial Paper Yield remains above its average, this double negative weighting is held until the first decline in the Discount Rate materializes.

TECHNICAL INDICATORS

Group Momentum

One important criterion for a sustainable rise in stock prices is market breadth. This is tracked in the barometer through the Group Momentum Indicator, which measures the percentage of a basket of 20 S&P industry groups that are above their six-month MAs. This data is in turn smoothed by a six-month MA, represented by the nonjagged line in Figure B.5. The plotted series has been further

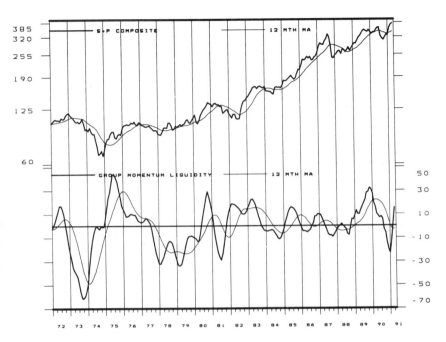

Figure B.5 S&P Composite and group momentum liquidity. (Source: *Pring Market Review*)

adjusted by relating the Group Momentum series to a smoothed rate of change of the Inverted Yield Curve (defined as 4 to 6-month Commercial Paper to AAA Corporates). Since the yield curve is a leading indicator of stock prices it has the effect of emphasizing the movements of the Group Momentum Indicator, and offering more timely signals of important reversals in equity prices.

The barometer's level is reduced when the Group Momentum Indicator is below its nine-month MA, and increased when it turns positive again.

The S&P Composite Nine-Month Deviation

This is the final barometer component. One point is subtracted when the S&P falls below its nine-month MA.

C

The Inflation Barometer

While it is possible to devise indicators that have a reasonably reliable long-term record of identifying peaks and troughs in commodity prices, none of them individually has a perfect record. To overcome this difficulty, we developed the Inflation Barometer, which consists of 10 individual indicators with a reliable 36-year track record of identifying bullish and bearish environments for commodity prices.

The barometer assumes that all 10 are in a bullish mode for commodities. As each one weakens to a point that is inconsistent with rising commodity prices, it is removed. A reading at or below 50 percent indicates a negative environment for commodity prices.

The choice of a commodity index against which to measure the barometer's performance is a difficult task since none of the published indexes offer a truly comprehensive picture of the level and direction of commodity prices. The main objective is to identify economic environments that are conducive to rising or falling interest rates, so indexes that include weather sensitive agricultural commodities are not suitable. This effectively limits us to two alternatives, the *Journal of Commerce* Raw Materials Index and the CRB Spot Raw Materials Index. The CRB Spot Raw Materials Index should not be confused with the more popular CRB Composite (Futures) Index, which is heavily dominated by weather sensitive agricultural commodities.

For most of the time there is very little difference between the movement in the *Journal of Commerce* Index and that of the CRB, but the CRB has been used because it is more widely publicized than the *Journal of Commerce* Index, and is therefore easier to follow. Since many of the economic indicators are reported with a lag of one month, their historic contributions to the barometer have also been lagged in order to better simulate actual conditions.

The components can be roughly divided into three categories: economic, technical, and business cycle sequence.

ECONOMIC INDICATORS

It is well known that tightening capacity in the economy results in upward price pressure, and vice versa. Accordingly, the barometer includes several indicators that attempt to measure tightness, both in the manufacturing and labor markets.

Capacity Utilization

Manufacturing capacity utilization is incorporated in the barometer as a deviation from a 12-month MA. It is shown in Figure C.1. The Capacity Utilization Trend Index is considered to be in a positive mode for commodity prices whenever it is above its zero reference line, i.e., the 12-month moving average. When it falls 1 percent below the average, its contribution is removed.

The Capacity Index (shown underneath the Capacity Utilization Index) is a combination indicator, constructed from both capacity utilization and vendor performance. Vendor performance data measures the percentage of vendors reporting slower deliveries and is, therefore, an alternative method of measuring tightness in the system. The combination of the two indicators offers a cross-check, confirming evidence of overall tightness in the system.

The Capacity Index is calculated as a nine-month rate of change

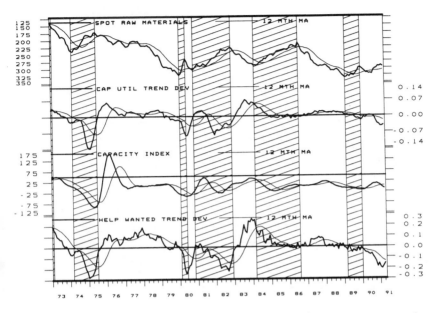

Figure C.1 Selected Inflation Barometer indicators—economic. Shaded areas represent periods of rising commodity prices. (Source: *Pring Market Review*)

smoothed by a six-month MA, and turns bullish for commodity prices whenever it is above zero. It requires a movement below −10 percent to trigger a bearish signal, which stays in force until it crosses above its zero line.

Help Wanted Advertising

Help wanted data is expressed in the fourth series of Figure C.1 as a deviation from a 12-month moving average. This indicator is considered bullish for inflation whenever it is above its zero reference line, but has to slip 2 1/2 percent below the average (shown as −0.025 in the figure) in order to be removed from the barometer.

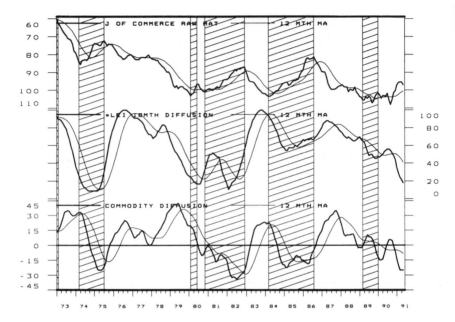

Figure C.2 Selected Inflation Barometer indicators—economic and technical. Shaded areas represent periods of rising commodity prices. (Source: *Pring Market Review*)

Leading Indicator Diffusion Index

The Leading Indicator Diffusion Index measures the percentage of 18 indicators with very long leading characteristics that are above their 18-month moving average. Since the raw data from this calculation is very volatile, the index has been smoothed by a moving average. Signals are generated by 12-month moving average crossovers. It is shown in Figure C.2.

TECHNICAL INDICATORS

The CRB Spot Raw Materials Index

The CRB Spot Raw Materials Index is considered to be in a bullish trend for commodity prices whenever it is above its 12-month moving average, and vice versa. A 1 percent decline below the 12-month moving average is responsible for the additional deduction of 10 percentage points. Crossovers of the 12-month moving average have been selected because these signals are usually valid and occur relatively close to the final peak or trough in the index. The data is plotted on a monthly close basis.

The *Journal of Commerce* Raw Materials Index

Since the construction of this commodity index differs somewhat from the CRB Spot Raw Materials Index, it offers a form of confirmation or cross-check. Bullish and bearish signals are generated by 12-month moving average crossovers.

The Commodity Diffusion Index

The Commodity Diffusion Index is constructed from a percentage of the 18 commodities used in the construction of the *Journal of Commerce* Raw Materials Index that are above their 12-month moving average. See bottom series on Figure C.2. The data is smoothed before it is included as a barometer component because it is quite volatile. A sustainable rise in the CRB Spot Raw Materials Price Index is not likely unless supported by an expanding number of commodities that are above their 12-month moving average, i.e., in positive trends.

Since the Commodity Diffusion Index tends to peak and trough ahead of the Raw Materials Index itself, zero crossovers offer useful benchmarks for major commodity turning points. In this context, the zero line represents the demarcation between the point at which 50 percent of the commodities are in a rising mode and 50 percent are declining. Historically, when the Commodity Diffusion Index has been able to cross, and hold, decisively above zero, it has almost always signaled a major advance in commodity prices.

THE BUSINESS CYCLE SEQUENCE

The three remaining indicators are included as a cross-check to ensure that commodity prices are acting in a manner consistent with their normal chronological sequence in the business cycle.

AAA Bond Yields

Bond yields (see Figure C.3) are included in the barometer because they reflect inflationary pressures. When the AAA Corporate Bond Yield is above its 12-month moving average, i.e., above zero on the chart, it suggests that the basic trend of yields is up and that the bond market is fearful of inflation. When the yield falls 1 percent

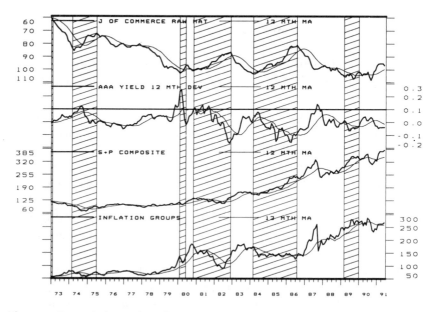

Figure C.3 Selected Inflation Barometer indicators—sequences. Shaded areas represent periods of rising commodity prices. (Source: *Pring Market Review*)

below its average, it signals a bearish trend and 10 percentage points are removed from the barometer. It is also important for short-term interest rates to confirm a decline at the long end, so the bearish AAA signal does not affect the barometer unless the four-month Commercial Paper Yield also falls below its 12-month moving average.

Equity Prices

Equity prices typically peak and trough ahead of commodity prices because they discount future economic activity. The S&P Composite has been included as a barometer component, using 12-month moving average crossovers for signals. (See third series on Figure C.3.)

The Inflation Group Index

Another equity component is the Inflation Group Index. It is constructed from several inflation sensitive S&P stock groups, such as copper, gold, domestic oils, etc., and they are included because rises in inflation sensitive stocks should be discounting higher commodity prices, and vice versa. Barometer signals are triggered by 12-month moving average crossovers. (See fourth series on Figure C.3).

D

Historical Market Performance and the Six Stages

The illustrations in this section represent market action in each of the six stages. Figures D.1 through D.12 show the stages as defined by the peaks and troughs of the markets themselves, while Figures D.13 through D.24 reflect the stages as defined by the barometers. By and large, stage classification as defined by market action is quite straightforward. However, there are some exceptions. For example, in 1961 the actual commodity peak was made in the spring, ahead of the stock market high. Since the secondary commodity peak, achieved in December, was only slightly below the spring peak but followed correctly in sequence, the December peak was used.

The 1976–1980 period also causes concern. The actual stock market peak associated with the business cycle occurred in sequence in 1980. However, the market experienced a substantial decline in 1977 and early 1978. This suggests that a minicycle rotation may have occurred, but since commodities did not decline substantially and money market prices never rose, it would appear that the equity sell-off represented an unusually large intermediate-term decline. If this view is taken, then the market peaks and troughs fall into a perfect sequence. Unfortunately, there is a further complication in that the barometer model did go through a complete cycle. This example demonstrates that the mechanical extrapolation of the market cycle sequence is far from perfect. Even so, if an investor had given weight to such factors as high stock yields and some of the inflation/deflation indicators described earlier, an investment policy oriented away from long-term bonds and toward inflation sensitive equities would undoubtedly have resulted.

The only other period that may have caused problems was between October 1987 and the end of 1990. This is because the October 1987 equity low developed *before* the 1989 commodity top and money market bottom. The stock market subsequently went on to make a new all time high. In this instance the 1987 top has been treated as the orthodox peak. The crash was an unusual two-to-three week affair, and the subsequent rally was supported by the biggest stock retirement of all time, whether measured in actual dollars or as a percentage of outstanding capitalization. In this respect it could be argued that the 1987–1990 rally was an intermediate-term advance in an overall bearish trend. In fact, a substantial number of stocks lost a considerable amount of their value in this period. Under this interpretation equities peaked in August 1987, and commodities topped out in early 1989 along with a bottoming in money market prices. Equities then bottomed in the middle of the recession in October 1990. This scenario also fits reasonably closely to the barometer model.

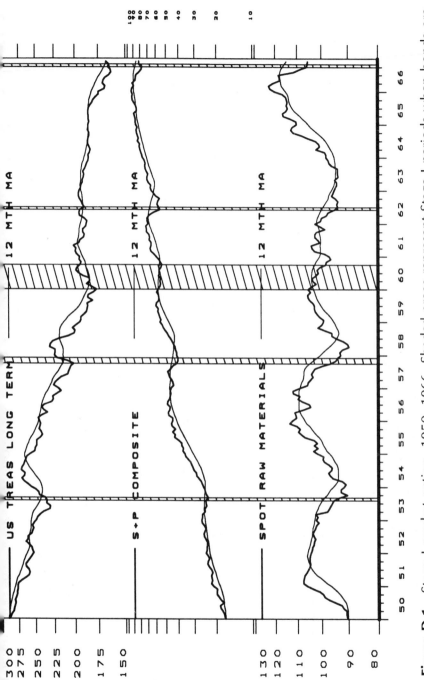

Figure D.1 Stage I market action, 1950–1966. Shaded areas represent Stage I periods when bonds are bullish; stocks and commodities are bearish. (Source: *Pring Market Review*)

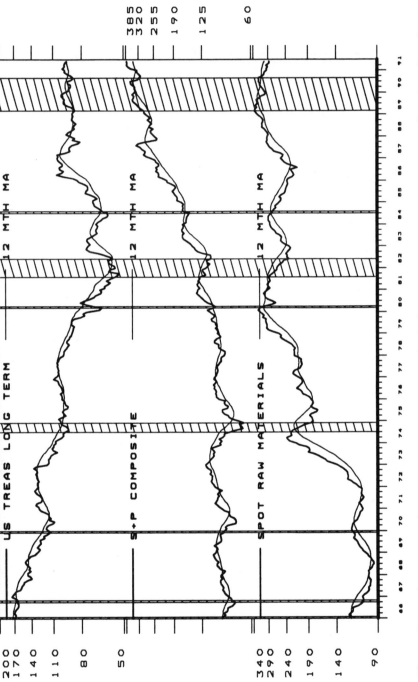

Figure D.2 Stage I market action, 1966–1991. Shaded areas represent Stage I periods when bonds are bullish, stocks and commodities are bearish. (Source: *Pring Market Review*)

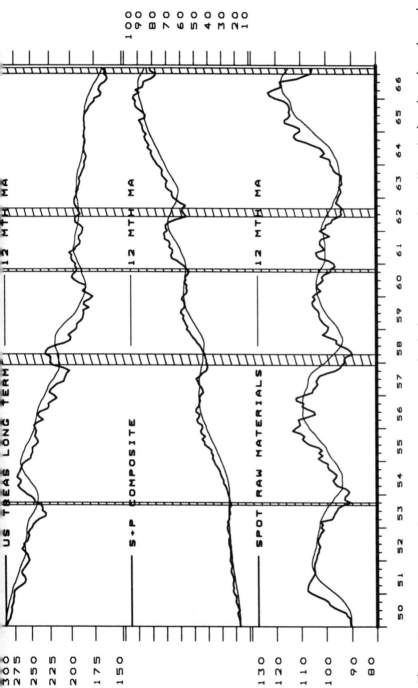

Figure D.3 Stage II market action, 1950–1966. Shaded areas represent Stage II periods when bonds and stocks are bullish; commodities are bearish. (Source: *Pring Market Review*)

313

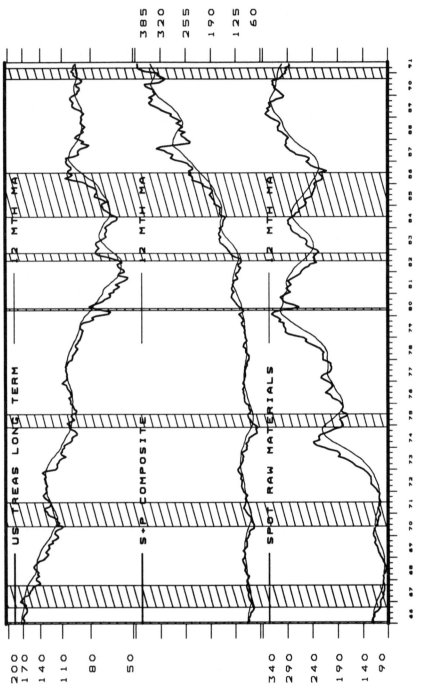

Figure D.4 Stage II market action, 1966–1991. Shaded areas represent Stage II periods when bonds and stocks are bullish, commodities are bearish. (Source: *Pring Market Review*)

314

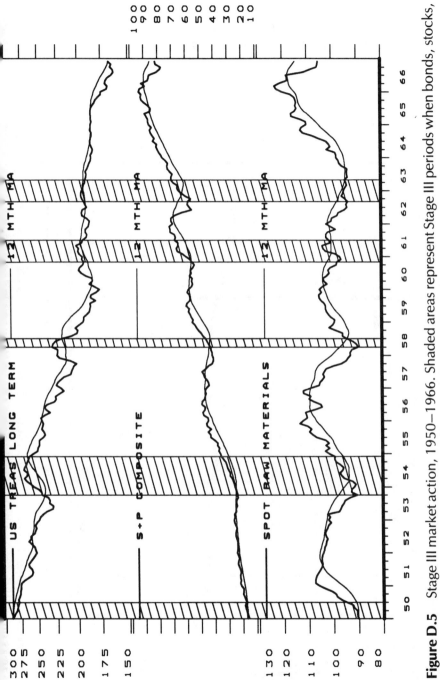

Figure D.5 Stage III market action, 1950–1966. Shaded areas represent Stage III periods when bonds, stocks, and commodities are bullish. (Source: *Pring Market Review*)

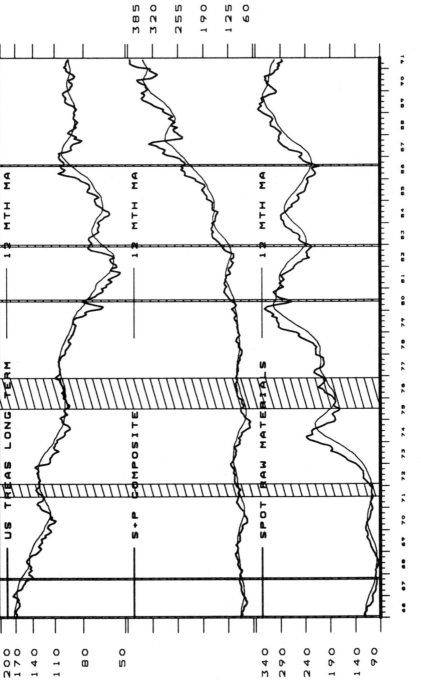

Figure D.6 Stage III market action, 1966–1991. Shaded areas represent Stage III periods when bonds, stocks, and commodities are bullish. (Source: *Pring Market Review*)

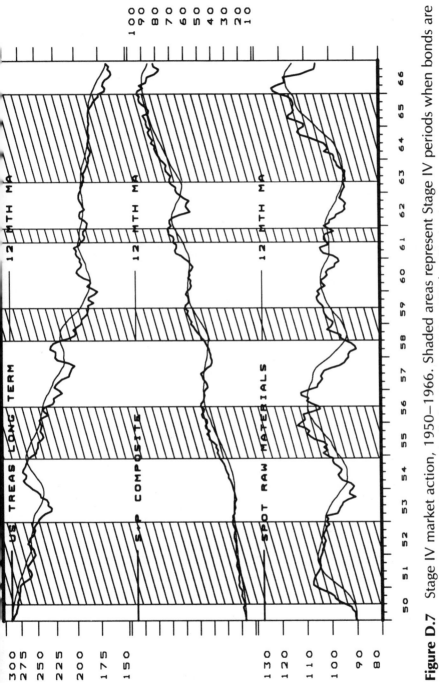

Figure D.7 Stage IV market action, 1950–1966. Shaded areas represent Stage IV periods when bonds are bearish; stocks and commodities are bullish. (Source: *Pring Market Review*)

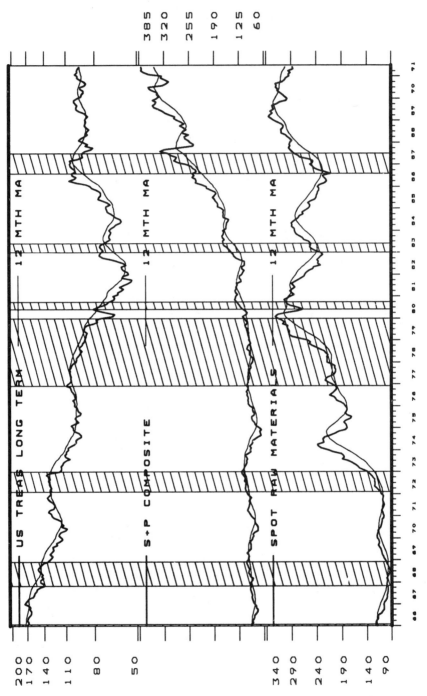

Figure D.8 Stage IV market action, 1966–1991. Shaded areas represent Stage IV periods when bonds are bearish; stocks and commodities are bullish. (Source: *Pring Market Review*)

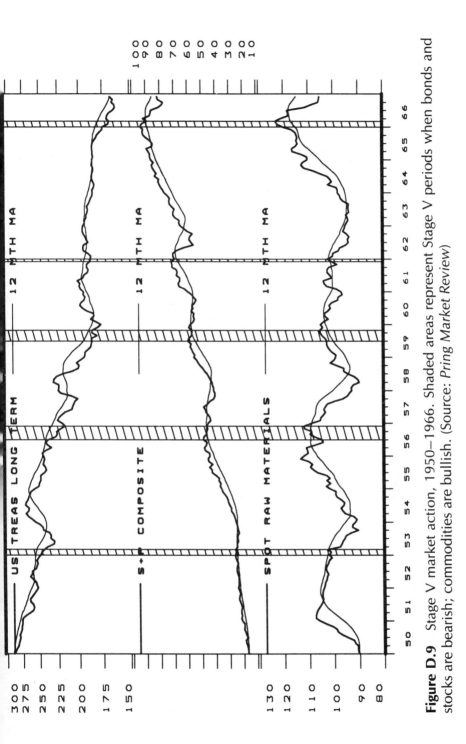

Figure D.9 Stage V market action, 1950–1966. Shaded areas represent Stage V periods when bonds and stocks are bearish; commodities are bullish. (Source: *Pring Market Review*)

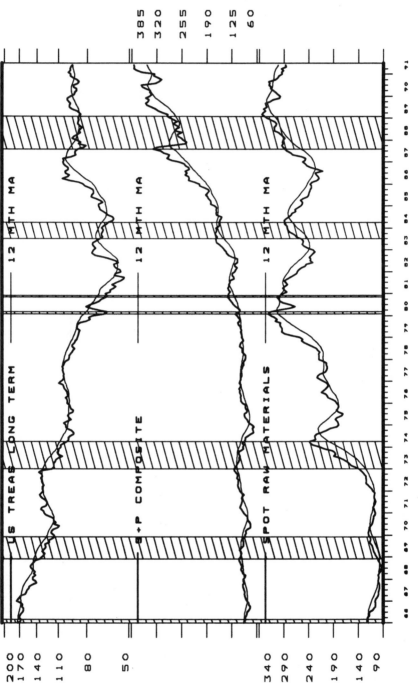

Figure D.10 Stage V market action, 1966–1991. Shaded areas represent Stage V periods when bonds and stocks are bearish; commodities are bullish. (Source: *Pring Market Review*)

320

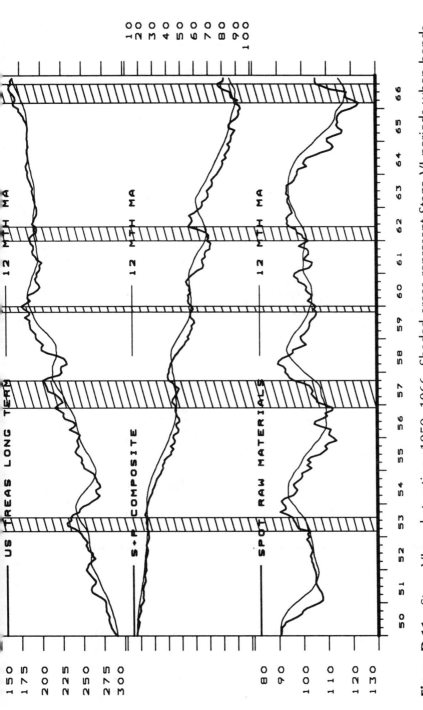

Figure D.11 Stage VI market action, 1950–1966. Shaded areas represent Stage VI periods when bonds, stocks, and commodities are bearish. (Source: *Pring Market Review*)

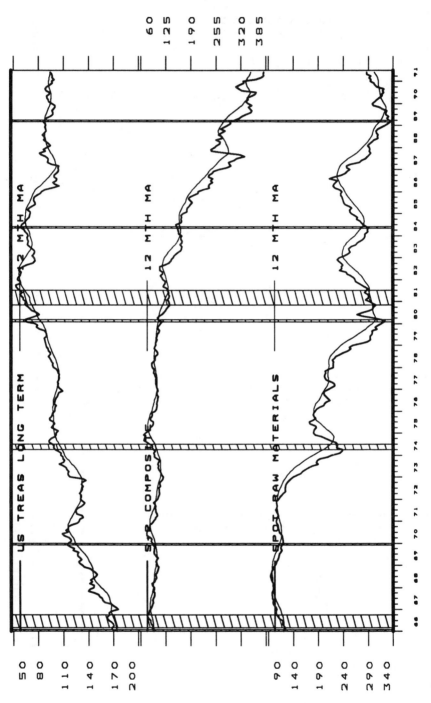

Figure D.12 Stage VI market action, 1966–1991. Shaded areas represent Stage VI periods when bonds, stocks, and commodities are bearish. (Source: *Pring Market Review*)

322

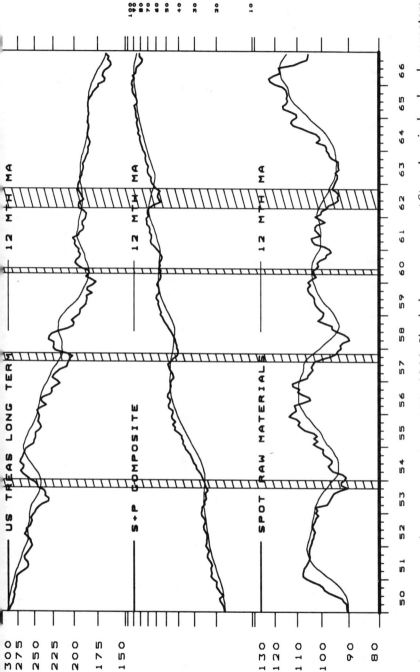

Figure D.13 Stage I barometer action, 1950–1966. Shaded areas represent Stage I periods when barometers for bonds are bullish; stocks and commodities are bearish. (Source: *Pring Market Review*)

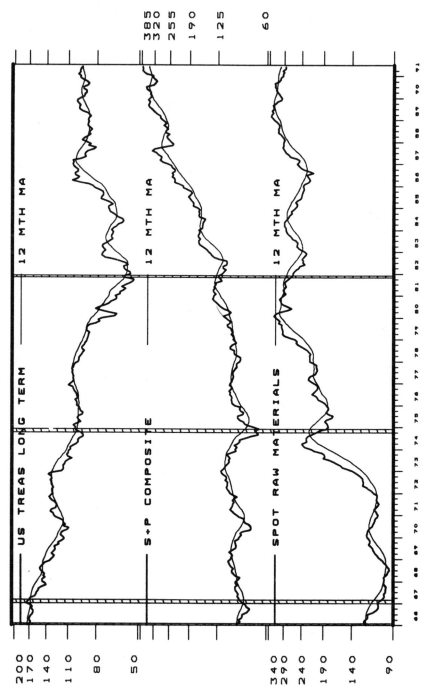

Figure D.14 Stage I barometer action, 1966–1991. Shaded areas represent Stage I periods when barometers for bonds are bullish; stocks and commodities are bearish. (Source: *Pring Market Review*)

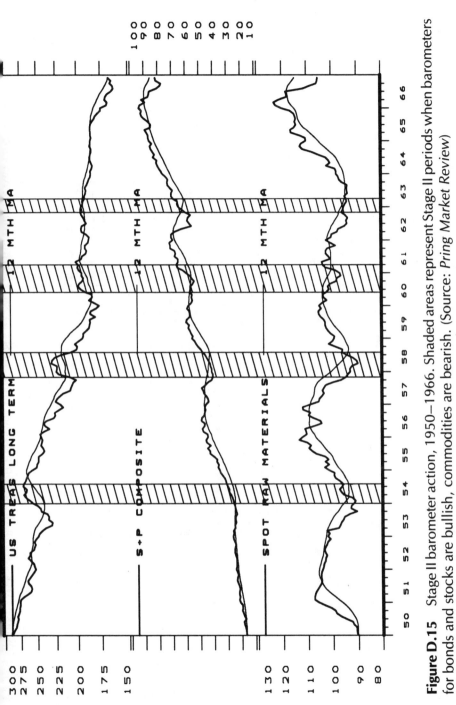

Figure D.15 Stage II barometer action, 1950–1966. Shaded areas represent Stage II periods when barometers for bonds and stocks are bullish, commodities are bearish. (Source: *Pring Market Review*)

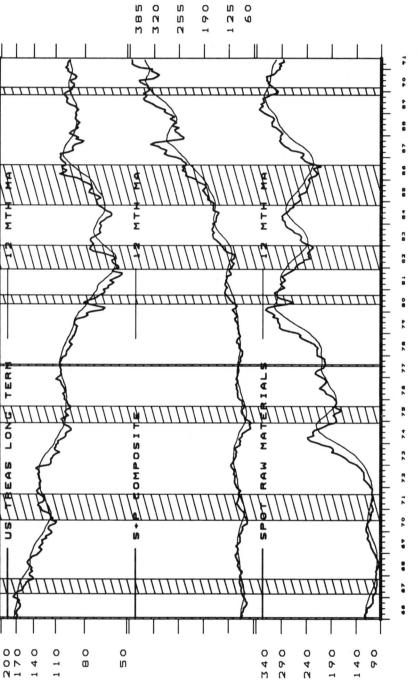

Figure D.16 Stage II barometer action, 1966–1991. Shaded areas represent Stage II periods when barometers for bonds and stocks are bullish; commodities are bearish. (Source: *Pring Market Review*)

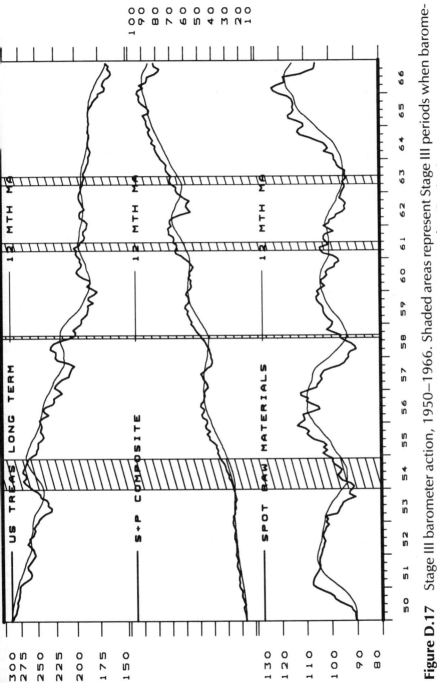

Figure D.17 Stage III barometer action, 1950–1966. Shaded areas represent Stage III periods when barometers for bonds, stocks, and commodities are bullish. (Source: *Pring Market Review*)

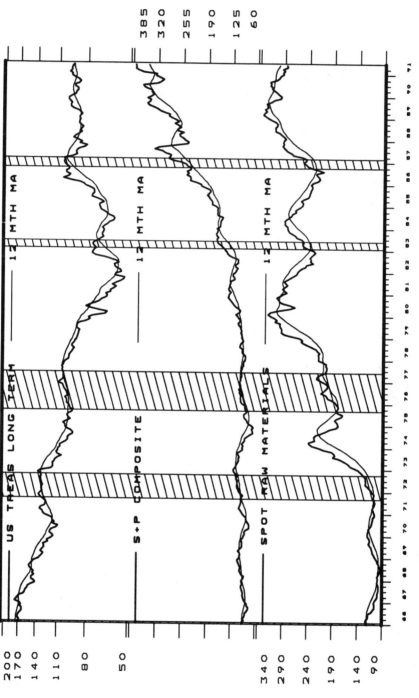

Figure D.18 Stage III barometer action, 1966–1991. Shaded areas represent Stage III periods when barometers for bonds, stocks, and commodities are bullish. (Source: *Pring Market Review*)

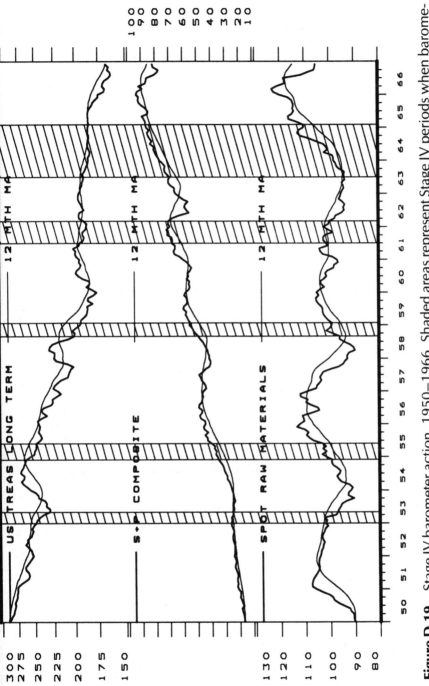

Figure D.19 Stage IV barometer action, 1950–1966. Shaded areas represent Stage IV periods when barometers for bonds are bearish; stocks and commodities are bullish. (Source: *Pring Market Review*)

329

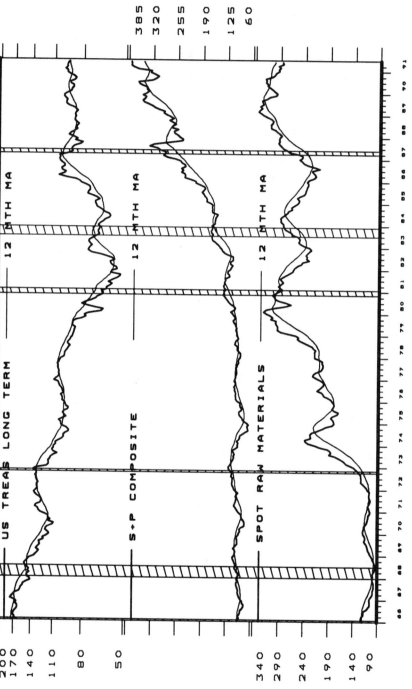

Figure D.20 Stage IV barometer action, 1966–1991. Shaded areas represent Stage IV periods when barometers for bonds are bearish; stocks and commodities are bullish. (Source: *Pring Market Review*)

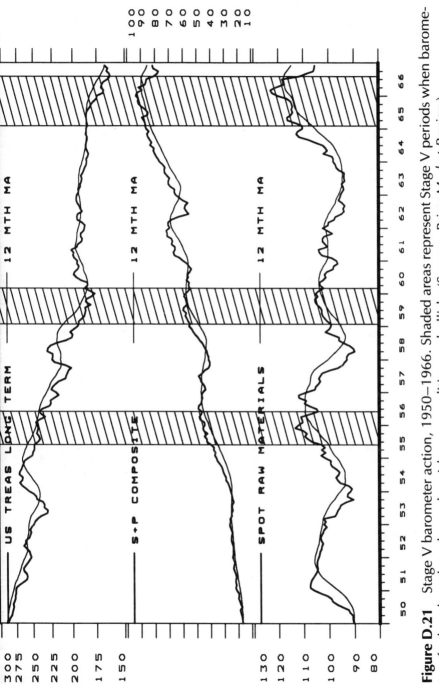

Figure D.21 Stage V barometer action, 1950–1966. Shaded areas represent Stage V periods when barometers for bonds and stocks are bearish; commodities are bullish. (Source: *Pring Market Review*)

331

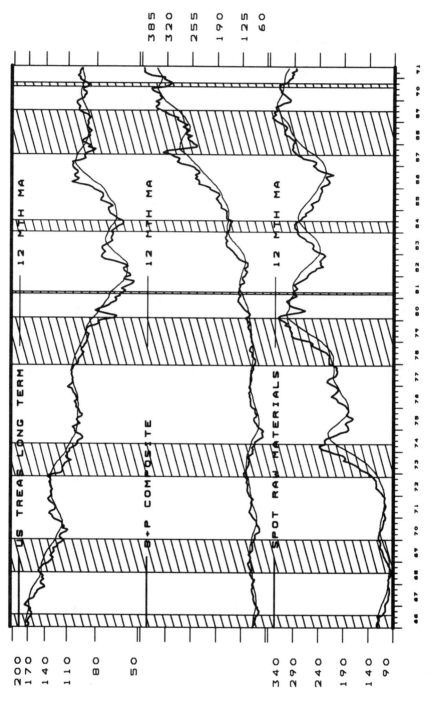

Figure D.22 Stage V barometer action, 1966–1991. Shaded areas represent Stage V periods when barometers for bonds and stocks are bearish, commodities are bullish. (Source: *Price Market Review*)

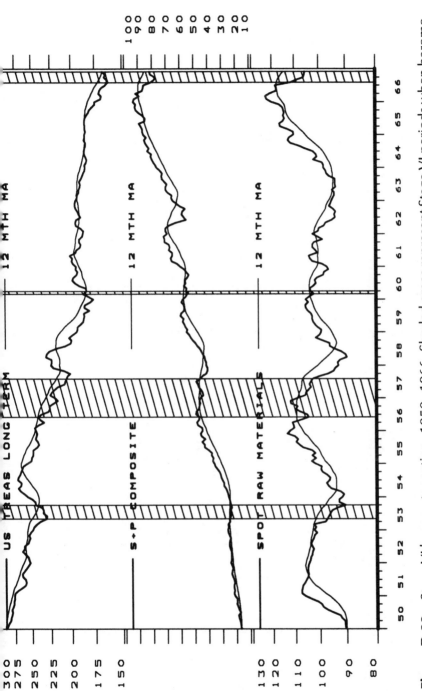

Figure D.23 Stage VI barometer action, 1950–1966. Shaded areas represent Stage VI periods when barometers for bonds, stocks, and commodities are bearish. (Source: *Pring Market Review*)

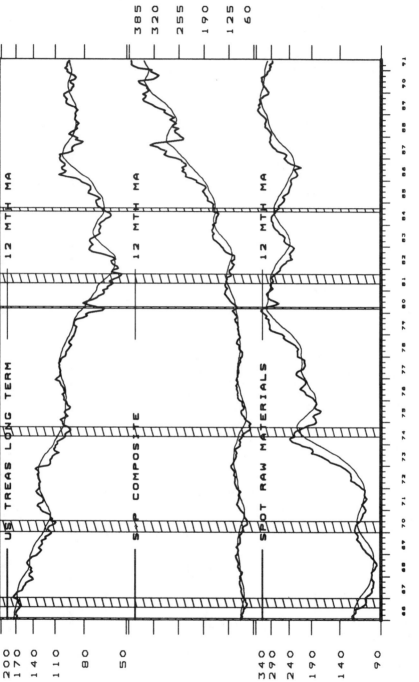

Figure D.24 Stage VI barometer action, 1966–1991. Shaded areas represent Stage VI periods when barometers for bonds, stocks, and commodities are bearish. (Source: *Pring Market Review*.)

334

INDEX

Special Introductory Offer:

A three-month subscription for $45.00 of the Pring Market Review for readers of this book (coupon must be enclosed).

Name_____

Company Name_____

Address_____

City_____State and ZIP_____

Telephone_____

❑MC ❑ Visa ❑ Amex ❑Check Enclosed

Card No. _____

Expiration Date_____

Signature_____

In U.S. Funds Only!

Comments or Specific Interest:

_____
_____
_____

Return to:
International Institute for Economic Research
P.O. Box 329
Washington Depot, CT 06794
203-868-7772   Fax 203-868-2683